Sibling Rivalry

Sibling Rivalry

How Mexico and the US
Built the Most Contentious,
Co-Dependent Feud in World Soccer

Hal Phillips

BLOOMSBURY ACADEMIC
NEW YORK • LONDON • OXFORD • NEW DELHI • SYDNEY

BLOOMSBURY ACADEMIC

Bloomsbury Publishing Inc, 1359 Broadway, 12th Floor, New York, NY 10018, USA
Bloomsbury Publishing Plc, 50 Bedford Square, London, WC1B 3DP, UK
Bloomsbury Publishing Ireland, 29 Earlsfort Terrace, Dublin 2, D02 AY28, Ireland

BLOOMSBURY, BLOOMSBURY ACADEMIC and the Diana logo are trademarks of
Bloomsbury Publishing Plc

First published in the United States of America 2026

Copyright © Hal Phillips, 2026

For legal purposes the Acknowledgments on p. xi constitute an extension of this copyright page

Cover design: Dustin Watson

Cover image: © LatinContent Editorial/Jam Media via Getty Images

All rights reserved. No part of this publication may be: i) reproduced or transmitted in any form, electronic or mechanical, including photocopying, recording or by means of any information storage or retrieval system without prior permission in writing from the publishers; or ii) used or reproduced in any way for the training, development or operation of artificial intelligence (AI) technologies, including generative AI technologies. The rights holders expressly reserve this publication from the text and data mining exception as per Article 4(3) of the Digital Single Market Directive (EU) 2019/790.

Bloomsbury Publishing Inc does not have any control over, or responsibility for, any third-party websites referred to or in this book. All internet addresses given in this book were correct at the time of going to press. The author and publisher regret any inconvenience caused if addresses have changed or sites have ceased to exist, but can accept no responsibility for any such changes.

A catalog record for this book is available from the Library of Congress.

ISBN: PB: 978-1-5381-9619-9
ePDF: 979-8-8818-6407-1
eBook: 978-1-5381-9620-5

Typeset by Deanta Global Publishing Services, Chennai, India
Printed and bound in the United States of America

For product safety related questions contact productsafety@bloomsbury.com.

To find out more about our authors and books visit www.bloomsbury.com and sign up for our newsletters.

Contents

Foreword by Seamus Malin vi
Acknowledgments xi

1 Rivalries Don't Just Happen 1
2 Stuck with Each Other: Rivalry as Codependence 21
3 A Friendly Meditation: Fear, Loathing, and Argie Worship in The GDL 43
4 Of Moles and Molé: How Mexico Seized Unlikely Control of the North American Derby 65
5 Envy and Scorn in the Borderlands 89
6 Soccer Made in America (or "How to Wander in the Footballing Desert for a Century") 111
7 The 1990s Changed Everything: The Potent Politics of Identity and Myth 133
8 Veni. Vici. Venue. Where Tribe, Home Ground, and Hashtags Collide 159
9 The Accidental Confederation: How Soccer's Best, Brightest, and Richest Have Come to Covet CONCACAF 183
10 The Unlikely, Once-Marginalized Custodians of a Rivalry Most Fierce 203

Notes 229
Bibliography 245
Index 255
About the Author 266

Foreword
Seamus Malin

Seamus Malin *was ABC/ESPN lead color commentator for the World Cup telecasts of 1994 and 1998. From 1982 to 2002, he traveled widely while covering the US Men's National Team from Vancouver to Guatemala City and the Heartland of Columbus, Ohio, to the cauldron of Estadio Azteca in Mexico City.*

Growing up in Dublin, Ireland, amidst a company of soccer-crazed pals, I came to share their fervent belief that the only national team we ever wanted to beat was . . . England! Problem was, it never happened. At least not in the years I lived there, before moving to Boston, Massachusetts, in 1958. It wasn't so much that England routinely thrashed us on the playing field; to us, the sad reality was that they simply refused to play us!

The attitude of the English gurus running the game in London when it came to regional competitive opponents could be summed up as follows:

Scotland? Well, I suppose, if we must.
Wales? They seem harmless enough.
Northern Ireland? Off island, but probably okay.
Republic of Ireland? Who? Never heard of them!

The soccer gods changed all that when the 1958 World Cup qualifying draw put Ireland and England in the same group. A 5–1 thrashing at London's Wembley Stadium humbled us all, but the return match in Dublin was a match for the ages. I was among the 46,000 fans jammed into Dalymount Park that day, standing on the terraces behind the goal where Ireland took the lead in the third minute. Tragically, that advantage was nullified in the cruelest of fashions: in the 90th minute, when England scored a fortunate goal and the roaring crowd suddenly lost its voice. A journalist writing in the next day's paper offered the feeling that the silence in the stadium could be heard in downtown O'Connell Street.

Descending upon Boston a mere few months after that traumatic loss, to begin a new life in a new country, provided the opportunity to shift gears sports-wise. I quickly found to my dismay that international soccer competition was virtually nonexistent in the United States. But my sports addiction was quickly fixed by baseball and the passion of fans in Boston. I think it took all of two weeks for me to develop a deep distaste for the New York Yankees. In a subconscious way—motivated by undercurrents of envy and scorn (two ideas that animate this book, dear reader)—the Yankees had merely replaced England in my emotional firmament.

Patience was required, and that patience paid off in surprising ways over the decades to come, as the sport of soccer began to establish itself deeply in United States culture. England even came to our shores for some exhibition games and, on one occasion, in 1993, was convincingly defeated by the US Men's National Team in Foxborough, Massachusetts, just outside Boston.

New continent, new culture, new life. But in the world of international soccer, so far as my new national team was concerned, it seemed the same old story: Another super soccer power in the neighborhood, preventing us from making the World Cup finals. No longer England but equally intimidating as far as the United States was concerned: Mexico.

That fateful summer of 1958 had witnessed the emergence of an astonishingly gifted seventeen-year-old Brazilian—Pelé, who announced himself at the World Cup in Sweden. Among the small field of sixteen countries participating, fully four hailed from the United Kingdom: England, Scotland, Northern Ireland, and Wales. The latter side had the dubious privilege of conceding the only goal that Mexico managed to score during their three games in Sweden, and that goal came in the 89th minute. Definitely not glory days for *El Tricolor*, but at least they were there!

Not so the United States (nor the Republic of Ireland either, to be honest). In fact, once I'd arrived in North America, the very marginalized Yanks did not make a World Cup appearance until 1990, in Italy. Mexico, meanwhile, was blithely qualifying for World Cup after World Cup, completely heedless of the United States and its sorry-ass record.

In my lively discussions with Mexican fans between 1958 and 1990, I encountered only contempt, and occasionally paternalistic bemusement when the subject of US soccer arose. The US team, such as it was, was no threat and thus could be easily lampooned. Fans of the US team, few though they were, could only look at Mexico with jealousy or repressed resentment. For more than thirty years, these attitudes seemed virtually frozen in place, the embodiment of envy and scorn. For the die-hard US soccer fan (often, in fact, born in another country), the national soccer landscape presented a virtual wasteland.

Then gradually the tables began to turn. The United States hosting the World Cup of 1994 had a major influence in this process. From that point forward, magically, the national team north of the border started getting results against Mexico. The ultimate obstacle had become a bona fide rival—and was despised as such.

US national team players of the 1970s and 1980s, those who invariably faced Mexico in its oppressive national stadium—the Azteca—told me they would mainly encounter bemused Mexican fans, who displayed contempt for the US team by showing up in smaller numbers. Such a match, such an opponent could not be taken seriously. However, there was change in the wind. By the mid-1990s, I found the atmosphere in Mexico virulently hostile, insulting, and dismissive. But compete they did, and the belligerence turned to hysteria at the prospect of losing to *El Norte* folk!

Now here was a proper fan reaction, one that reminded me of Dublin 1958!

My experience calling games at the Rose Bowl in Pasadena, California—where the United States met Mexico in several exhibition matches during the fateful 1990s—also evolved, often in seemingly contradictory ways. Walking through the parking lot before matches, I was often smilingly welcomed by tailgating Mexican fans raising a bottle in the air and inviting me over for a drink and a chat. This was a heartwarming and affectionate recognition that now, we US folks had become true soccer converts with a half-decent team to represent us!

Once inside the stadium, however, everything changed. Insults were hurled (not bottles thankfully). Hostile chants reverberated, and the fists of blame-gaming Mexicans were raised threateningly in the general direction of our broadcast booth whenever a referee's difficult decision went the wrong way. A far cry from *"Dos Equis, amigo?"*

My experience with the American players from 1990 onwards confirmed that the Mexican rivalry had quickly ascended to almost mythical proportions, even if the US fan base took its time to reach the point of raucous *Dos a Cero!* chants. I especially welcomed those in snow-covered venues where Mexican players shivered, and American fans simply helped themselves to another brew. By this time, in a new century, the US fan base was committed to and savoring the rivalry along with growing United States successes on the field.

Not all US sports fans have climbed aboard. In 2017, while visiting Big Bend National Park on the Rio Grande, I asked several Texans about their feelings on the US-Mexico futbol rivalry. The typical reply was, "I don't know much about that. The only football team I care about are the UT Longhorns!" (These were the locals whose trucks had bumper stickers saying, *No Effing Wall. Love your neighbor.*)

Later on, I chatted with a twenty-five-year-old who had arrived from Mexico at age two. I asked him to designate which national soccer team he now supported. He was clear-headed and definitive, *"El Tri,* of course!" When pushed for an explanation, he smiled and answered, hand on heart, "I have no choice."

Between World Cup 1994 and all the friendlies I worked there, Pasadena is the place I most strongly associate with the North American Derby. I spent many days and nights there savoring lively exchanges with Mexican and Mexican American hotel staff. Loyal to the Mexican national team, to a fault, they gave begrudging credit to the US team after its stunning 2–1 win over pre-tournament favorite Colombia. When I quizzed them about the US team's future prospects against Mexico, their colorful answers took me back in time. They reminded me of the response I heard a well-known British sports journalist give when quizzed about Ireland's chances against England: "If England don't win easily, Ireland might tie." There was also enthusiastic agreement that if Mexico lost to the United States, their fans would demand that the coach be fired!

When I changed the subject and touted the success of the US Women's National Team, they were unmoved: "That's only because no other decent soccer country cares about female football!"

Many years ago, before US-Mexico had become more evenly balanced, I was covering an exhibition match between the two nations. As usual, the crowd was heavily pro-Mexico, and the US team squeaked out a late tying goal to secure a 1–1 result. The small number of Americans there rejoiced, but the Mexican fans were devastated. A sympathetic bilingual American woman in the press box exclaimed somewhat sadly, "But the outcome is so much more devastating to *them*; in the U.S. we have everything, but they need their team for daily joy so much more."

Those days are gone. Today the rivalry is equally but unpredictably bitter and joyous, balanced with incredibly high stakes and perfectly credible expectations on both sides. Can the day be far away when an American fan might be heard to say: "If the U.S. doesn't win easily, Mexico might tie!" Or, perhaps: "If the U.S. can't beat Mexico, our manager is toast!"

How does that sound?

S.M., February 2025

Acknowledgments

During the summer of 2022, when my first soccer book was newly released, I sent a copy to Grant Wahl. We didn't know each other from Adam, but if you want to sell a futbol book in the United States, it's better to get the once and future dean of US soccer writers on board. As luck would have it, he required little convincing. Grant showed himself to be a great friend and champion of *Generation Zero: Founding Fathers, Hidden Histories & The Making of Soccer in America*, the story of how "US soccer" in the space of two decades finally graduated from ironic oxymoron (think "Jamaican bobsledding") to a rightful place among proper footballing nations.

Generation Zero generated a lot of nice phone calls, texts, emails, and published testimonials from friends and professional contacts alike. But Grant's response was a cut above. For starters, he actually read it (not a given, even among family members and reviewers), which was obvious from the content of our very first conversation. Over the next six months, the man went out of his way to praise and link the book online, share its notice with other futbol-media gatekeepers, and introduce me to folks who might further spread the good word. His was a study in professional altruism, one I will spend the rest of my days seeking to emulate.

As you probably know, Grant was covering the Argentina-Holland quarterfinal at World Cup 2022 when he suffered a fatal cardiac event in the press box at Qatar's Lusail Stadium. It's difficult to overstate this tragic loss. Grant Wahl wasn't just the finest soccer writer this country has yet produced. He was the American game's foremost cultural interpreter, a role he had only recently transcribed to the world of documentary film. He was only forty-nine.

•••

When we last spoke, on November 10, 2022, Grant and I recorded the conversation for his podcast. On air, so to speak, we discussed a brief passage in *Generation Zero* where I essentially pitch this book here, the one you're holding in your hands. While *GZ* charted the critical maturation of American soccer from 1970 to 1990, it's basically impossible to do that research and tell that history without tripping over massive quantities of competitive and emotional baggage attached to the US-Mexico rivalry. I didn't devote more than a meaty paragraph to explaining why a savvy publisher should commission me to write such a work of nonfiction. But I did make the case. In print.

Many thanks to the entire team at Bloomsbury for heeding the call.

Researching and reporting *Sibling Rivalry*, I was fortunate to forge dozens more relationships with kind, knowledgeable, gracious people, only a few of whom I already knew, each of whom loves soccer and the two countries that straddle our shared border. I want to take a moment to thank them all here, while reserving special commendation for Stephen McDermott Myers, my primary editor on this project. To the extent the language here has been strengthened and refined, Esteban and his skills as editor, poet, scholar, shaman, and Spanish-language grammarian are responsible.

Esteban and I played college soccer together at Wesleyan University, where, on the day we showed up for double sessions, I was immediately saddled with a nickname I didn't much like: Bluto. Because the moniker fit physically, and *Animal House* so strongly informed the collegiate zeitgeist in August 1982, it stuck. My Wes teammates still tend to call me that, though, true to form, Esteban would refine and strengthen it. He soon took to calling me Senator Blutarsky—then Senator, full stop. It's a habit he maintains, to my delight, well into the twenty-first century.

●●●

When Grant Wahl and I sat down to record that podcast, he knew something I did not: He had just completed a docuseries for Amazon called *Good Rivals*, scheduled for streaming release later that November of 2022. Off air, he informed me of all this—and playfully gave me mock shit for pitching a book idea that ripped off his forthcoming documentary! I volleyed back that *he* should be ashamed of himself, as a print journalist, for stealing an idea I committed to the page two years before. Then making something so vulgar as a *film* with it!

But wait. This gets better.

Grant then apologized, in advance, because he was already planning his next project, what became *Billion Dollar Goal*, a docuseries aired posthumously by Paramount Plus in November 2023. As many viewers have since pointed out to me, this doc basically follows the story told by *Generation Zero*: how a plucky, unlikely group of young Yanks qualified for a World Cup and single-handedly launched the Modern American Soccer Movement—the billion-dollar enterprise cited in the title.

It's a pretty good title, though I never got the chance to tell him so—or ride him, in jest, for ripping off *GZ*. Exactly a month post-pod, he was gone.

For all the serendipities and relationships *Sibling Rivalry* has enabled, however, few proved more elevating and cross-pollinating than my interactions with Grant and his professional legacy. Not just the *Good Rivals* doc, which I cite throughout this book, but the extensive body of reporting work he left behind, mainly in print but now online.

So, Grant: I hope you can get your hands on a copy of *Sibling Rivalry*. Yes, the embedded book pitch worked a treat. Maybe, from across the astral plane, you might avail yourself of a digital or audio version. I do wish you were still here on this mortal coil, so that we might laugh again and feign outrage at all the unlikely symmetries and mutual exploitations we've wrought.

Hal Phillips, May 15, 2025

1

Rivalries Don't Just Happen

Late in November 1980, during the final days of Jimmy Carter's one-and-done presidency, the US Men's National Team defeated its Mexican counterpart, 2–1, in a World Cup qualifier played in Fort Lauderdale, Florida. The Americans hadn't beaten their southern neighbors at soccer since 1934, a span of forty-six years and twenty-four matches. Curiously, there were no fitting celebrations outside the modest, rain-soaked confines of Lockhart Stadium, where a mere 2,200 folks showed up to watch.

In the decades since this outlier result was recorded, American soccer fans and media have labored to frame it as a historic breakthrough, a landmark victory. Forty-six years is certainly a very long time. In every other respect, however, this was a meaningless encounter. Two weeks prior, inside *Estadio Azteca*, the same Mexican national team had embarrassed Team USA, 5–1, delighting the 90,000 in attendance and ensuring the United States would miss its eighth consecutive World Cup. Disappointment with that result had not registered in the minds of American sports fans in the slightest. Neither had the subsequent victory in Fort Lauderdale. What made US headlines that Sunday before Thanksgiving? The Philadelphia Eagles beat the Oakland Raiders in a late-season preview of Super Bowl XV.

In 1980, US sports fans remained largely indifferent to world soccer. The victory at Lockhart Stadium—what amounted to a consolation prize for an invisible national team—didn't appear anywhere on domestic television.

In 1980, for every stateside fan of the World Cup, there were three or four whose feelings toggled between ignorance and contempt. To this day, in fact, most Americans struggle to process the elemental *idea* of international team competitions. The sporting enterprises we follow closely and strongly prefer—the National Football League, Major League Baseball, the National Basketball Association—are 99 percent domestic.

During the 1980s, the United States wasn't equipped to maintain an international soccer rivalry with anyone.

The Mexicans? They were very well equipped, and they sure as hell had a rivalry with us.

David Brett Wasser can attest to this imbalance. While the November 1980 victory in Florida didn't air on American TV, the Mexican network behemoth Televisa did broadcast the match live across Mexico. Wasser is the preeminent video archivist of US soccer, which hasn't made him famous. Hunting down obscure, half-petrified VHS tapes hasn't made him rich, either. (His primary gig: administration of a non-profit that supports investment in animal-cruelty-free corporations.) The man is bloody dogged, though. His pursuit and digitization of Team USA footage has borne considerable fruit: Today Wasser's got some 250 match films in his collection, which he stores at his Austin, Texas home in a room he calls The Tomb of US Soccer.

But here's the thing: Televisa has flat-out refused to provide Wasser a tape of the Fort Lauderdale qualifier, despite repeated, increasingly exasperated requests over the course of twenty years.

"It's very frustrating," Wasser told me. "The full tape is in the Televisa archive, but I've never been able to find anybody who can get it out of there. All that has been released is a 10-second clip of one of the USA goals. It starts at 11:48—but it's not much. It's a really historic moment for the U.S. national team, but who knows if we'll ever get to watch it."

So, why does the Mexican broadcasting monolith refuse to share the tape with Mr. Wasser?

Here's a clue: Once the United States had been eliminated from the 1982 World Cup qualification—on account of that 5-1 thrashing inside the Azteca—Mexico was already through to the next stage. This reality reduced the succeeding encounter to something resembling an exhibition, a dead rubber.

Yet Mexican manager Raúl Cardenas and the *Federación de Futbol Mexicano* (FMF) sent a first-choice team to Florida two weeks later.

This brand of national-team decision-making drives soccer club administrators crazy. Why risk injury to a star goal-scorer, for example, when there's nothing concrete at stake? US midfielder Ty Keough played in the 5–1 blowout, but he missed the Fort Lauderdale match because his indoor club, the St. Louis Steamers, needed him back. Hugo Sanchez was the finest Mexican striker of his era, perhaps the entire twentieth century. He scored in Mexico City; his club, UNAM Pumas, would have preferred he skip the Florida encounter. Instead, Cardenas played him all 90 minutes. Why did he even make the trip? Why did Mexico go all out to win this irrelevant encounter? And why has Televisa hidden away the match tape?

Because a futbol match with the United States has never been irrelevant or meaningless—not in Mexico.

The result in Fort Lauderdale eventually cost Cardenas his job with the *Federación*, but not his reputation. The man remains a legend south of the border. He managed the national team at the 1970 World Cup, a tournament event still cherished by the Mexican futbol community. As a player, Cardenas represented his country at three earlier World Cups; he later coached two of the nation's iconic clubs, Club América and Cruz Azul, with great success. When Cardenas passed away in 2016, none of his obituaries referenced the notorious November 1980 loss to the United States. Try researching this fellow even today: All mention of this match has been scrubbed from his online profile.[1] Out of respect.

The US Soccer Federation went a different way. It celebrated the historic upset by sacking the *winning* manager, Walt Chyzowych, and not scheduling another US Men's National Team (USMNT) match for the better part of two years.

•••

Here's a useful thought experiment: Imagine that ABC actively withheld tape of the Soviet Union's wildly controversial victory over the US men's basketball team at the 1972 Munich Olympics. Here was another preposterous upset with clear nationalist overtones—the first time the Americans had ever dropped an Olympic basketball game, to anyone, and the victor just happened to be an Evil Empire. National pride combined with a Cold War fixation *could* have led a reactionary American Broadcast Company archivist, and maybe a confederate or two, to place an unofficial embargo on such a tape—had a video curator in Kursk started sniffing around twenty-five years later, looking for footage. But the network did not hide that game film away under lock and key.

Media reaction to events at Lockhart Stadium underlines both points. North of the border, the result caused barely a ripple outside the tiny space devoted to soccer in 1980. Again, the game wasn't televised anywhere in the country. According to Wasser, no USMNT match would be broadcast nationally until four years later, when, in October 1984, NBC chose to air a preliminary World Cup qualifier against a country that no longer exists. Hello, Netherlands Antilles.

Further south and west? Well, the November 1980 upset in Fort Lauderdale was covered like every match contested by *El Tricolor*, the iconic national futbol team better known as *El Tri*. Starting in the 1960s, every national team match was the subject of great fanfare and broadcast live from Oaxaca to Tijuana. Those footballing confrontations with the Americans? Front-page news, especially in *La Afición*, the only daily newspaper in the pre-internet age dedicated entirely to Mexican sport.

Not surprisingly, *La Afición* responded to the shock loss with a rather unhinged combination of finger wagging and pearl clutching. "A Sad Reality for our Futbol: It could not be worse. The national team fell—to the US!" That was the headline package. The story read, "We are mired in total disappointment. And worse still, in a disorientation. Because the team does not advance, because it does not have international prestige, because it does not know how to play when not at home."[2]

Again, the United States hadn't beaten *El Tri* (pronounced *el tree*) since 1934! Mexico had toyed with the hapless Americans for decades, all through the 1960s and 1970s, when the North American Soccer League was a thing—when the standard of US play was supposed to have benefited from legitimate first-division football. (It didn't.) Why did Mexican sporting media respond to this blip with such apocalyptic handwringing?

Because rivalries don't just happen. They simmer for decades, feeding off broad cultural feelings of envy and scorn. They are further informed by historical grievance and geopolitical arrogance, when they're not the subject of historical amnesia or resolute denial. In other words, these long-term antagonisms often have nothing to do with soccer at all.

What's more, the competitors themselves, those who control on-field events, cannot know how a result like Fort Lauderdale will inform sporting relations between the two nations—supporters and media wield far more influence in this respect. For that reason and a dozen more, the emotional stakes that *make* a rivalry rarely take hold in the psyches of either party at the same time, with the same levels of intensity, according to the same sentimental logic. Perfectly symmetrical relations are hard to identify, actually. One party always cares a little more than the other, and that's where US vs. Mexico stood in 1980. Up to that point, and for the next ten years, the Mexican futbol community considered the United States a rival—but only in the way boxers consider the punching bag a rival.

Should the punching bag suddenly strike back? Well, imagine the surprise.

•••

Once we consider the economic, cultural, and military histories that Mexico shares with its northern neighbor, we better appreciate how much Mexicans enjoyed hammering the United States over and over again for sixty years. We can also understand why, during the 1990s, when the Americans really did start to compete as soccer equals, Mexicans weren't so sure they wanted this rivalry anymore. Come the debacle of World Cup 2002, such ambivalence gave way to the six stages of Mexican grief: denial, anger, tequila, bargaining, depression, and acceptance.

Not only did *El Tri* and its massive fan base accept and recover, the communal trauma of 2002 galvanized the nation in a new way. Twenty-four years later, on the cusp of a World Cup they will host together, Mexico and the United States have developed a serial competition unlike any on Earth, in any sport.

On the pitch and off, national team wins and losses continue to come at extraordinary cost—a strange, psychic brew animated by blood, sweat, and tears, by honor and ridicule, by envy and scorn. In every other way, however, the two countries have built and come to *share* a North American futbol culture where their respective leagues, federations, clubs, fans, and broadcasters grow ever more intertwined. Some might describe these delicate relationships as codependent.

Because long-term rivalry is nothing if not an intimate form of interdependence.

Upon closer examination, it's clear the Mexican National Team and its transnational fan culture remain torn between these fascinating realities and the unyielding, persistent idea that their primary soccer relationship is somehow beneath them.

Which does nothing but up the ante each and every time the two nations take the same field.

National populations commonly engage in such mass self-deception. The Cato Institute, *Politico,* and *Al Jazeera* don't agree on much, but they each acknowledge that US armed forces maintain approximately 750 military installations in a minimum of eighty countries around the world.[3] Millions of Americans believe this commitment is necessary to "keep the peace."

Sporting matters are hardly immune to this phenomenon. Famously, the English still project themselves as a dominant, indispensable soccer nation, despite not having won anything since the 1966 World Cup, a trophy claimed on home ground, via an overtime winner highly disputed to this day. In golf, the US Ryder Cup Team can't seem to process or accept the idea that its European foe is, at the very least, an equal—equal enough to win ten of the last thirteen biennial competitions.

Many Mexicans consider themselves too good for their futbol competition with the United States because the idea of America as an equal, in soccer, undermines their self-image as an elite footballing nation. Fans of *El Tri,* especially those living in Mexico, firmly believed in their inherent superiority when this contention was obviously true, between 1937 and 1991.

And they believe it still today, when it's clearly not.

And so, when the proverbial push did come to shove that fateful afternoon on June 17, 2002—when the new realities of US vs. Mexico were made globally obvious, at the World Cup held in Japan and South Korea—they landed south of the border like a physical trauma. The Americans eliminated their North American siblings from the competition that day in Jeonju, 2–0, a resounding result that soon became a taunt and a cheeky badge of honor among the growing US fan base. (*Dos a Cero!*)

From that point forward, the potential for Mexican shame began to animate the rivalry like never before. When the heavy bag punches back, in the most public way possible, entirely new coping mechanisms are required.

"Losing to the United States doesn't bother me. It infuriates me," recalls Javier Aguirre, the manager in charge of *El Tri* in South Korea. As fate has it, he leads the national team yet again, ahead of World Cup 2026. "I know that many won't forgive me for that loss. Myself included . . . I've cried twice in football, and one of those times was out of sadness after losing to them. It was one of my lowest moments, and I paid the price for it." [4]

One wonders whether Aguirre and Cardenas ever sat down and compared notes. They'd have had lots to talk about.

•••

The timing of *El Tri*'s 2002 reality check could not have been worse. Fresh off winning FIFA's second-most prestigious men's tournament, the 1999 Confederations Cup, Mexico viewed the World Cup in Japan/South Korea as its inevitable coming-out party, the opportunity to officially join the ranks of futbol's global nobility. For such a robust soccer culture—one that had hosted World Cups (1970, 1986), one that sustained a rich and influential professional league (the Mexican *Priméra*, est. 1943)—those ambitions were understandable. As was the full and rapt attention of virtually all Mexicans, from one end of the country to the other.

North of the border, soccer has come a very long way *since* 2002. It has passed hockey as the nation's fourth major sport, fueled by successful, expanding professional leagues for both men and women, in addition to popular national team programs. For the iconic US Women's National Team—which has grown into a cultural touchstone and a threat to win the World Cup each time the tournament is played—"popular" amounts to faint praise.

Today, American soccer fans can sit down on a Saturday morning and read about the US game and listen to dedicated futbol podcasts into the night. They can choose to live-stream matches from a dozen different foreign leagues at their whim. It is precisely soccer's digital maturation, its unisex and international scope, that has allowed the game to take ice hockey's place in our major-sport pecking order.

None of these factors were in place back in 2002. Futbol in the States remained a niche enterprise at the turn of the century, followed only by a die-hard minority and covered by a proportionally pint-sized media corps. MLS had been around for a mere six seasons; the quality of play and fan ethos remained, as the Irish like to say, a bit manky. After an embarrassing, winless showing at the previous World Cup in 1998, the American players and fan base were happy enough just to qualify for Japan and South Korea. To wash the stink off.

Soccer had obviously developed very differently in these neighboring countries, due to their distinct but uniquely intertwined histories.

For instance, when the millennium turned, Mexico's media apparatus—the means by which the sport got delivered to and consumed by the masses—was already highly developed and pervasive. The broadcast sector had also become uniquely invested in the country's futbol fortunes. Mexico is a vast country by any standard, home to 134 million people, the most populous Spanish-speaking nation on earth. (Second largest? the United States, with 56 million.) Mexico also possesses the most robust Spanish-speaking *economy* in the world, and its television industry, corporate culture, and soccer federation had all evolved cooperatively to foster and monetize the public's soccer cravings.

Here's an illustration of just how effectively and intentionally things had been managed out of the country's media hub, Mexico City. Through much of the twentieth century, *beisbol* competed quite ably with soccer. Many in the far north and south of the country considered it the national sport. By the mid-1970s, that contest was over, thanks to a strategic partnership of television executives at Televisa and the FMF. One sport was on TV all the time—futbol. *El Tri* matches. A full schedule of programming from the *Priméra*, Mexico's first division. Select games from half a dozen leagues across the Spanish-speaking world.

Over time and by design, baseball—a game closely associated with *yanqui* culture—receded from the airwaves and, eventually, the popular consciousness. A lot of people got rich investing in and promoting futbol in Mexico. Televisa rakes in the ad dollars from match broadcasts, naturally, but it also owns Club América, the nation's most popular club. The broadcaster owns the national treasure where *Las Aguilas* and the national team play the lion's share of their home dates: *Estadio Azteca*. Meanwhile, the *Federación* owns and operates Liga MX, the twenty-first century incarnation of the *Priméra*. This loosely formed oligopoly has dominated Mexican futbol since the 1960s. In the 1970s, it quickly matured into an efficient, soccer-centric hype machine and money printer.

Was it coincidental that all these powers-that-be funded and televised the one sport where Mexico utterly dominated the United States? Nope.

American corporate media is no less influential, calculating, or profit-driven, of course. There's no doubt the National Football League dominates US sporting culture today in ways analogous to Mexican soccer. Yet American football still shares the media space and the recreational space with a larger, more diverse sporting universe: basketball, baseball, soccer, and hockey, golf and tennis, track & field, adventure sports, motor sports, even the bizarre programming phenomenon that is cornhole. This more varied sporting culture also extends to collegiate versions of all the so-called "major" sports. What's more, multiple networks—fierce competitors in their own right—all bid to broadcast this all-you-can-eat buffet to the domestic audience, as profit margins encourage and allow.

Through the years, for better and worse, the Mexican formula has established itself as far more concentrated, centrally planned, and reliant on one game. The promotion of soccer to Mexicans was no accident of culture, but rather a particular corporate media strategy that leveraged this irresistible fact: Here was the one North American arena—sporting, economic, or cultural—where Mexico consistently made mincemeat of the United States.

Which is all to say, when the United States and Mexico drew each other in that first knockout round of World Cup 2002, no one in Mexico City, no one in Guadalajara or Ciudad Juarez or Puebla, no one in provincial towns north, south, east or west entertained the idea that *El Tri* would lose the match. Not on the largest imaginable stage. Not with an elusive "fifth match" in the quarterfinals at stake. Not to the damn *gringos*, who merely dabble in the Beautiful Game.

But it wasn't 1980 anymore. The USMNT that qualified for the first Asian World Cup had matured into a dangerous opponent, *El Tri's* primary continental rival—even if most Mexicans didn't seek such a rival. Not this one anyway.

"The press was saying we were already in the quarterfinals," Aguirre told the journalist and documentarian Grant Wahl, "that we'd already beaten the Americans—and there was no way we could lose." [5]

Note Aguirre's carefully calibrated sentiments above. Mexican *media*—our friends at Televisa, plus hundreds of newspaper folk—had created most of those outsized expectations ahead of all those World Cups. Supporters of *El Tri* had enthusiastically consumed all that media. In June of 2002, so far as Mexican journalism and fans were concerned, the national team (*La Selección*) was a hemispheric power on the verge of greatness, destined for a likely next-stage encounter with the mighty Germans. The upstart United States was superfluous to this heroic progression, almost incidental to this national narrative—to this prophecy so frequently foretold.

If *los americanos* could be slayed yet again along the way, perhaps embarrassed? So much the better.

•••

Dr. Joe Cobbs studies sports rivalry at Northern Kentucky University in the curiously redundant town of Highland Heights, just over the river from Cincinnati, Ohio. It's a compelling deep dive, this study of why athletic associations form and gather intensity, and why they don't. According to Cobbs, while captivating long-term confrontations can start out quite lopsided, inequality eventually kills them or renders them devoid of cultural value. What does "value" mean in a competitive context? It's about identity, mainly. Every installment of a rivalry—what many English and Italian speakers call a derby, what Spanish speakers call a *clásico* (the German riff: *Der Klassiker*)—brings with it the risk that results may damage or enhance the shared self-image of one set of supporters or the other. These flashpoints shine brighter than in normal games because the risks and rewards are heightened. And baked right in.

This ongoing, unpredictable tension can set any individual *clásico* alight. Over the course of decades, this combination of suspense, apprehensions, vanities, and hostilities can even produce the rare and vaunted *superclásico*.

Such as it was, the North American Derby back in 1980 resembled US vs. Mexico in the women's context today—only in reversed roles. In February of 2024, the Mexican women's national team shocked the United States 2-0 (*Dos a Cero!*) in Carson, California. There was a great deal of November 1980 in this result: The Americans had entered the match 40-1-1 all-time against *El Tri feminil*. The takeaway? A sterling achievement for Mexican women's soccer. Maybe a sign of things to come. But for the time being? No contest. Not quite yet.

The early 1990s finally attached actual meaning—read: the clear and present risk of identity damage—to the men's derby, even if the Mexican sporting public and media establishment would not acknowledge the facts of the case until 2002.

The first brick in that wall was laid in 1991, roughly a year after the United States had qualified for its first World Cup in forty years. Here again, economic incentives and corporate actions proved crucial to the evolving equation. As soon as the Stars & Stripes had graduated from "hapless" to "competitive", CONCACAF—the regional body that administrates soccer in North America, Central America, and the Caribbean—created the Gold Cup, a confederation championship including all the best *selecciones* in North America. Lo and behold, in July of 1991, the Yanks shut out Mexico, 2-0, in a Gold Cup semifinal held inside the Los Angeles Coliseum. Out of nowhere, the 1994 World Cup hosts were looking feisty.

CONCACAF is no one's favorite collection of futbol bureaucrats. But they recognize box office when they see it. FIFA recognizes six such confederations around the world, and their various championships are typically quadrennial. From the beginning, the Gold Cup was conceived, as a *biennial* tournament—to maximize opportunities to stage and televise the United States against Mexico. The 1993 Gold Cup final was held in Mexico City, inside *Estadio Azteca*, where *El Tri* avenged the 1991 loss in dominant fashion, 4-0. A year later, in the final World Cup warm-up for both teams, the USMNT prevailed, 1-0, before a largely Mexican American crowd of 90,000 at the Rose Bowl in Pasadena, California.

Still, the Mexican press, the country's futbol establishment and fan base were not convinced. They didn't *want* to be convinced. Their national team had gone decades—most of the twentieth century—without losing a single time to the United States. That one-off in November 1980? An embarrassment, no doubt, but pure aberration. The North American Soccer League went out of business in 1984, for heaven's sake. It wouldn't be replaced for twelve years. Even by 1994, Mexicans largely stuck by their long-held assessment: *So what if they are improved, these americanos don't care about futbol. This is a phase, a series of rogue events. It will pass . . .*

"In our research, we've found that the growth of rivalries relies on key ingredients. We call this one *disparate values*," Dr. Cobbs explains, citing Mexico's contention that it loves futbol and Americans do not. "It's hard to know whether these attitudes are supported on purpose, but we know they make it harder for each side to empathize with and respect each other—because they don't share these important values. Which means I'm more willing to exhibit prejudice toward you. I'm more willing to discriminate against you in relationships between the two groups of fans."

By the close of World Cup 1994, however, the men competing on Mexico's national team itself had developed a different perspective. They saw the writing on the wall.

For professional players and coaches, nothing is ever gained by underestimating the opposition. After dropping a high-profile quarterfinal to the United States at the 1995 *Copa América*, the South American continental championship, this much had become clear to the *El Tri* rank and file: Here was a national team opponent clearly on the rise, worthy of respect. And oh, *by the way*, it's a next-door nemesis representing a nation of 300 million aggressive and organized souls, the industrious engine of the planet's lone superpower and largest economy. *Los Yanquis* are good at most everything else—why would soccer be any different? Certainly Mexico City's partisan press corps could see this, too.

Ahead of a home World Cup qualifier in April 1997, Mexican captain Alberto García Aspe verbalized this assessment. He warned that the United States was "no small rival any longer." He went on to note that no one should expect the upcoming match to be a work of art. Yet here's how *La Afición* relayed and interpreted *el capitán*'s level-headed sentiments, in print: "In summary, the Mexicans instead of turning to the dress coat should put on the overalls and become embroiled in a battle without mercy against the Americans, as if they were recovering the Alamo, or Texas."[6]

Hello! Them's what we call "fightin' words".

Over the top? Maybe. But pre-game hype doesn't mean the underlying emotions aren't authentic or grounded in shared cultural memory. According to Dr. Juliette Levy, professor of Latin American History at the University of California, Riverside: "Every soccer match between the U.S. and Mexico is a replay of the Battle of Churubusco [1847]."[7]

Churubusco was the critical battle of the Mexican War, and it took place in the heart of Mexico City. According to Levy, who spoke her piece to the producers of *Gringos at the Gate*, a documentary film released in 2012, every soccer contest between the two nations is fraught beyond American understanding. "The complication for the U.S.-Mexico rivalry is that history," she continued, "It's very unique. If Mexico loses the match, the U.S. walks into Mexico City and plants its flag all over again. And if Mexico wins, it's an ability to regain the greatest territorial loss in Mexican history."

Little of this context has been absorbed or acknowledged in the United States. Yale scholar Greg Grandin points out that the Mexican War is not much taught in American schools, not in any depth.[8] Grandin published the Pulitzer Prize-winning *The End of the Myth* in 2019. North of the border, he argues, the Mexican War is treated as something less than consequential—even though these hostilities essentially created the western United States. For the record, future Civil War general and President Ulysses S. Grant took part in the conflict. He also saw fit to call it "the most unjust war undertaken by a powerful nation against a weak one."

As the millennium turned, low-key warnings like those from García Aspe fell on increasingly deaf ears. Fans of *El Tri* didn't want to hear anything like straight talk about this coming futbol force from *El Norte*. Belief in Mexico's footballing superiority was not a subject for debate or historical introspection. It was, rather, a matter of *identity*, an act of communal defiance. Even in 2026, the idea that *El Tri* and the USMNT are somehow soccer equals does not compute—not for citizens of Mexico, not for millions of expatriates spread across North America. Any such computations on that subject remain taboo, or better left unsaid. For Mexican partisans to verbalize such a sentiment, or to write about it dispassionately, would represent a cultural betrayal.

Are the resulting appraisals of each national team realistic? *Not at all*. Are those rose-colored irrationalities yet another psycho-social pillar of this kick-ass North American Derby? *Oh, yes*.

•••

The benchmark 1991 US Men's National Team was the first to beat *La Selección* in a game that truly mattered. No wonder the loss made such an unwelcome impression on the Mexican psyche. This Gold Cup semifinal stuck in the craw of *El Tri* players, coaches, media, and supporters for another reason: The American squad that evening had been coached by Bora Milutinovic, a pivotal individual in the evolution of Mexico as a footballing nation.

Bora is one of those figures—Pelé and Eusebio, Pep and Mou, Stalin and Zlatan, Marta and Mao—for whom just one name is required. The Serbian national was never a dominant on-field talent, though. His career as a journeyman defensive midfielder was unremarkable. But it showed him the world: from the old Yugoslavian first division to *Ligue 1* in France, to four years with UNAM Pumas in the Mexican *Priméra*. When Bora hung up his cleats, he moved straight into the role of Pumas manager.

Different cultures have developed specific diction to describe the unique dominion enjoyed by male futbol coaches. In the United Kingdom, he is a "football manager," though players often refer to him as "the gaffer." Germans prefer the more generic *fußballtrainer*, while the French prefer *entraîneur*, the Portuguese, *treinador de futebol*. Spanish-speakers often use the vaguely deferential *Mister*. In Mexico, in this specific role, Milutinovic showed himself to be the furthest thing from unremarkable. He was enormously popular from the get-go. He had already married a local. His curious Serb-inflected Spanish, the pirate-captain good looks, and all the victories quickly won hearts throughout his adopted country.

Mostly the victories. *El Mister* led Pumas to a league title in 1981, with Hugo Sanchez scoring the goals. Together they captured a *Copa InterAmericana*, beating Nacional of Uruguay later that year—a remarkable double. The InterAmerican trophy is no longer contested. In Mexico, it fell from favor in the late 1990s when *Priméra* clubs started competing in South America's more prestigious club competition, the *Copa Libertadores*. However, the tournament remained a very big deal in 1981. Then as now, whenever domestic clubs enjoy success against South American competition, *el pueblo mexicano* sits up and takes notice. Be it club or country, Mexican fans in search of prestige tend to look south, while owners, the FMF, and broadcasters tend to look north—in search of American dollars.

The *Federación* named Bora manager of the Mexican national team in 1983, a critical moment. He assumed control of *El Tri* following a very bad run of form—and just when Mexico had replaced Colombia as host of the 1986 World Cup.

Back in 1970, under Cardenas, when Mexico was a first-time World Cup host, tournament organizer FIFA—an acronym originally coined from the French *Fédération Internationale de Football Association* (for International Federation of Association Football)—adroitly placed *El Tricolor* in a soft group. In a 16-team tournament, finishing second in such a group meant an automatic berth in the quarterfinals, where the Mexicans bowed out rather meekly to Italy, 4–1.

The national team entrusted to Bora through 1986 would reckon with far higher expectations, and the Serb delivered. *El Tri* won its group, beating eventual semifinalist Belgium in the process. Then it disposed of a very capable Bulgarian side in the Round of 16, before falling in the quarters to tournament runner-up West Germany. On penalties, no less.

Mexico has never again ventured so deep into a World Cup tournament. As any fan of *La Selección* will point out, with great snark, the national team has never again advanced beyond the Round of 16, to a so-called "Fifth Match." For all his sideline wizardry during the summer of 1986, for the belief and self-love he instilled in his Mexican charges—in the Mexican people writ large—Bora got elevated to an exalted status somewhere between national hero and saint, a standing he would maintain even when he led neighboring Costa Rica at its first-ever World Cup in 1990.

No nation's fans could possibly feel proprietary toward Bora, so well-traveled was the man. He left *El Tri* following the '86 *Mundial*—what Spanish-speakers call the FIFA World Cup—landing first at Club Atlético San Lorenzo de Almagro in Argentina, then Udinese in Italy. He returned to the Mexican league with Tecos of Guadalajara, then led Veracruz. Remarkably, he would eventually manage eight different national teams around the world, though he's famous for being unintelligible in only five languages.

Most American fans recognize Bora as the fellow who coached the US at the 1994 World Cup. But he was hired in 1991, and his introduction more or less created the US-Mexico rivalry from whole cloth.

"So you've got a former coach of the Mexican national team, married to a Mexican woman, and all of a sudden he's our coach," says Sunil Gulati, the former US Soccer Federation chief and FIFA Executive Committee member. "In a very real sense, the rivalry starts and changes in the way it's perceived when Bora comes to the United States. And the Gold Cup in '91 kinda shows that. That's a turning point for sure."[9]

Ahead of that tide-turning Gold Cup encounter with Mexico, the first time the two countries had played an official match since 1984, Bora sailed right past the issue of his having coached the old adversary. He didn't mention how well Mexico had performed under him in 1986. In fact, he waved away fifty-seven years of history, the entirety of the continental derby up to that point.

"So, Bora walks through the locker room and says, *You're going to beat them. You are better than they are*," recalls US striker Eric Wynalda. "That was everything. We actually said, as a group, *Yeah, he's right! We can beat these guys!* Nobody's giving us a snowball's chance in hell, but our mentality flipped because of him. We had the guy who coached them telling us we were better than them. That was a monumental moment for us, in how we addressed the rivalry."[10]

Bora did prove an uncommon and wonderfully transformative figure. He delivered to his northern charges exactly what he had to *El Tri* the decade prior: belief and results. Under his leadership, the US played Mexico four times, posting two wins, one loss, and a draw. Against the cream of the crop, at the World Cup 1994, he coaxed Team USA to the Round of 16, where it lost to eventual champion Brazil, 1–0. Is it any surprise that clubs and national federations kept hiring the guy before he finally stepped away from coaching in 2014?

Yet Bora did something else extraordinary in service of this Sibling Rivalry: He bravely passed through a previously untested portal that connects the two soccer communities. Milutinovic was the first modern futbol figure to demonstrate this delicate, transnational maneuver. Before embarking on Phase IV of his international coaching odyssey, Bora even returned to coach *El Tri* from 1995–97.

Post Bora, individual players and coaches, fans and media have more often seen the opportunity to similarly dance back and forth across the border—a frontier that, for much of the twentieth century, had more strictly segregated one national identity from the other. Thirty years removed from our time in The BoraSphere, his example continues to resonate. The interdependence of this US-Mexico interaction—its soccer-specific confluence of talents and economies, of opportunities and migrations, of loyalties and cultures—has only multiplied.

Today the national teams representing both countries, male and female, don't settle for the mere hiring of coaches across this formerly great divide. They routinely court and compete for players whose mix of ethnic heritage allows them to play for either combatant.

And so, hundreds of athletically gifted young men and women on both sides of the border must annually do what only a handful had been asked to do prior to 1991: They must choose.

•••

With his scholarship, Dr. Cobbs leans heavily on an understood social dynamic between two very human qualities: envy and scorn. Cobbs was first introduced to these terms, in the sports psychology context, by Dr. Andrei Markovits. He's the author of several seminal works on sport and society; his 2017 paper used envy and scorn to better understand rivalry in US college football culture, specifically. Yet the mother of all this scholarship is Princeton psychologist Dr. Susan Fiske, who doesn't mention sports fandom at all in her work. Even so, her pioneering research totally nails the root nuance beneath why and how we support our teams, in addition to why and how we so despise our arch enemies. "Comparison compels people, even as it stresses, depresses, and divides us," Fiske wrote in her 2010 paper, *Envy Up, Scorn Down: How Comparison Divides Us*.

> Comparison is only natural, but the collateral damage reveals envy upward and scorn downward, and these emotions, arguably, poison people and their relationships . . . If comparison contaminates, envy and scorn are worse, but for better reasons. Comparison at least can be adaptive, providing information and motivation, but the feelings that follow can be poisonous. Envy says, *I wish I had what you have*, but it implies, *And I wish you did not have it*. Scorn says, *You are unworthy of my attention, but I know you are down there somewhere*.[11]

Until I read Fiske, I had never heard the *clásico*, any *clásico*, so clearly explained and explored—using such familiar emotional goal posts.

For much of the twentieth century, Mexican football fans scorned US soccer as a rival unworthy of their attentions, while perhaps envying American affluence and influence. On the flip side, US soccer fans for many years envied Mexico's place in the larger futbol world: its national team prowess, its mature first division, its flamboyant, enthusiastic fan culture, its consistently gorgeous game jerseys. At the same time, the larger US culture was dismissive of the sport—a particularly ugly, peculiarly American affectation that drove Mexicans crazy with rage, especially once the USMNT started beating *El Tri* in the 1990s.

When we think of Michigan vs. Ohio State, or Red Sox vs. Yankees, this dueling combination of envy and scorn feels fairly typical. But it's highly unusual to find it on the international soccer front. "There's nothing that Spain envies about Portugal, nothing the Portuguese envy about Spanish culture," Markovits says. "With international rivalry, there is no envy. It's all scorn."

That Mexico vs. the United States *does* provoke so much envy and scorn, in both directions, is yet another reason this derby has grown into such a richly textured, utterly intense struggle. In this way, the *El Clásico Norteamericano* has what distinguished members of the world futbol pantheon—Spain-Portugal, Germany-Holland, Argentina-Brazil—simply do not.

While media and supporters produce and verbalize most of the envy and scorn, it's the national team players themselves who effectively embody and humanize this dynamic. Consider the path taken by María Guadalupe Sánchez Morales, born and raised in Nampa, Idaho, just west of Boise. She never played "premier" youth soccer, yet she flourished at the college level, which is when the FMF recruited her to play for Mexico. She has scored thirteen times for the country of her parents' birth. This choice may ultimately limit her World Cup fortunes, but not her professional livelihood. She joined the National Women's Soccer League's Chicago Red Stars in 2019, then switched to Chivas of Guadalajara in *Liga MX Femenil*, before returning to NWSL in 2024 with the San Diego Wave.

Striker Brandon Vasquéz was born and raised south of San Diego in Chula Vista, California. He trained as an academy prospect across the border with Club Tijuana, but he eventually built his goal-scoring credentials in Major League Soccer for F.C. Cincinnati. Also the child of first-generation Americans, the strapping Vasquéz formally committed to the Stars &Stripes before signing, in early 2024, with *Liga MX* giant Monterrey. A year later, he was back in MLS with Austin FC.

In 2026, every month without fail, a dozen more young A-listers—most of them Mexican Americans, all of them products of a futbol culture the United States shares with Mexico—make the same momentous choices. It's fitting that cutthroat competition for this transnational talent will continue right up through the shared World Cup, scheduled to run from June 11 through July 19, 2026.

The North American Derby has come a very long way since November 1980.

Awkwardly, the citizens of North America also share the burden of Donald Trump, whose re-election to the White House has the potential to grievously disrupt the world's biggest sporting event. At this writing, in May of 2025, the deportations and tariffs he soft-pedaled on the campaign trail continue to strain geopolitical relations between the United States and Mexico—between the United States and its other co-host, Canada. As early as January 2025, the *LA Times* was reporting on "mounting concern" at FIFA that the US government was "not ready to welcome the more than 6 million visitors who will flood North America" for the event. [12]

Say what you like about the president's emerging authoritarian track record, but his second administration, if nothing else, is better aligned today with the previous two tournament hosts (Qatar, Russia) and the one slated for 2034 (Saudi Arabia). An epic irony that is perhaps lost on FIFA. Or perhaps not.

2

Stuck with Each Other
Rivalry as Codependence

For much of the twentieth century, Mexican law did not sanction dual nationality. That changed in 1998, with an amendment to Article 37 in the country's Constitution. Futbol interests, of course, had little to do with this development. The federal government, then led by the Institutional Revolutionary Party (PRI), was more concerned with preserving and enhancing the flow of money that traditionally travels over the border, mainly north to south, among family members. Considering that an estimated 35 million Mexican Americans reside north of the border, that's no small amount of remittance. The legislation was also passed to encourage Mexicans living abroad to vote in domestic elections back "home"—to preserve, value, and participate in their Mexican identities, regardless of whether they've also adopted a US identity, citizenship, location, or lifestyle.[1]

This is a soccer book, but the reader may have noticed already that law, politics, and culture frequently intrude—adding all sorts of relevant spice and specificity. Today, the unflinching, speculative economics of modern futbol in North America push and pull players in *both* directions, north and south. Which brings us to Martín Vásquez, the Jalisco-born defensive midfielder who made three friendly appearances for the Mexican national team between 1990 and 1992, only to secure US citizenship and earn seven senior caps beginning in 1996.

In the twenty-first century, hundreds of youth national team members have competed at the U-17 level for one national team, only to sample the rival national team at the U-21 level. This maneuver is allowed and, in a strange way, encouraged by both federations. Once a player formally chooses a senior national team, the rules further allow him or her to petition FIFA and request a final, one-time change of nationality. By my reckoning, Vásquez was the first to perform this North American tribe-swap at the senior level.

However, his example—and all the succeeding examples—reflect a further, crucial wrinkle: namely, the extent to which US and Mexican soccer communities increasingly interact as separate-but-cooperative components of a single, continental futbol organism. This kinship comes into focus when we recognize how far from the actual border the organism operates. Jalisco, the western state that includes Guadalajara, is nowhere near the US border. Neither are Boise, Idaho, nor Santa Rosa, California. Nevertheless, Americans and Mexicans are always circling back to the border and the regions on either side. We can't help it. Folks want this shared ecosystem to *mean* something.

"People from the border region complain about that all the time. I don't think many of us understand the border. It's almost a separate country unto itself," says Amy Glover, the US-born CEO and cofounder of Agil(e), a strategic communications firm based in Mexico City. "I mean, Washington, D.C., doesn't understand the border. That's obvious. In Mexico City, most people don't understand it—make no *effort* to understand it, actually. It truly is a completely distinct culture, a dramatic meeting point that is distinct from both countries. And that's the thing that's hard, particularly for Americans: because the border develops their viewpoint of Mexico. But it's a very specific and limited viewpoint.

"Footballers have to play for one national team or the other," Glover points out, "but it's interesting to watch that evolve. More and more people, especially from that border region, have this dual identity today, which is particularly relevant from a sports perspective. And an economic perspective. And a political perspective."

These dualities, these movements through the border region and back again, have, for centuries, lent romance, mystery, and conflict to this shared real estate—what *yanquis* consider the Southwest, what Mexicans refer to as *El*

Norte; what certain ancestors dubbed *Nueva Espana*; what others call *Dinétah* (Navajo) or *ni'* (Apache, for both land and mind). For centuries, its only constant has been the kinetic ebb and flow of humanity, mainly northward and southward, over shifting boundaries formed and maintained by tribe, by politics, by military engagement, or business interests. Nonetheless, these divisions continue to be fudged or ignored by bloodlines, personal ambitions, agricultural cycles, wartime employment, and other capitalist realities.

In 2024, when border politics were white hot, more than 112,000 pedestrians and 272,000 personal vehicles, in addition to 16,000 goods-bearing trucks, legally crossed the US-Mexico border headed north every day of the week[2]—evidence that, come what may, folks on both sides are in this together. We've *always* been in it together, as siblings more or less, living on either side of a territory the majority of US citizens and Mexican citizens seem determined *not* to understand.

Top-notch footballers born in and around the border region—folks like striker Ricardo Pepi, who hails from El Paso, Texas; or USMNT teammate Alejandro Zendejas, born across the river in Ciudad Juarez—still face the same personal dilemma: to play, as Glover says, for one national team or the other. In 2026, these defining decisions are made by young athletes across the country. Such is the growing popularity of soccer in the United States. Such is the size and breadth of the Mexican American community here. So fierce is the contest for their services and allegiance.

While Martín Vásquez preceded him by nearly thirty years, Jonathan Gonzalez may have been the player who first crystallized this new, broader reality for fans in both countries. The attacking midfielder was born to Mexican nationals in 1999, six-hundred miles north of the border in Santa Rosa, California. He quickly matured into a sought-after product of the US national youth development system—until 2018, when he suddenly and rather surprisingly declared for *El Tri*. Today, after stints in both *Liga MX* and Major League Soccer, he plays his futbol in Ciudad Juarez, unofficial capital of the border region. He ended up making just three appearances for the Mexican National Team, the last in 2019.

Americans tend to think of human movement between cultures as exclusively north-going. The choices and subsequent careers of Gonzalez,

Pepi, Zendejas, and hundreds of others argue otherwise. After starting out in Major League Soccer, Pepi competes in the Netherlands for PSV Eindhoven. The diminutive Zendejas starts in midfield for Club América in *Liga MX*, where half a dozen US players join him.

When the parents of Jonathan Gonzalez went north, little did they know their son would end up in Juarez. Navigating the border is never simple or straightforward, and the professional stakes, the emotional stakes, the existential stakes have always proved impossibly high. The grandfather of *El Tri* legend Rafa Marquez went north in the 1960s—and never came back. His grandson has not yet forgiven him.[3]

•••

Parsing dual identities is a time-honored practice in world football because national eligibility standards have continually evolved since the 1920s. That's when the modern Olympic movement, then the World Cup tournament, started using citizenship to divide us up into teams. The rules governing such things? Fast, loose, and ever shifting. Residency matters, as does a "clear connection" to the country one wishes to represent. For much of the twentieth century, a single grandparent of Italian heritage was enough to make one eligible for the Italian national team, so far as FIFA was concerned.

Beginning in the 1930s, the US Soccer Federation (USSF) eagerly poached and handed out green cards to European, Mexican, and Central American natives—such was the scarcity of legit world-class players north of the border. Mexicans only rarely resorted to such roster-building. They were too proud to engage with US-born players in this fashion and, frankly, there wasn't much talent to poach. Through 2023, *La Selección* has fielded just fifteen naturalized players in its history.[4] Save two examples from the 1950s (Spaniard José López Herranz and Cuban-born Jorge Romo), these imports are largely a post-1998 phenomenon. Counted among the remaining thirteen: eight Argentinians, three Spaniards, two Brazilians, and zero Americans.

Today, however, the *Federación* and *Liga MX* clubs routinely raid Major League Soccer academies and other US Soccer Federation youth programs looking for potential transnational talent. One reason why: Article 37. Here's another reason: In 2004, FIFA ruled that dual nationals could compete, say, for the Mexican U-17 national team one month, then the US U-17s the next month. It's complicated. In 2026, such dual nationals might be first-second-or third-generation Mexican Americans.

France deals with a similar situation. Its population is loaded with the talented sons and daughters of first- and second-generation immigrants who have arrived from former colonies or holdings in Africa. Many elect to play for *Les Bleus*; others for Cameroon or the Ivory Coast. But here's the difference: France does not maintain a border, or a border rivalry with Mali, with Senegal, with Algeria or Madagascar. In fact, they play each other only sparingly.

After fifty years of competing sporadically, North America's sibling rivals now compete with each other constantly—for victories, for talent, for television ratings and dollars, for glory. These priorities can effectively mask all the examples of their mutual reliance, including player development and the creation of televised futbol content. There's nothing quite like these symbiotic relationships in international sport. In the end, they lift US vs. Mexico to the top echelons of world futbol. No two nations of this quality continually perform such a politically volatile, culturally complicated dance. No top-tier footballing adversaries play so frequently. These matches, their far-reaching implications, the envy and scorn demonstrated from both sides, the juicy narrative twists, the transfer of on-field talent back and forth: All these factors just keep accumulating over time.

"On purpose, we call these 10 elements *ingredients* because it's sort of like a recipe. You've got to have enough ingredients to make the rivalry work," explains Dr. Cobbs, who conducts his derby research in partnership with Dr. B. David Tyler of the University of Massachusetts at Amherst. Their findings, data, and surveys are available at knowrivalry.com. "If you just have one or two ingredients, a true rivalry is probably not going to develop. But once you layer on a third and fourth, now you've got enough of a narrative for one opponent to mean more than other opponents.

"One of our ingredients is the consistency of competition. If you have really low consistency of play—meaning, if the U.S. doesn't play Belgium very often—the consistency's just not there. As a result, I, as a fan, have a lesser sort of dissonance about cheering for both clubs. But if they start playing each other over and over, then they meet in a World Cup semifinal, or they're in the same group a couple times? Then a narrative with real conflict starts to develop. It's not a rivalry without conflict."

Other nations, more established futbol nations than Mexico and the United States, maintain top-class soccer rivalries. Think Germany vs. Holland, or Spain vs. Italy. In terms of championship implications, Argentina vs. Brazil puts the North American Derby to shame. They've won eight World Cups between them, for heaven's sake. Their decades of competition are littered with conflict. The two countries speak different languages and share a long border.

Still, that physical demarcation has never been so highly politicized or militarized as the one separating Mexico from the United States. Did we mention that NAFTA is up for renewal in 2026? Nearly 10 percent of the US population can claim Mexican heritage; neither Brazil nor Argentina share expatriate populations (or supply chains) on anything like this scale. More to Cobbs' last point: Today, in the Age of Messi, the two South American foes play each other only when they must—during World Cup qualifying, maybe in a *Copa América* setting. What's more, this indifference has prevailed since the heydays of Pelé and Garrincha, Kempes and Passarella.

World Cup titles matter. When those are at stake, they represent one hell of an ingredient. But they're quadrennial—up for grabs every fourth year. Do the French now enjoy a credible, vibrant *klassiker* with Argentina, in the wake of the 2022 final in Qatar? They may never play each other again. The truth is, frequency matters. Trade relations matter. Cultural interdependence, past military engagement, passion, language, borders, and politics: They all matter, too. Over the last ten years, Trumpism has pushed the American right to new heights of political hysteria on immigration issues, much of it aimed squarely at Mexicans in Mexico and Mexican Americans here in the States. You think that doesn't matter?

For all these continuous synergies and antagonisms, which combine to verge on codependence, today's *Clásico Norteamericano* is hard to beat.

"If it's about passion and intensity and excitement and pressure, I absolutely think U.S.-Mexico is no. 1 around the world," former USMNTer Alexi Lalas told his podcast audience in March 2024. "Whether it's about language, or whether it's about our politics—where each and every day there is some public, controversial political reference made toward Mexico, and *vice versa* .

.. Whether it's our culture: entertainment, music, movies and food. And then obviously, when it comes to the matches themselves. It's subjective, of course, but I'm going with U.S.-Mexico." [5]

Lalas mentioned pressure, and that's revealing of his perspective as a former player. American national team members deal with a typical amount of media and fan pressure to win, to qualify for World Cups, and to impress on the biggest stage. Mexican national team players? They deal with enough for three or four national teams.

"There is no national team that is under more pressure, regardless of the situation, than Mexico, especially when the opponent is the U.S.," Stars & Stripes alum Herculez Gomez said on the *Futbol Asada* podcast in March 2025,[6] ahead of the Nations League semifinals.

"I can tell you from personal experience, from playing in the Mexican league, from playing against the Mexican national team. It's what rules their world. The pressure revolves around those guys 24/7. It's relentless—whether you're coming off a big win or have not won in forever . . . We could say Mauricio Pochettino comes in and, you know, it's the first time the U.S. has ever had a manager of that caliber, and that's a certain type of pressure. But regardless of the state of the Mexican national team: no players, no national team, no entity deals with that type of pressure. Not in CONCACAF. And it's not even close."

•••

When studying the matches *El Tri* and the United States have contested since 1991, it's clear that Mexican fans and especially the press have been reluctant to use the word *clásico*. They were not prepared to honor this particular opponent with this ceremonial, almost solemn term—not before 2002. Many Mexicans feel much the same way today, in 2026, on the eve of hosting a World Cup alongside their continental cousins. At the same time, Mexican Americans specifically have bought into our shared soccer community. They want it to succeed and have already played a key role in its modern success.

For the record, don't be thrown by the accent above the "a" in *clásico*, or anywhere else in these pages. In written Spanish, that simple grammatical cue merely tells the reader which syllable to emphasize. The word futbol often has one over the "u," but this particular term and this spelling have been adopted and altered by so many languages and cultures that we use it here unadorned.

What's more, on the subject of cross-cultural soccer vocabulary: Mexicans and most Spanish speakers use the word "revenge" a bit differently—with less malice than English speakers. Here's an oft-cited phrase: *El fútbol siempre da revanche.* "Soccer always allows for revenge." In English, "revenge" means something visceral and menacing. Not so in Spanish, in the athletic context, where it can mean a simple rematch, including an opportunity for redemption.

Soccer is littered with these foreign-language terminologies. It is the world game, after all, the most popular sport on Earth. We don't shy away from Spanish-language terms in this book. They lend even more spice and specificity. For much of the twentieth century, however, scholars of American sport argued that the popularity of soccer abroad—indeed, the popularity of futbol among Mexican expatriates and dozens more immigrant populations living in the United States—had damaged or delayed the game's American acceptance and integration. From the close of the Second World War through the 1980s, soccer in the United States was considered, and broadly derided as, a "foreign" sport invented and played primarily by "foreigners."[7]

"I remember playing Mexico one time in the Santa Ana Bowl," remembers California native Paul Krumpe, who debuted for the US national team in 1986. "I had my whole family there, and my wife's family had not seen a lot of soccer. They were completely surrounded by Mexican fans! The only other time I played Mexico was at the Coliseum in Los Angeles. Again, 60,000 people there, and 55,000 were cheering for Mexico. That's what U.S. Soccer did at the time because they needed to sell tickets."

The US Soccer establishment eventually learned not to trade home-field advantage for gate receipts. It took the entirety of the 1990s to figure that out, but ultimately the actions of Mexican American fans forced the Federation's hand. Were it not for all these US-based fans of *El Tri*, the USMNT would not have moved qualifiers to places like Columbus, Ohio. And without Columbus, there is no *Dos a Cero!*

Over and over again, Mexican American fan culture, now fully integrated into US soccer culture, has moved our shared soccer community forward. Here's more of what I mean: Before MLS started streaming most of its games via Apple TV in 2023, league broadcasts on the Spanish-language network Univision routinely posted better Nielsen ratings than those on English-language ESPN or the Fox cable outlet, FS1. Translation? Spanish-speaking US residents support soccer on TV in prodigious numbers, no matter who's playing. And no entity benefited more from this demographic fact than Major League Soccer.

Notably, in August of 2023, MLS first staged a month-long tournament in partnership with *Liga MX*, the Mexican first division that replaced the 70-year-old Mexican *Priméra* in 2013. During the inaugural "Leagues Cup," US-based supporters of Mexican clubs showed they would travel hundreds of miles to support their favorite *club* teams, not just the national team. When Club América played a thrilling knockout match at Nashville FC, *Américanistas* from across the Mid-South sold out the city's 30,000-seat Geodis Park. There to welcome them in the parking lot with a spatula in one hand and a Modelo in the other? *La Brigada De Oro* ("The Gold Brigade"), the host club's original Latin American supporters group, formed in 2019.

Based on total attendance, Major League Soccer today ranks sixth among the largest leagues in world futbol.[8] Impressive. But MLS truly shines in the realm of fan culture, on display at venues from Atlanta to Los Angeles, by way of Austin, Charlotte, Seattle, and Salt Lake City. A great deal of the rockin', feel-good atmosphere is borrowed (like so many MLS club names) from European football culture: the scarves, the singing, the kvetching ("Berhalter Out!") minus the right-wing hooliganism. At the same time, these vital, viral strains of US fan culture owe an equal amount to the high bar and shared experience that Mexican American supporters have helped create. Not the harassing of opposing goaltenders with homophobic slurs, or raining bags of urine down on opposing fans. (We'll get to all that.) But rather, engaging in creative futbol cosplay, and working that portable grill in the parking lot.

"As soccer grows in the USA, the Mexican American community has embraced tailgating. By adopting the tailgating tradition, Mexicans are going through the acculturation process:[9] they are adopting beliefs and traditions of a culture different from their native or ethnic culture," wrote Roxane Coche and Oscar Guerra, two contributors to *Perspectives on the US-Mexico Rivalry:*

Passion and Politics in Red, White, Blue & Green, a 2016 collection of essays edited by Jeffrey Kassing and Lindsey Meân.

"People experience a two-fold process of social and cultural adaptation when migrating to a foreign culture. They adopt beliefs and behaviors of the new culture, which is known as *acculturation*—and they evolve in their native cultural group, a process known as *enculturation*. Acculturation and enculturation happen over time through various cultural experiences, including sport, which can greatly influence interactions between communities."

•••

Meet Gabriel, a Mexican American buttonholed by Coche and Guerra outside the Rose Bowl at a derby clash in 2015. According to Gabriel, tailgating at US-Mexico matches requires routine culinary code-switching—and diplomacy. "Well, I'm doing *carne asada* and some of the other guys are going to do hamburgers and hot dogs—and I don't agree with that," he reported. "This is a *Mexican* tailgate, so we are going to have tacos! But hey, we're in the USA so I guess we have to deal!" [10]

This writer can speak to similar thought processes. I spent much of the 1980s and 1990s seeking out satellite-delivered soccer programming in ethnic eating and drinking establishments from coast to coast. Because there was next to no futbol on American television. When the United States competed at the 1995 *Copa América*, down in Uruguay—where they beat *El Tri* in a bruising, derby-boosting quarterfinal—I watched the slugfest inside a Mexican restaurant just north of Boston in Somerville, Massachusetts. US-based soccer fans did much of the code-switching back then. We had to be creative and tactful. When the newly emboldened Yanks eliminated their sibling rival from the *Copa*, via penalty shootout, I respectfully thanked the proprietor, paid my bill, tipped big, and got the hell out of there.

In his 2024 master's thesis, "*Existimos porque resistimos*: Navigating identity through soccer as a Chicanx in Southern California," Erick Calderon argues that Mexican American fans purposely walk a far more complicated path:

> Choosing the Mexican national soccer team is a yearning [for] ethnic attachment, rather than a coup attempt to dismantle American culture.

Existimos porque resistimos ("We exist because we resist") is a statement to that truth and an indicator of how important sports are to a community who has been historically oppressed and marginalized. Soccer is central to the construction of the identity of Mexican Americans and has provided a window in which we can further explore the ever-changing dynamics to that identity. [11]

In a melting pot, the desire to maintain cultural ties with the "old country" is commonplace, and every individual negotiates the matter differently. "A number of Mexican Americans feel deprived of a genuine connection to their Latin American past, to their heritage, and to their ancestors and therefore become fixated in becoming accepted to their diaspora," argues Calderon, who teaches in the Ethnic Studies Department at Shasta College in Redding, California. "That and the marginalization they encounter that further make them feel like 'others', are pull factors . . . in efforts to keep their ethnic attachment."

In the main, Mexican Americans grow up in families that form a specific US subculture, one that prepares them to follow futbol *and* support the Mexican national team. New generations may support the USMNT with increasing enthusiasm. Others may hold to their heritage and support *El Tri*. Either way, the existence of Mexican Americans has assisted the larger, shared US soccer culture to grow and establish its own shared identity.

The process has taken time. Broadly speaking, American futbol during the 1990s remained a minor sporting concern. Major League Soccer, born in 1996, did not offer up a decent on-field product until 2010. Yankee television networks, unlike Televisa and Univision, didn't yet understand how to make money broadcasting the game—not without commercial interruptions.

Most relevant, futbol is a game greatly enhanced by its international components: *amistosos*, or friendly exhibitions; regional championships like the Gold Cup and *Copa América*; the regional rivalries used to qualify for those tournaments, including the ultimate object of all these national teams, passage to and participation in the FIFA World Cup.

Unfortunately, and true to this day, there exist precious few international elements to American team sports. As a result, outside of US vs. Mexico, there isn't a single American comp for this sort of long-term, international derby. Consider the rivalry comps that *do* exist in our sporting consciousness: Giants and Dodgers, Packers and Bears, Celtics and Lakers. These timeless sporting feuds are very good fun, but they are contests between domestic cities, regions, and fan bases. There is no US vs. Cuba *clásico*, for example; no rivalry with Japan, not in baseball—our national pastime. Ditto for American football, the most popular US sport. No one outside our borders, other than a few thousand Canadians, even plays the game.

Beginning in the 1990s, the men's and women's national teams—aided by millions of Mexican Americans—have slowly but surely taught US citizens how international team sports function. These efforts have shown us how fabulously entertaining such spectacles can be. And, how freakin' gripping the resulting rivalries can become. The novelties still attached to these competitions, in the United States, play to futbol's advantage: Americans today follow their national futbol teams with special vigor and enthusiasm, precisely because they are the only sporting outlets for our not-insignificant nationalism.

•••

Let's not forget: This evolution took time. American sports fans spent most of the 1990s discovering how the World Cup and the US-Mexico derby *worked*. How nation vs. nation competition worked.

By contrast, the months leading up to the 2002 World Cup were among the most successful and promising in the history of Mexico's national team. In the summer of 1999, *El Tri* appeared to have answered all outstanding questions as to who, in fact, was the giant of CONCACAF. "Nineteen ninety-nine was an important year because the Confederations Cup was played in Mexico," central defender Rafa Marquez said, in 2021.[12] "The tournament being here in Mexico, we felt obligated to win." And they did win.

The Confederations Cup is the second most prestigious tournament administered by FIFA. Its unique field includes the host nation, the World Cup holders, and the six reigning continental champions. *Estados Unidos*, qualifying as 1999 Gold Cup winners, eventually met host Mexico in the semifinal. "We could never allow the U.S. to win at the Azteca," recalls the ever-blunt Alberto

García Aspe, speaking in 2021. "To this day, the U.S. cannot and should not win there. Because Mexico has to be the favorite at home. That was very clear to us [in 1999], but it wasn't easy." [13]

A gritty, scoreless draw finally turned when mercurial striker Cuauhtémoc Blanco scored the only goal—in sudden-death overtime (what world football has insisted on calling a "golden goal" in "added extra time"). Back in that moment, the victory appeared to have quelled all south-lying anxieties relating to US vs. Mexico. Yes, the Americans were a vastly improved opponent. But they clearly lacked the skill and pedigree to play with *El Tri* in the big moments. Here was the proof.

The Mexican victory netted the hosts something else, too: a major tournament final, on home soil, against exactly the sort of derby company Mexicans have always dreamed of keeping. Mighty Brazil. Now *there* was a side worthy of Mexico's competitive aspirations, an adversary that had finished runner-up to France at the 1998 World Cup, just the summer before—a side that would win it all four years later in Japan and South Korea.

Here we should acknowledge a subtle but important segmentation among *La Selección* supporters: Those who reside in Mexico itself tend to fret most about how their national team measures up with the likes of Brazil, Argentina, and European powers. Mexican Americans care deeply about these leading lights as well, but they are equally concerned with supporting *El Tri* as a means of reconnecting with their own heritage—and beating the United States. For this expatriate community, defeating the United States, anywhere north of the border especially, presses emotional buttons that folks in Mexico City cannot quite imagine.

Against the vaunted *Selecao* in the 1999 Confederation Cup final, Blanco yet again accounted for the deciding goal, crowning a singularly impressive 4-3 performance before more than 100,000 inside the mystical confines of *Estadio Azteca*. This result—so stylish, so impassioned, so obviously world class—thrilled all Mexicans, at home and abroad. The victory changed the way Mexicans thought about Blanco, who went from "mercurial" to "talismanic." For one brief shining moment, it also changed Mexico's self-image as a footballing nation. "It's an important title for the national team," Marquez said. "The most important one so far."

Twenty-three months later, playing under Javier Aguirre, *El Tricolor* went out and nearly won the 2001 *Copa América*, falling to host Colombia in the final. Aguirre's side would have been the first from outside South America ever to win world soccer's oldest international trophy.

Mexican futbol had never ridden quite so high. The United States and Mexico would always be regional rivals—trapped together in CONCACAF, where opportunities to test themselves against hemispheric titans were sadly rare. But only one side was capable of winning trophies. This much was clear and obvious to Mexican partisans early in the summer of 2002. "All the dedication and devotion of the Mexican fans had been awakened by that team," recalls Marion Reimers, a Spanish-language journalist and football commentator for TNT Sports.

As another World Cup loomed, Marquez—already the face of Mexican soccer (today the national team's *Mister* in waiting)—prepared to join F.C. Barcelona, the biggest, glitziest club on the planet. *Dos a Cero!*, that ultimate rejoinder to all those intimidating pro-Mexican crowds on US soil, was not yet a thing. Following a typically grueling World Cup qualifying process, wherein the two national teams traded home victories, *El Tri* and the USMNT each advanced to Japan and Korea.

The idea that these adversaries would meet there, as part of the planet's biggest, richest, most prestigious sporting event? Not on anyone's radar. According to Landon Donovan, that's just not how the World Cup generally works. "It is entirely possible," the California native told Grant Wahl in 2021, "that for the next 50, 100, 200, 300, 500, 1000 years, we don't play Mexico again in the World Cup." [14]

●●●

Donovan's appreciation of the North American Derby extends well beyond these century-long odds. Not because he played internationals against Mexico nineteen times, but because his childhood was spent marinating in the multicultural, bilingual influences that dominate futbol life in the border region. He was raised in Redlands, "Where people who can't afford to live in L.A. go," he asserted in 2021. His mom was a teacher, his dad an electrician—a hockey player, born in Canada. "My parents, neither of them made a lot money. We lived well but, by American standards, we grew up quite poor." In this way, he was more like the Hispanic kids he competed with and against growing up, not the wealthier, whiter suburbanites who still dominate premier club systems in Southern California and across the country.[15]

By the time Donovan's speed and field vision started turning heads—first as a member of Cal Heat, a youth club based in Rancho Cucamonga; then as a 15-year-old member of the US Olympic Development Program—he was fluent in Spanish. "I grew up an hour and a half from the border. I know that culture . . . When I started playing club soccer, our team was predominantly white but all the teams we played that were very good? They were all Hispanic. When I started to play, my attitude was, *These are the kids I want to play with. They're good. They know how to move and pass.* They were a big influence on me."

At every critical stage, Donovan's futbol fortunes would intersect with those of Mexicans. At the 1999 U-17 World Cup in New Zealand, where his American squad defeated *El Tri* 3-2 in the quarterfinals . . . On the occasion of his senior USMNT debut, in 2000, when he came on to score and secure a friendly *dos a cero* at the L.A. Coliseum . . . In every World Cup qualification campaign and Gold Cup tournament contested from 2001 to 2013.

These bouts with Mexico framed his entire international career.

So far as his opponents were concerned, Donovan often played the villain. Why? Because he scored goals. He converted six times in the senior Derby. No one from either side has scored more. In 2004, prior to an Olympic qualifier in Guadalajara, he relieved himself in a pitch-side shrub—the Mexican media horde never let him forget it. And yet, that same press corps knew they could also come to this baby-faced assassin for a thoughtful comment. Here was a *gringo* who understood Mexicans because he *understood* them in their native tongue. As a Californian, Donovan had also puzzled out the nuance inherent to bigger pictures. "For me the border is really interesting because you're literally saying to people, you're not welcome here," he told Wahl. "And by the way, it does not go both ways. Americans going into Mexico? Yeah, no problem."

There are moments for this brand of civilian reflection. And there are moments for cutthroat confrontation, when ranks must be closed. In June of 2002, as World Cup group play drew to a close, "It was like, *Oh wait, we could* play Mexico. Then it was, *Oh fuck yeah—we're playing Mexico. We're going to war, man . . . It felt like we were going to war.*" 16

• • •

The United States didn't just defeat Mexico in the Round of 16 match in South Korea—by the now-familiar score of *Dos a Cero!*, thereby advancing to a quarterfinal against Germany. The American victory traumatized an entire nation.

The 90 minutes themselves, staged in the provincial capital of Jeonju, were predictably unpredictable and fiercely contested. The unfancied Americans scored early through striker Brian McBride, and *El Tri* did not respond like a team that believed it had joined world futbol's best and brightest. As their plucky opponents grew in confidence, the Mexicans withdrew.

Mexican manager Javier Aguirre didn't help matters. He subbed off midfielder Ramon Morales before halftime—opting for the more attack-minded Luis Hernandez and a new formation, featuring three strikers. When a futbol manager makes *any* sort of substitution before the interval, one that isn't occasioned by injury or a hail of conceded goals, it's a tacit admission that he got the tactics wrong.

"I think we crushed them psychologically—that they were making a tactical change in the first half," US manager Bruce Arena told the press afterward. Marquez more or less agreed: "That substitution made by Javier surprised us all," he recalled in 2021. "It was so premature."17

Luis Hernandez himself articulated, to Wahl in 2021, exactly how damaging the substitution proved within the team, in the moment: "I questioned him [Aguirre]: 'You're wrong to take out Ramon. Take out a central midfielder instead. He should be sacrificed.' But he was blinded because he planned out the game badly." 18

Donovan would pot the second goal shortly after halftime, and the match transitioned to meltdown stage. Not like an ice cream cone. More like a nuclear reactor. Embarrassed and desperate, the Mexicans lashed out at their rivals physically, as often happens when expectations drastically outpace performance. Even the imperious, impeccably behaved Marquez lost his shit in a spasm of shame, helplessness, and despair. He was red-carded in the 88th minute for a studs-up headbutting of US midfielder Cobi Jones. British match announcer John Helm called it "a dangerous and cowardly challenge."

"It was dispiriting to go down 2-0. They hurt us and they did it easily," Marquez remembers. "We tried to slow down the opponent by being more aggressive, because we weren't playing well. You start to think about what everyone will say. That we're failures—who lost to our neighbors . . . As they rightly say, I lost my mind."

That sending-off, those 90 minutes, this next Round of 16 dismissal, against this specific foe, before a worldwide audience: Taken together, these happenings produced a pivotal moment in the footballing association that Mexico shares with the United States. For a little more than a decade, the two national teams had sparred more or less as equals in tournament play on this continent and around the world. But the Mexican futbol community willfully, even blindly, refused to acknowledge this parity. Only the players went there, very quietly and indirectly.

This result changed everything, and there was no going back.

• • •

Brothers in a family may squabble or grow covetous of rank, material possessions, or affections within a household. But they do not effectively compete until they grow to be developmental or physical equals. Here, the family dynamics of rivalry are universal and unbending—until they do bend, and perhaps rupture, in the face of cold, hard truths. (Whereupon all hell often breaks loose.)

For most of the twentieth century, the soccer relationship between the United States and Mexico was not a rivalry at all. In pointed contrast to the cultural, military, and economic hierarchies recognized by each country, the Mexican national team didn't just play the role of footballing Big Brother. Mexican players and fans *fetishized* their domination of the United States, their richer, more populous, frequently overbearing neighbor to the north.

The above might sound like psychobabble, but any of us raised with brothers and sisters will recognize this emotional framework. On June 17, 2002, Little Brother established himself as an equal in the most public and convincing way possible. The USMNT moved the ground beneath everyone's feet, shattering

Mexico's self-image and seeding the field for a new, co-equal *status quo*, a derby more fierce and more passionate than anyone could have imagined in 1991 or 1980.

For many in the US futbol community, the scale and peculiar emotion of an international *clásico* registered for the very first time. They found it exhilarating.

In Mexico, where world futbol derbies were well understood, the after-effects proved nothing less than seismic.

"It was a slap in the face for Mexico," recalls Argentinian play-by-play legend Andrés Cantor, perhaps the most recognizable soccer voice in the Western Hemisphere. Cantor has called a dozen World Cups, but he's also worked hundreds of Mexican league and national team matches since the early 1990s. "Every time Mexico loses to somebody that they deem inferior to them, it's a tragedy. They're stuck, because of the pressure to always perform and beat teams that are now catching up to them. That is the reality."[19]

Here Cantor refers not merely to the national team itself and the *Federación* that administers *El Tri*. He's also referring to the Mexican press, to the fans, to the entire futbol culture. Waking up the morning of June 18, 2002, Mexican sportswriter Martín del Palacio could not have agreed more.

"It has been a long time since I was so depressed," he wrote in *La Afición*.[20]

> The sadness of June 17th . . . will be hard to forget for quite some time. Mexico lost to the United States. An entire country, that awaited with eagerness the result, lived with bitterness the replaying of our ancestral defeats . . . It was a catastrophe, and the people are living it as such. It is eight thirty in the morning and I have not yet gone outside but I already have the faces of the people carved in my mind . . . During four years we will remember with a hole in our stomachs and a knot in our throats yesterday's tragedy. But the history of football is also cyclical and we will have a lot of time for revenge.

There's more going on here than mere despair. Mexican futbol history reveals an underlying, long-term anxiety related to June 17, 2002: the base fear of being found out. It's one thing to lose to the United States, the Old Enemy, in the one arena where untouchability had been claimed. But such a public beating potentially revealed *La Madre Patria* as something else: a fraud, a sovereign nation bestriding very little, not even the modest confederation known as CONCACAF.

There's a famous, perhaps apocryphal saying adopted by many Mexican fans following losses. It's attributed to legendary striker Alfredo Di Stéfano, an Argentine who paired with another godlike figure, Hungarian Ferenc Puskás, to pioneer the *Galacticos* tradition at Real Madrid. Though it's supposed to have come from the irresistible Di Stéfano, his quip is burdened by grim resignation: *Jugamos como nunca y perdimos como siempre*—"We played better than ever and lost same as always."

Call me crazy, but that just doesn't sound like a fan who believes his team is The Giant of CONCACAF. The historical record actually reveals something very different: a regional soccer brand built largely on twentieth century bullying of the United States. (We'll get to all that, as well.) A cynic might well ask: Once that out-of-date credential is removed, what is left?

The day after the day after, *La Afición* writer Xavier Velasco offered up an answer: "There are some things that cannot happen to us. Not because they are not possible, but because we are in no way willing to permit them to happen," he wrote, under the forbidding-but-delectable headline, *Remember the Alamo*.

> That is, if they were to occur, they would cover us with disgrace, making our faces grim perhaps forever. And even if the entire world was not aware of this suffering, our ego would live for years diminished before the black memory of that inadmissible embarrassment. Evidently, all this perspective does not reflect with precision the deep prostration that would take hold of the national ego if it were, disastrously, precisely the *Gringos* who knocked us out of the World Cup.[21]

Mexico's South Korean exit was no mere embarrassment. It was a dark and sober reckoning, resulting from public humiliation.

But here's the thing: Shock and distress can precipitate great change. And each is pretty great fodder for upping the ante on arch enemies.

●●●

The trauma of loss has frequently altered the course of national sporting destinies. In the realm of world soccer, such cataclysm—magnified by the unyielding dynamics of long-term envy and scorn—can ultimately etch those new realities in stone.

Our best example in the worldwide footballing context might be the proprietary way the English looked upon soccer played outside its borders through the Second World War. They had skipped the first three World Cups, scornfully judging the rest of the world unfit to compete with Mother England in a game she had invented. This condescension started to fizzle out prior to the first Brazilian World Cup, in 1950. First, the English Football Association agreed to send a team. But then, in far-away Belo Horizonte: Yikes! An inexplicable 1-0 defeat to the lowly Americans—and a failure to advance from group play. When the immortal Puskás and his high-flying Hungarians visited Wembley Stadium in November 1953, and ran their hosts off the park, 6-3, the sum total of indignities proved more than the British sporting psyche could bear. Magically, their scorn lifted. The English were all in on international football.

American indifference toward Olympic team competitions fell away in a very similar fashion, early in the 1990s. A bronze medal in men's basketball at the 1988 Seoul Games—not the gold medal Yanks consider their hoop birthright—had convinced USA Basketball and the NBA that only the nation's best professionals should compete at world championships and Olympic Games. Not college kids. As it happened, the formation of the so-called Dream Team prior to the 1992 Barcelona Olympiad didn't just recapture gold. The spectacle captivated our sporting public.

So it was with Mexico and its footballing struggle with the United States. Until *El Tri* had suffered such a jolting defeat in the glare of a World Cup, the nation could not and would not consider the Americans a worthy, primary rival. The result on June 17, 2002, flipped the script.

"That doesn't make Mexicans hypocritical," Reimers told me, "but it is interesting to me that when you talk about European rivals, in futbol, the big rivals are those who can *beat* you. That's what *makes* them a rival."

Players have always understood this basic truth, even if fan and media cohorts might resist it. First-rate athletes recognize and deal with these situations routinely, from the earliest days of their careers. But supporters? Journalists? Not so much. Their indomitability is largely a pose, a conceit, a rallying cry, a performance whose sheer momentum can carry it forward for decades.

Professional footballers understand something else: The emotional logic of rivalry produces perfectly reasonable anxieties. But these are fears that only geek up a previously humbled opponent to turn the tables—to humble their rivals in turn. Because, as we know, *Futbol always provides for revenge.*

"What I'm going to say might sound like a betrayal to many. Because honestly, we will never *say* that we're equals," Reimers admits. "But the truth is that the U.S. has grown a lot. And I believe that it has kept Mexico on its toes. The distances are shorter. Mexico really needs to get its game up. Not only in terms of the sport as such, in terms of results, but also in terms of infrastructure growth and understanding a global and younger audience."

Make no mistake: In 2026, the US Men's National Team also harbors aspirations beside and beyond beating Mexico. Its own Federation desperately wants to compete with established soccer nations, too, especially those from Europe. Gregg Berhalter's side went seven games unbeaten vs. *El Tri* (five wins, two draws) between 2021 and 2024. That's Younger Brother's best-ever run in The Derby, and there was a time when that sort of success would have meant indefinite job security for an American head coach. In 2024, however, his failures versus futbol's upper tiers got him fired. In fact, Berhalter's side beat just one world-top-20 opponent during his 5-year tenure, *Estados Unidos Mexicanos.*

At the same time, US-Mexico has evolved into much more than a series of national team games. Today, MLS and *Liga MX*—the entities that produce and polish talent for both national teams—compete for eyeballs and television ratings on the same networks. In the Leagues Cup, they compete as straight-up partners. Every day of the year, the two federations cross swords to sign the hottest, most promising young talent. Controversially, *La Selección* continues to play most of its international friendlies in the United States. It's a revenue stream the FMF and the merged entity TelevisaUnivision (TUDN, est. 2022) cannot resist.

World Cup 2026 will be co-hosted by Mexico and the United States, along with up-and-coming Canada, an arrangement that *has* quietly encroached on the binary nature of the continent's top derby. Precocious Kid Brother plays under a talented and outspoken American coach, Jesse Marsch, who has forcefully supported the idea that fifty United States are more than enough.

Still, it's difficult to see how US vs. Mexico will ever be diminished by third wheels. Mexico's stubborn stance—never outwardly acknowledging the United States as an on-field peer—does nothing but elevate and intensify the household joust. Each post-Jeonju encounter has grown increasingly fraught with heat and consequence, triumphalism and tragedy. And the politics? As recently as 2006, George W. Bush had courted Mexican Americans in search of a so-called permanent Republican majority. It feels like ancient history. By 2009, the Tea Party happened. Then Donald Trump happened, seeking votes by hurling politically expedient, quite scurrilous accusations at his neighbors to the south—to say nothing of the 50 million Latinos living in his own country. Since 2016, border relations between these two NAFTA partners have grown steadily more nativist and politically hysterical.

Bad for geopolitical détente.

Pure gold for this eternal, ever-escalating athletic confrontation.

Even as both countries aspire to bigger, more glittering international things, the narrow nature of Mexican sporting obsessions, to say nothing of geography, guarantees the North American *Clásico* will remain radioactive. By the same token, when I asked Professor Cobbs what meaningful international rivalries the United States maintains outside of soccer, he was blunt: "I really don't think we have any. I mean, the closest would be Canada, in ice hockey."

In other words, like brothers and sisters in a sprawling continental family, by turns dysfunctional and intimate, we need each other. And we're stuck with each other.

3

A Friendly Meditation

Fear, Loathing, and Argie Worship in The GDL

The main road to *Estadio Akron* leads north and west out of central Guadalajara to the suburbs. The annual mid-October procession honoring Our Lady of Zapopan follows roughly the same path, beginning near dawn at the Cathedral of Guadalajara and concluding five hours later at Our Lady's famous Basilica. In 2024, this feast day—which annually attracts 2 million adherents along the cortège route—coincided with the Mexican national team's first visit in a generation. Just three days after the parade, 50,000 faithful followers of *El Tricolor* headed north, then west, to mark the 78th renewal of Mexico vs. United States.

I was determined to be there, to experience the final scheduled clash of sibling rivals prior to the World Cup, the one they'd be hosting. Together.

All the pageantry associated with the North American Derby had been very much expected. But a feast day devoted to *La Reina y Madre de Jalisco*? That's what we call *gravy*.

My foursome had arrived the night before in time to find the first of several spectacular restaurants in the city's leafy, upscale Americana district. Our Lady's parade route cut directly through our *colonia*, or neighborhood, that Saturday morning before the Tuesday-evening match. I grew up in Greater Boston where such feast-day events were annual fixtures in the decidedly

Italian and Catholic North End. Still, it's borderline miraculous to wake up in one's Airbnb to discover thousands gathered along the boulevard outside, applauding and taking the morning sun, while 30,000 dancers and dignitaries escort a small statue through the streets.

Three days later, during the Uber drive to *Estadio Akron*, it only *seemed* as though there were 2 million Mexicans on the road to Zapopan. Outside the stadium, at the pre-match presser, in the restaurants and bars, a peculiar malaise had noticeably settled over the country's third largest metropolitan area, complicating the vibes ahead of the *clásico*. *El Tri* had not beaten the *gringos* in seven consecutive meetings—Mexico's longest drought in the duel's 90-year history. Futbol will always provide for revenge, and this next meeting was a home game. However, while the match had sold out in three hours, the crowd's nervous anticipation felt tinged with another, more pointed resentment: The national team had not appeared in Guadalajara since 2010.

Walking through the random maze of tailgaters outside the Akron, few whiffs of indignation could be readily identified. Only the succulent smell of *carne asada* on portable grills. Mexican futbol tailgates would be perfectly recognizable to most US citizens, though I did notice a multitude of RVs: a sign of folks who had come a great distance and planned on reveling until morning.

The tailgating urge is fairly bulletproof, but the natives here were clearly restless. *El Tricolor* manager Jaime "Jimmy" Lozano had just been fired for his insupportable transgressions: another loss to the Yanks (a Nations League semifinal in Spring 2024) followed by an impotent showing during the summer's *Copa América*. The FMF replaced him with Javier Aguirre, a Basque whose heritage explains his nickname, *El Vasco*. His third stint with the national team had not started well. A thumping of harmless New Zealand had been followed by a scoreless draw with rising CONCACAF power Canada.

In Puebla, two days prior to the US match, Spanish club Valencia, sitting 18th in the *La Liga* table, had been strategically lined up to give *El Tri* and the new coach a confidence-building result. Instead, Mexico fell behind 2–0 and struggled to salvage a 2–2 draw. The local press erupted in volcanic howls of indignation.

Traipsing about in the GDL, I learned that dissatisfaction with *La Selección* here is more nuanced, more personal than what one might read in the papers.

For much of the twentieth century, Guadalajara stood as Mexico's second city, a futbol-mad region that was home to Club Deportivo Guadalajara, better known as Chivas, "the Goats." Chivas is the only outfit that vies with Club América in terms of national profile and following. This western metropolis, 7 hours' drive from the capital, is also home to plucky cross-town club Atlas, the city's first *Priméra*-winning side (1951). Atlas is known nationwide as "The Academy," for having developed modern legends like Rafa Márquez, Jared Borgetti, Pável Pardo, and Oswaldo Sánchez. On the night we showed up, the Mexican Federation feted the pending retirement of long-serving *El Tri* midfielder Andrés Guardado, another Atlas graduate.

Monterrey recently supplanted the GDL in terms of population, but this is no backwater. Greater Guadalajara is home to 5 million *tapatíos*. It will host four World Cup games come 2026, including Mexico's second group match.

However, since a disappointing 1–2 loss to Ecuador in 2010, the *Federación* had not returned to Jalisco State. It saw fit instead to stage friendlies in less prominent cities such as Torreón and Querétaro (2011), Tuxtla Gutiérrez (2014), Toluca (2015), the Monterrey suburb of San Nicolás de los Garza (2018), and Mazatlán (2023).[1] Imagine if the US Women's National Team did not play in L.A. or Chicago for fifteen years. The public would perceive that as a slight. In fact, the only reason the FMF had delivered *El Tri* to *Estadio Akron* in October 2024? The Azteca was undergoing pre-World Cup renovations.

At first glance, *Estadio Azteca* in Mexico City makes perfect sense for World Cup qualifiers and friendlies, especially vs. the United States. For supercharged fixtures like these, why mess with success? The United States has won there just once. Ever.

The bigger picture is more thorny. Guadalajarans and fans across the country recognize that *La Selección* and the FMF had long ago forsaken much of Mexico. The national team has played 172 friendlies since 2005; 124 of those have been staged in the United States (!). In the nineteen years Guardado represented his country, *El Principito* played just twice in his hometown. Over the same stretch, *El Tri* played thirteen times in Arlington, Texas, and ten times in Glendale, Arizona.[2] Where Mexican American supporters pay in US dollars.

The FMF and its broadcast partners maintain a party line on this arrangement: They argue that it's a way to reconnect expats with their native country—clearly a priority for the Mexican government since amending the Constitution in 1998. Be that as it may, this stance comes off to many Mexicans as a front for simple economic exploitation, enabled by first ignoring fans in Mexico itself.

Aguirre is a good soldier, enlisted by the *Federación* to right a listing ship. On this issue, speaking to the media ahead of the October 2024 friendly, he walked a fine line: "Mexico wants to see its national team. It's been years since we came to Guadalajara. It had been a while since we played in Puebla. Morelia asked us to go there. León, Juárez . . . They want to see their national team."

Before the game, I made a point to tip a few beers with members of the American Outlaws, the official US Soccer fan group. These guys show up. They support the Stars & Stripes wherever they may play. But this was their first visit to Guadalajara, too. We met up in a faux British watering hole called the York Pub, on Avenida Chapultepec. When I remarked on their small numbers, they explained that north of the border, tickets for this match were made available *only* to them. Because membership has its privileges, and ticket demand in Guadalajara was so very high. What's more, those Outlaw tickets were sold exclusively through US Soccer's corporate partners at Ticketmaster for $165 a pop.

When it comes to attending the planet's most quarrelsome, lucrative futbol rivalry, it's hard to keep anyone's hands clean.

●●●

Imagine for a moment that Argentina plays host to a friendly against its northern neighbor in the capital, Buenos Aires, and 70,000 Brazilians, expatriate and otherwise, just happen to show up across the River Plate. Massive resentment and dangerous bedlam would surely ensue—just as chaos would bust out if New York Yankee fans ever so markedly outnumbered Red Sox fans at Fenway Park.

Of course, neither of these scenarios has ever taken place. Nonetheless, this awkward dynamic plays out routinely in the United States whenever Mexico is the opponent. *Unless* the US Soccer Federation strategically schedules the match at a small, MLS-owned stadium where ticket access can be restricted — that's what the USSF does for must-win dates like World Cup qualifiers. It's the reason Columbus, Ohio lives so strongly in our American soccer consciousness. Apart from that—for friendlies, for Gold Cup and Nations League encounters—the Federation lines up the largest stadium it can find because it knows that at least 70,000 free-spending Mexican expatriates will show up. Greenbacks in hand. Ready to party, inside and outside the stadium.

In this and so many respects, the North American *Clásico* has been disproportionately stoked by the actions of these dual nationals. And sometimes, echoes of that influence actually work against Mexican citizens, in Mexico. Why return to Guadalajara when the FMF and TelevisaUniversal (TUDN) can rake in so much more money in Las Vegas?

"It is a very particular scenario: Mexico is the only national team in the world that plays at home in two different countries!" notes Marion Reimers, the journalist and football commentator for TNT Sports. "Consistently, I mean. Brazil will play games in Europe, you know, because they have so many players there—but not over and over and over again!"

Remember the wider context here: This Mexican American demographic is a culturally distinct immigrant population around which political, economic, and cultural recriminations continue to swirl. Any North American who has experienced either Trump administration understands how intensely the mere presence of Mexicans is felt north of the border. And yet, the Mexican national team plays nearly all its friendly internationals on US soil—because the States are home to so many *Tricolor* partisans. Who pay in dollars.

This "foreign" fan base has demonstrated itself to be an extraordinarily powerful entity, comprising millions of souls eager to express their Mexican identity via ticket sales and distance traveled, via tailgate cuisine and *lucha libre* masks—the striking headgear associated with Mexican freestyle wrestling.

To be clear: Friendlies are international *exhibitions*, matches that aren't part of World Cup qualifying or any specific tournament competition. They're official FIFA-sanctioned competitions, but only just. Let's also be honest: Outsized Mexican influence on this rivalry can also be traced back to money. The FMF and its chummy Mexican broadcast partners do take in far more revenue situating these friendly internationals in Dallas or Denver, as opposed to Puebla, León, or Guadalajara.

While Mexican expats well appreciate this cross-border curiosity—perhaps more than they did in 1997, on account of those changes to their Constitution—the home citizenry are decidedly more skeptical. Reimer continues:

> I don't mean this in a demeaning way, but it's symbiotic—and so obvious. From a Mexican perspective, we have always seen this relationship with a sort of jealousy and some disdain, I believe. I'm going to use a bit of strong language here. Even though my vocabulary in English might not be the broadest: But this is a sort of *down-washing*, a sort of prostitution of our Mexican identity, not playing matches in Mexico, or so often playing the men's national team in the United States, in addition to other exhibitions.
>
> It hurts, because it feels as if not playing in Mexico has a purely economic interest behind it. These matches should be played in Monterrey. They should be played in Guadalajara. They should be played in Toluca. In terms of friendly matches, they should be taken someplace else. I do believe a lot of people resent this."

The out-of-balance, interdependent circumstance Reimers describes in frank terms is indeed unique in world futbol, if not in all of international sport.

The closest cultural comp for Mexico vs. US right now is probably Türkiye vs. Germany, owing to the presence of 7 million persons of Turkish heritage living and working there. Türkiye matches during the last European Championship, hosted across Germany in June 2024, posed approximately zero loyalty issues for the largest immigrant population there. "Only Turkey," brothers Erkan and Tahla Ayka told *The New York Times*, in unison, when asked whom they'd be supporting at Euro 2024. "We live here. We were born here. But our hearts are in Turkey." [3]

This confluence of cultures, the consequence of economic migration, makes an international *klassiker* more impassioned wherever it plays out. It's the migrant position of Turks, many of them former or current "guest workers," that also sparks a familiar sort of resentment among Germany's growing right-wing political movements.

But Turks and Germans don't share a border; they've not fought wars or surrendered territory on account of one. Though Türkiye and Germany are members of the same European soccer confederation (UEFA), they don't play often enough to give the antagonism a lasting, contentious life of its own. The

United States and Mexico have faced each other thirty-eight times since 2000. The Germans and Turks? Just six, half of them friendlies. As our rivalry scholar Dr. Cobbs points out: not enough conflict to create a serious derby.

Furthermore, the Turkish futbol federation for damn sure isn't scheduling friendlies in Dusseldorf over and over again. Ditto the Algerian Football Federation with regard to France, where 6 million folks of Algerian heritage make their homes today. Accordingly, Reimers' implicit critique of the Mexican federation, of Mexican broadcasters, of their partner promoters at Soccer United Marketing—a controversial, US-based firm that, until 2021, counted both the US Federation and the FMF as clients—is well taken.

"We have always seen this as a way in which Mexican immigrants are sort of abused, no?" Reimers argues.

> They are used to paying for everything in dollars. They are being used to broaden the treasure chests of the Mexican Federation. And sometimes journalists here in Mexico can be quite hard on that aspect. At the same time, I do believe these friendlies have the ability to *strengthen* the Mexican identity in the U.S. They help immigrants not to forget their home country. They help them to connect with something that they left behind, something they miss.

Mexico remains a special case. Turks love their futbol and their country of origin, but Mexico is a nation so futbol obsessed, so enamored of its national team, it will sell out stadia everywhere: in Houston, at Giants Stadium in North Jersey, and naturally anywhere in Mexico itself—but also halfway around the world in Doha, where *El Tri* supporters turned Qatar crowds green for three World Cup dates in November 2022. Mexican national team fandom knows no physical boundaries. If left unchecked, it will transform US home fixtures into away matches, something it's been doing routinely for decades.

In short, the whopping-big Mexican American population in the United States wields extraordinary influence on this sporting contest, its economics, and its respective cultures. I mean, is there anything more indicative of identity than tailgating in stadium parking lots? According to Lindsey J. Meân and Raquel Herrera: "Sport is a significant site for the construction and maintenance of national, regional, and local identities and communities," they observed in the *Perspectives* anthology.[4]

This is not simply because sport represents a country and its people on an international stage in a way that has powerful political, geopolitical, and ideological implications, but because sport is a primary form through which *nation* manifests as a shared, imagined community. Sport usefully and easily unites vast populations of different and diverse people into communities with a shared sense of patriotism, pride, belonging.

•••

To visit Mexico in any capacity is to discover and invariably debunk a series of stereotypes perpetuated by US media, politicians and, sad to say, too many of my fellow citizens. We can start with the premise that life in Mexico is a never-ending hellscape perpetuated by warring drug cartels—a charge that felt rather absurd on the ground while dining *al fresco* in cafés throughout Colonia Americana and Zapopan.

Nevertheless, that morning of the match, I went out hunting for grocery staples with a friend and fellow traveler who picked up a local tabloid in the check-out line. The grisly lead photo—five headless corpses found in the desert, 600 miles away, five months before—freaked him out. His reaction read like the early pages of Robert Andrew Powell's excellent-but-unsettling 2012 book, *This Love Is Not For Cowards: Salvation and Soccer in Cuidad Juárez* (which, we can agree, is one helluva great title). Powell paints a sobering, often-gruesome picture of life just south of the border; he's also great on the Mexican fan experience in the pre-*Liga MX* era. Yet our own week-long experience in Guadalajara was delightful. Never did we feel the least bit threatened. Still, this one travel companion wouldn't shut up about his tabloid-enabled brush with cartel mayhem—an annoying, dubious stance for anyone who resides in the United States, where, according to the Pew Research Center, an estimated 40,886 deaths resulted from gun violence in 2024. Which works out to 786 per week.[5]

Also from the Mexican Trope Dept., and far less disturbing: that Tuesday evening we strolled through the main entrance of *Estadio Akron* only to encounter a 7-piece *mariachi* band entertaining a large crowd in the lobby. The moment seemed a bit on the nose—just the sort of scene some ignorant Yank might have expected.

Only later did this writer properly bone up on the matter. *Mariachi* refers not to the music but rather the ensemble—typically violin, trumpet, guitar, and acoustic bass. The genre they play is called *ranchera*, a regional folk strain that rural residents of Jalisco brought with them to urban Guadalajara in the late nineteenth century.[6] The lineup and music are strongly associated with this specific part of the country, even if *mariachi* eventually spread to Mexico City and has become a broad and vibrant symbol of national identity—to Mexicans and Hollywood *gringos* alike.

So, it was perfectly appropriate, in fact culturally faithful, that a *mariachi* band would greet futbol fans as they entered the Akron for the region's first international friendly in fourteen years. In this context, I was a bit surprised at the sedate atmosphere inside the stadium. With all that had been written—one local press report pointed out that *El Tri* showed up in 2010 only because the Akron had just opened—I had expected something louder and more festive.

We *americanos* are more familiar, frankly, with the scenes inside and outside US stadiums when the Mexican national team comes calling. During the 1990s, as the *clásico* first started to pierce the US consciousness, the flamboyant Mexican fan uniform of choice was a giant sombrero, perhaps complemented by an improbably bushy fake mustache. We can agree that (1) Mexican fandom relies heavily on costume; and (2) wrestling masks are an improvement in terms of style, eccentricity, and the sight lines of those sitting directly behind.

However, these are the "away" kits, which *El Tri* supporters are more apt to wear when the game is being played in Dallas or Pasadena. There were no *lucha libre* masks in evidence at the Akron (scheduled to be renamed *Estadio Guadalajara* prior to the 2026 World Cup). Fans generally wore their preferred *La Selección* jerseys, just like home fans do anywhere. Additionally, outward assertions of identity were few. Veteran, traveling fans will tell you: That's an act more logically associated with showing up to support one's futbol team in enemy territory.

It breaks down this way: US-based Mexican Americans attending *El Tri* matches are more concerned with projecting their partisan fidelity to friend and foe in the crowd, to those watching on TV. Whereas ticketholders in

Mexico are more concerned with the country's footballing identity and reputation, weighed against Argentina and other global powers.

"I'd agree there wasn't as much performance in Guadalajara as there has been at other games, on either side," says Matthew Eison, a resident of South Carolina and one of the American Outlaws who traveled south for the October 2024 friendly. "As far as the cosplay is concerned, you may have a point. For our part, Eagle Man and Wonder Woman weren't there either—they *always* dress up. I have a friend who dresses as Elvis, but only for World Cups. I do remember a lot of cosplay at Azteca qualifiers. All fans, especially *El Tri* backers, bring the outfits for the World Cup."

Adds Philadelphia-based Outlaw Craig Hahn:

> I've definitely noticed the same thing. There's more thought put into the "outfit" when you're abroad or in an away setting. Especially for big tournament atmospheres and bigger games, like the World Cup or *Copa América*. For a normal Mexico friendly in the U.S. or Mexico, it seems to be more causal. I've also noticed that the over-the-top *lucha libre* stuff just isn't so big with *El Tri* fans in Mexico, compared to in the U.S.

I would add that home crowds don't need to assert or perform their identities. They *know* who they are. The surrounding tribe does, too. They typically dominate the stadium, where the assumption is obvious: *We're all here for the same reason.* Conversely, visiting fans must be performative in order to stand out, to be provocative: *Here we are!* During a big qualifier, away supporters feel the obligation to take it up a notch. Cue the guy in the rhinestone-studded pantsuit.

No such interplay revealed itself among fans inside or outside the Akron. The US contingent was too small. Moreover, the overriding vibes among locals instead centered on *El Tri* having been away too long, side by side with the traditional hysteria relating to national team failures. During Gregg Berhalter's tenure as Team USA manager, Mexican anxieties weren't at all misplaced. His national teams finished 5-0-2 against *El Tricolor*. In the previous meeting, Berhalter's squad throttled *El Tri* in a March 2024 Nations League final, 2-0.

"While the U.S. continues to work toward becoming a team that is greater than the sum of its parts . . . the path forward is less clear for Mexico," wrote

Texan Jon Arnold in March 2023. His excellent Substack, *Get CONCACAFed*, covers the current feud and the region better than anyone.

> The players in the [Mexico] squad who you'd expect to provide those moments of magic, the unbalancing of a defense, seem to either have hit a ceiling (Chuckie Lozano, Uriel Antuna), haven't shown at the international level what they've done with their clubs (OK, this is pretty much just Santi Gimenez) or are unable to push past their current levels to even reach the national team (Diego Lainez, Cesar Huerta). Right now, the U.S. has the sauce. Mexico is missing flavor. Until that changes, the balance of the rivalry will stay the same. [7]

There was another reason for evident unease in the GDL. Mauricio Pochettino, in charge for just his second match that October of 2024, had brought with him something new for a US skipper—the cachet of having led big clubs in Europe: Chelsea, Paris St. Germain, Tottenham Hotspur. Even more relevant: fans inside the Akron are like futbol *aficionados* across the Americas; they are hyper-aware and admiring of the Argentinian coaching pedigree.

Turns out they had nothing to worry about, not this night. The roster Pochettino originally assembled for this international window was B-level at best. Then, ahead of kickoff: Five US players, including in-form captain Christian Pulisic, were sent home—some at the request of their covetous European club teams, others to guard against injury and overuse. Ten minutes into the match, the American B Team appeared well out of its depth, while the opponent looked very much in the mood.

Aidan Morris, a promising young defensive midfielder newly signed away from Columbus Crew—by Middlesbrough in the English Championship—bore the brunt of this difficult situation. His foul led to a free-kick *golazo* from Raul Jiménez in the 22nd minute. Before the match, Morris may have sat third on the Team USA depth chart at defensive midfielder behind Tyler Adams and Johnny Cardoso, maybe fourth, if we consider Weston McKennie's ability to serve in that role. Morris had played well in the previous friendly vs. Panama, three days before in Austin, Texas, Pochettino's very first game in charge. Inside the Akron, he looked like a young player still trying to make his name with a middling second-division club. Which is to say, outclassed.

Just after halftime, the Mexicans sealed their own *Dos a Cero* when Jiménez again victimized Morris, stealing the ball in the box and setting up César Huerta for an easy finish. With that, the crowd relaxed and enjoyed itself via another time-honored Mexican gift to stadium crowds everywhere. The Wave had been introduced to a global audience at the 1986 World Cup. With the result in hand, Guadalajarans inside *Estadio Akron* indulged in this signature celebration over and over again—with light hearts, thanks to *El Tri*'s dominating performance.

• • •

That morning of the match, still full of optimzism for US fortunes, my posse of New Englanders headed out for another outdoor brunch on a tropical terrace. Our stomachs well lined, we walked to the edge of Americana, down the Avenida Niños Héroes, then north a few blocks on Chapultepec to the York Pub. That's where we met up with a dozen or so American Outlaws gathered for their pregame. Hahn and Eison were seated at the next table (their US soccer garb gave them away). Across the narrow bar, a quartet of Mexican fans sat quietly with their beers, drinking in the oddly red-white-and-blue atmosphere.

Eison's T-shirt was particularly eye-catching and appropriate. It depicted former USMNT defender Graham Zusi in Pauline fashion—as in St. Paul, the apostle. His decision to honor "San Zusi" was not made by accident, as it recalled one of the warmest and fuzziest moments in the history of US-Mexico futbol relations. Perhaps Eison was looking to make a good impression on those *El Tri* fans across the bar, then inside the Akron.

It's a good story, the how-and-why San Zusi got canonized. October 15, 2013: the final matchday of World Cup qualification. The United States was playing in Panama City with its place at Brazil 2014 already secured. Not the case for the hosts, who needed a draw to keep their World Cup dreams alive—and to dash those of mighty Mexico. Panama has since grown into one of CONCACAF's strongest sides, but *Los Canaleros* remained mere up-and-comers in 2013. A result against the Americans would have meant a World Cup debut and the country's full-on coming-out party. In the dying moments, they clung to a 1–1 scoreline, just enough to see them through—and to crush the World Cup hopes of *El Tri*.

Zusi scored late in the Panama match to rescue all three points for the United States and send the 20,000 fans inside *Estadio Rommel Fernández* home heartbroken. His goal also delivered *El Tri* to an intercontinental playoff with New Zealand and ultimately to the World Cup finals in Brazil. That's why Eison's T-shirt read, "San Zusi," or St. Zusi. The instant sainthood was bestowed by Mexican broadcasters in appreciation of his miraculous 92nd minute strike in Panama City.[8]

I had read about this righteous-if-temporary outpouring of affection. I'd heard about the T-shirts, but I'd never seen one.

"Certainly, it was a big deal at the time, but I'm not sure it's been remembered in Mexico," Eison says, my eyes fixated on the winged, beatific Zusi spread across his chest. "I would be surprised if any Mexico fans remember his name for what happened."

There are no such verifiable consequences in play with a friendly, a mere exhibition. For that reason, Eison and his mates were not expecting trouble that evening back in October 2024—inside the York Pub or the Akron. Yes, the crowd jeered and whistled during the Star-Spangled Banner, but they reserved far more lusty catcalls for Alex Zendejas, the Mexican American midfielder who chose the USMNT over *El Tricolor* and plays for Chivas' archenemy, Club América.

"To be honest, the crowd in Guadalajara was probably the most behaved I've seen," Eison told me after the match. "I mean the *puto* chants continued, for a bit, but we had no security around the section. That *never* happens. And we had no misbehavior toward us whatsoever."

Maybe it was the shirt? "Ha! I doubt it. I don't know if that's more due to the match being in Guadalajara vs. Mexico City—or that this wasn't a qualifier, or that Mexico beat us. But it was definitely a first!"

Eison has, for the record, seen more US-Mexico matches than you've had hot dinners. He has attended four such confrontations south of the border dating back to 2009—all of them at the Azteca, all of them World Cup qualifiers. As such, he has witnessed an evolution: "Maybe it's the post-COVID effect or decreased expectations, but recent games vs. Mexico in the Nations League have been less intense in terms of atmosphere. Other things may be affecting this. But the Mexico crowds have become more sedate over time in general, for me."

It's here that match frequency may have taken some of the edge off US vs. Mexico. Fans want more encounters. So do the federations and broadcast bean-counters. Is it possible that the economics of playing so many matches, so many friendlies, so many Nations League finals, and Gold Cup semifinals have taken a toll? Familiarity *can* breed contempt, of course, but the opposite may apply to twenty-first-century rivalries where content—in the form of match after match, after match—is king. Argentina and Brazil play only when they must; neither entertains the idea of dress rehearsals to fill the coffers of eager TV partners. In the long term, when it comes to the preservation of contempt, they have it right.

Or maybe the Argentinians in particular have a knack for sowing and preserving contempt.

•••

Walking through the tailgate scene outside *Estadio Akron*, I stopped a few times to chat up the locals—hoping to find English speakers to discuss the match and our multigenerational family feud. This search proved largely fruitless. Google Translate can only do so much. But those limited conversations, taken together, did underline one thing: Mexican fans were impressed and maybe a bit spooked by Pochettino's recent hire. Be it broken English or fluent Spanish, the man's name kept coming up.

As a fan of Tottenham, whom Poch managed from 2014–19, I don't disagree with the sentiment. He's clearly the most impressive, experienced coaching hire in the 108-year history of the US Men's National Team. But Pochettino is respected reflexively in Mexico because he's Argentinian, and Mexican admiration for Argentinian futbol culture runs deep. And a bit eccentric.

The fixation dates back to the origins of soccer in the Americas, as *La Albiceleste* exhibited world-class form from the very beginnings of the international game. Their national teams immediately gained finals. They leveraged their European heritage to win finals, sometimes in Italian shirts (!). After claiming the 1978 World Cup, they officially took their place among the game's global aristocracy—a pedigree underlined by one legend at the Azteca in 1986, and then again at the 2022 World Cup in Qatar, courtesy of another.

It makes sense that Mexicans envy Argentinian skill, tournament success, and high standing. For their part, Mexicans take great pride in the fact that Maradona reached his potential in *their* country. They feel the same way about Pelé.

Also well established as fact: No country exports coaching talent on the scale of Argentina. Tata Martino managed Mexico at the 2022 World Cup, after all. In September 2023, as qualifying for World Cup 2026 got underway in South America, all but three of the ten national teams were led by Argies. In Guadalajara, Jon Arnold pointed out to me there were just three Mexican managers in the 18-team *Liga MX*. The number of Argentine skippers? Seven.

Mexicans admire something else sky blue and white: An in-your-face, hyper-masculine M.O. that fans of *El Tri* especially perceive, in their heart of hearts, as totally bad-ass and weirdly admirable. If there's a single Spanish word to describe and inform this cultural phenomenon, it's *desmadre*, which translates as "motherless," implying that people without mothers have no manners, and therefore behave badly. *Desmadre* can also translate as "chaos." In the specific Latin American soccer context, I think another useful English-language comp would be "shithousery," laced with heavy doses of homophobic chest-beating.[9]

Everyone in Latin America, especially the Mexicans, acknowledges that Argentinian players, clubs, and fans are masters of this peevish form. Not just supporters who seek to create unsettling pandemonium in and around stadiums. The national team and its players have proved equally... *resourceful*, when it comes to these dark arts. Be it Diego Simeone quaintly baiting David Beckham into a red card during the 1998 World Cup Round of 16; or Boca Juniors captain Rubén Suñé starting a bloody brawl with Sporting Cristal of Lima on March 17, 1971 (nineteen players were sent off); or Argentine clubs paying supporter groups, the *barra bravas*, to serve as violent paramilitaries—a twenty-first-century trend that has destroyed attendance in the country's first division.

These are small potatoes compared to the nation's Federation and brutal military junta allegedly collaborating to fix a match against Peru to ensure Argentina's place (at Brazil's expense) in the 1978 *Mundial* final. We witnessed another high-profile example in Miami, Florida, at the close of *Copa América* 2024, when Argentine internationals celebrated the title by singing a post-match, locker-room ditty that denigrated French national team players as hailing from all over the world. That is, everywhere but France. It wasn't sour grapes: Messi & Co. had won the *Copa* final—against Colombia. The singing was meant to troll their victims from the World Cup final held two years prior.

Win or lose, the Argentinian brand of *desmadre* never lets up and never forgets. For it has but one clear, universal goal: to gain an advantage by getting under an opponent's skin. The more coarse the language, the more overt the bigoted tones and physical intimidation, the better.

Admiration of this behavior would, at first blush, seem an odd fit for Mexican fans and the national population at large. In most walks of life, the Mexican people do not demonstrate these disagreeable traits at all. They are famously polite. "Mexicans would never insult *anyone*, especially to your face," attests Amy Glover, a dual citizen born in Michigan but a Mexican resident for thirty years. "It's just not their way, their culture. In twenty-five years of my living here, even though I look the way I do, no one has ever even been rude to me. Ever! Mexicans don't play that game. Americans are far more violent and rude, to be honest."

This subject matter has very little to do with Americans. It's more to do with Mexico's would-be rivalry with Argentina, alongside Mexico's age-old struggle to assert itself as a first-world futbol power. Without signature victories from *El Tri* or *Liga MX* clubs abroad, the optics of this striving can be unfortunate. Witness the dust-up between Mexican and Argentinian supporters following their group-stage encounter at the Qatari World Cup. "Social media videos showed Mexico fans provoking Argentines with insults over all-time top scorer Messi and their Falklands War defeat by Britain," Reuters reported in November 2022. "That led to street brawling that left some fans bleeding and injured, according to footage and photos." [10]

US soccer fans have surely noticed the in-stadium habit of *El Tri* supporters calling the opposing goalkeeper *puto*, or "fag." That's quintessential *desmadre* behavior, and it dovetails with this deep-seated Mexican cynicism about their own national team. Mexican fans normally resort to the chant only when *El Tri* is losing or not performing up to expectations.[11] It's an attempt to change the energy inside a stadium. To change the subject, as it were. In Guadalajara, the performance was good: Fans laid but a single *puto* on US keeper Matt Turner. Up 2-nil and riding high, their hearts just weren't in it.

Undertaken in homage to Argentinian bad behavior, the *puto* chant and other transgressive stadium behaviors also have a broader purpose. They're meant to supply the sharp edge that Mexicans and their national teams have lacked. Or, that is the perception among Mexican fans themselves.

The Major League Soccer community witnessed an unprecedented, telling dose of *desmadre* during F.C. San Diego's February 2025 home date vs. St. Louis. Frustrated by the proceedings, which produced no goals, FCSD supporters whipped out the *puto* chant on three separate occasions. This was a brand-new expansion club in the winter of 2025; this match was the second it ever contested in MLS, its home opener. It would be naïve to believe that this display from supporters was anything but an opening-night assertion of Mexican American identity and custom.

F.C. San Diego naturally denounced the chanting straight away. In the direct aftermath, *The Athletic* reported on what next steps might include:

> Mexico's football federation, alongside U.S. Soccer, has poured resources and manpower into combatting the issue, with mixed results. The Mexican federation has gone as far as instituting a "Fan ID" system in recent years, one that is capable of using facial recognition to catch people in the act. That sort of technology isn't actively used in MLS stadiums, though some of the league's clubs have dabbled in facial recognition in some form or another. Speaking on Tuesday, [F.C. San Diego CEO Tom] Penn was clear enough in suggesting that the club would absolutely remove any fan who can be clearly identified as having participated in the chant.[12]

On the social media platform Threads, Mexican American Herculez Gomez, the Team USA veteran turned pundit, was more blunt: *For years they would say it's a "Mexican National Team problem" or "It's a Liga MX problem." Well, here we are in "America's Finest City," and now it's a Major League Soccer Problem. Your move, MLS.*[13]

●●●

The language of *desmadre* is inherently, almost necessarily sexist and misogynist. True men, according to its unwritten rules, defend territory and honor club or country by dominating, demeaning, and/or emasculating the opponent, according to Patrick Thomas Ridge in his excellent *Perspectives* essay, "Mexico 'On Top': Queering Masculinity in Contemporary Mexican Soccer Chronicles." These so-called "ultras" do so by brawling with rivals, but more often by calling them out as, say, "cabaret bitches" or "penetrated" losers unworthy of honored places in the arena. In predictably twisted *machista* fashion, the penetrator is not a sexual deviant, only the violated party.[14]

This offensive stance can manifest by actually squaring off with opposing supporters inside or outside stadiums, and this does happen in Argentina. However, the chants best spell out what's really going on. Here's a common sentiment from supporters of the Buenos Aires club Atlético Huracán: *Le vamos a romper el culo!*, to wit: "We're going to ream your ass!"[15] Charming.

Mexican fans take these themes and run with them, but their chants and wordplay are nevertheless a bit more subtle and clever. Club América, as the richest and most successful club in *Liga MX*, is a frequent target. When *Los Aguilas*, "The Eagles," aren't being derided as *zopilotes* ("buzzards"), opposing supporters might create a derisive song that mentions *las chillahermanas*, or those who cry like little girls. Or they might go straight to *las huilas*, an abstract take on the old standby, "whores."

These multiple variations on vulgar themes should help US readers contextualize the whole *puto* thing. When on-field developments are going badly for *El Tri*, when a Mexican crowd is somehow embarrassed or bored by the performance, slinging homophobic slurs at opposing goalies comes straight from the *desmadre* playbook. The anonymity of the crowd, the desire to stir the pot and change the game, transforms hyper-polite Mexicans into transgressors.

Most everyone across the Americas finds the Argentinians generally, and their soccer fans specifically, to be shameless assholes who behave in a rude, brazenly underhanded fashion when it suits them. At the same time, Argentinians are keen to claim a more refined European lineage (read: whiteness) compared to their South and Central American neighbors. [Not surprisingly, this is the northern European hooligan dismissal of Italian and Argentinian *bravos*: All talk, not enough actual fighting.]

Mexicans and Mexican Americans, for all their good manners, would appear to respect and advocate for this crude conduct—in the futbol context, where they continue to embrace the foul-mouthed chaos and protection of the crowd. On either side of the border.

More important to our subject matter: In mimicking the cheeky misbehavior of Argentinian fan culture, Mexicans are actively aspiring to a higher rung of rivalry. Followers of *El Tri* want desperately to beat the United States. On this subject, there is no doubt. But when it comes to international futbol distinction, the Yanks do not have what the Mexicans most desire. *La Albiceleste* do, and Mexicans have carried a fervent case of Argentina envy for a very long time.

"It must definitely be Argentina, because Argentina is one of the best teams in the world," Reimers explained to me. "Mexico has been very close to beating them. They lost at the 2010 World Cup with a goal that was offside from Carlos Tevez. But culturally there is also a big, big feud between Mexico and Argentina.

We are on different sides of the spectrum in Spanish-speaking America. They are the deepest south and we are the furthest north—the two poles. Let me help my American friends understand what that means: We have so many countries that speak Spanish. We all share the same language. We all have variations of that language, but we kind of understand each other and our particularities. It's like a big brotherhood.

But since we understand each other culturally and linguistically, we know how they are—and they understand how we are. And Argentinians are famous for being very sour losers and even worse winners. Yet I've also heard Mexicans speak very glowingly about how Azteca is the place where Maradona was crowned and where he realized his greatest potential. They take pride in it."

Meaning, the Azteca is so mystically potent, it's a place where even nasty, cheating Argies can come to finish their hero's journey?

"*Claro*. It's a magical land. It's the land of the Aztecs! It's the land where everything happened . . . There's also this interesting feud because Argentina is one of the biggest economic markets in Latin America and Mexico is always bigger. *They* resent this. But in terms of football and other stuff, we hate *them* because they're arrogant and because, I mean, we're hurt by all the losses."

Remembering our rivalry scholar Dr. Cobbs, the narrative, cinematic factors most important to the evolution of any *clásico* are envy and scorn. (Call them, "Worst Supporting Actors in a Dramatic Series.") It appears the Argentina-Mexico derby embodies and obeys these critical signposts. And yet, they are not competitive equals, and it ain't even close. Nor do they play often enough to make a rivalry work.

"Absolutely," Reimers says. "That makes all the sense in the world. I do love those two concepts."

For his part, Leo Messi remains mystified by the whole relationship, specifically the jeers he received when Inter Miami visited Monterrey during the 2024 CONCACAF Champions Cup. "I don't know what happened with the Mexicans, when that anger started, because I always felt very loved by the people of Mexico," he told the Associated Press in January 2025. "I never disrespected anyone, but they took a position of having a rivalry with us that doesn't really exist. There is no comparison between Argentina and Mexico." [16]

●●●

Devotees of US professional sport might have difficulty in recognizing or absorbing all these visceral ideas about national rank and aspiration. For starters, as the world's preeminent state in terms of military, economic, and sporting might, most twenty-first-century Americans do not and will not acknowledge that we have any peers, let alone true rivals. But these biases are only part of the equation.

For much of the twentieth century, we *did* have a true rival: the Soviet Union, with whom we vied for geopolitical power and stature over the course of fifty years following the Second World War. Naturally, that Cold War extended to sport, and it's instructive to consider the focus we Americans placed on those battles. Forty-six years down the road we're still talking about those audacious college hockey players who beat the awesome USSR at the 1980 Olympics. Similarly, this great nation of ours demonstrated great quantities of envy and scorn in rooting for all those individual US figure skaters, gymnasts, and swimmers who "went toe to toe" with various communist counterparts over the course of decades.

Outside of the 2- or 3-week Olympic window, we can agree Americans don't care all that much about figure skating, ice hockey, or swimming. Back in the day, though, we got pretty gosh-darn emotional about them, if not fully invested, and furnished these confrontations with all sorts of cultural baggage. When rooting for "our" side, our "way of life," our place in the worldwide ranks, our identity as US citizens in a global setting mattered to us quite a lot.

Whom we choose or aspire to compete with is just another form of identity.

Suddenly it's not so hard to comprehend why Mexicans get so worked up about how their national soccer team stacks up—compared to world futbol's ruling class. Compared to a bullying Latin American familiar like Argentina. Compared to a cultural monolith, the Great White Shark on its northern border.

The difference is—and it's a critical distinction, especially vis-à-vis the Argies—Mexicans quite like Americans, despite their long history of apex-predator-like exploitation, land grabs, and racism.

According to The Pew Global Attitudes Survey for 2013, 66 percent of Mexicans had a favorable view of the United States, compared to 65 percent of respondents in the UK.[17] Ten years later, after a full decade of Trumpism, the Pew Global Attitudes Survey for 2024 found that 61 percent of Mexicans still had a favorable view of the United States, compared to just 54 percent of respondents in the United Kingdom and Canada, for example.[18]

Mexican views have remained remarkably stable and positive in this regard. Since 2000, according to Pew, their favorable feelings toward the United States never exceeded 68 and have never dropped below 52.

There was a telling dip in Mexicans' favorable views of America from 2017 to 2020, when they dropped to between 29 and 35. One might expect another Trump dip during the man's second term. [Note: The manuscript for this book was finalized in May 2025.] Taking the longer, broader view, we must acknowledge that a meaningful gulf exists between envy and admiration. Both attitudes can apply simultaneously, of course. To describe this dance as delicate and complicated is to understate the case. We'll need to explore the turbulent, incestuous history these neighboring countries share, on and off the pitch, to best process and understand it.

4

Of Moles and Molé

How Mexico Seized Unlikely Control of the North American Derby

Fifty miles east of Mexico City, in the mid-sized mining metropolis of Pachuca, a Neo-Gothic spire rises above the otherwise low-profile, Spanish-colonial skyline in the historic district. Dedicated in 1901, this Methodist church, *La Iglesia Metodista del Divino Salvador*, remains architecturally and religiously unique, not just here in the capital of Hidalgo state but in the whole of Mexico.

When imperial Spain ruled Mexico (1521–1821), there was no Methodism practiced in Pachuca, only Catholicism, along with the refinement of silver extracted from the surrounding landscape. By 1824, the mines had all flooded and fallen into disrepair. To revive the city's fortunes, investors formed the Company of the Gentlemen Adventurers in the Mines of Real del Monte. More than 130 mine workers and engineers arrived a year later from Cornwall, in the southwest of England. Many died at the port of Veracruz following an outbreak of yellow fever, but the remainder set out on the arduous 230-mile journey to Pachuca, which sits 8,000 feet above sea level. Aided only by donkeys, the Cornish lugged the unwieldy steam engines they would need to drain the mines. Many left when the job was finished, but many stayed to make their expatriate lives. These are the British subjects who brought Methodism to this remote corner of Hidalgo state. They also brought a taste for meat pies, or pasties.[1] And they brought futbol.

Soccer is the world game, but first it was an English game, one whose origins in Mexico are not diminished on account of that European heritage. Even today, in an age rife with anti-colonial sentiment, this old-world sporting influence is largely considered a feature, not a bug. British futbol roots remain a sign of authenticity across the Americas, where the sport was introduced in similar fashion all through the nineteenth century. There are, for example, seventeen clubs outside of North London that go by the name Arsenal—six in South America alone.[2]

In the United States, soccer empresarios today think nothing of appropriating the cachet of English club names. Major League Soccer is littered with them, but that's a relatively new exercise. Late nineteenth-century US culture? Notoriously *anti*-British when it came to sports acculturation. While South Americans were founding new clubs in homage to The Gunners, certain North American folk remained obsessed with developing what they perceived to be homegrown sports—even if baseball and gridiron can be traced quite directly back to rounders and rugby. This preference for authentically "American" pastimes, along with an aversion to games perceived as foreign, persisted through most of the twentieth century.[3]

The Cornish met no such resistance. They introduced cricket and Association football to this highland region, along with Protestantism. The same year their new chapel was dedicated, local British expats founded the Pachuca Athletic Club, whose early lineups were specifically comprised of Anglo mine workers living in the communities of Santa Gertrudis, La Blanca, and Real del Monte. Soon competitions were joined among similar clubs in and around expat communities in Veracruz and Mexico City. The Mexican League of Association Football was officially born on July 19, 1902. Its players, coaches, and administrators were entirely English, though some of the second- and third-generation players from places like Pachuca had already acquired Hispanic surnames.

To repeat: For all its colonial transgressions, the British Empire is not begrudged this formative role. Not in Mexico, where the effects of British military imperialism were never felt. Had those footballing miners and extraction engineers showed up in Hidalgo from, say, the Spanish quarry regions of Asturias or León (or perhaps Cornwall, Missouri!), the region and the remainder of Mexico may not have taken to soccer with such enthusiasm.

But take to it they did, and Pachuca is considered the birthplace of Mexican soccer. At this writing, early in 2025, its *Liga MX* entry, C.F. Pachuca, reigns as the top club side in all of North America, having claimed the CONCACAF Champions Cup in June 2024. One wonders whether Salomón Rondón—the unpredictable Venezuelan striker who arrived in Hidalgo by way of the English club West Bromwich Albion, and whose brace foiled Columbus Crew in the 2024 continental final—appreciates his fascinating place in this long history.

History, though, is a funny thing. Different parties, inside and outside a particular culture, tend to remember things quite differently—oftentimes on account of competing cultural agendas, and other times organically. In fact, we humans have a real knack for divining ways to mismatch our memories of a shared past. "Facts are not truth, though they are part of it," historical novelist Hilary Mantel has written. "Information is not knowledge. And history is not the past—it is the method we have evolved of organizing our ignorance of the past. It's the record of what's left on the record." [4]

Most American soccer fans, for example, presume their archrivals to have dominated North American futbol from the get-go. They are mistaken, mainly because our communal futbol memory extends, at best, no further than the arrival of Pelé in 1975. As it happens, the historical record also differs from what Mexicans have been telling themselves all these years.

•••

It took a bit of time for turn-of-the-century, native-born, Spanish-speaking Mexicans to put their own stamp on the game. Pachuca Athletic Club was formed following the 1895 merger of Pachuca F.C. with the Pachuca and Velasco cricket clubs. The first Mexican player to appear for Pachuca A.C., David Islas, didn't debut until 1908. By then he was suiting up in the newly formed *Priméra División*, a competition first undertaken in July 1907. This league still featured amateur sides with names like the Mexico Cricket Club and The British Club, each based out of the capital. Even Albinegros de Orizaba of Veracruz, a club owned and operated by Scottish steel magnate Duncan Mac Comish Mac Donald, was an entirely British enterprise, on-field and off.[5]

Prior to the First World War, this was the working model found most everywhere across Central and South America: British expats would seed these foreign fields for soccer and, just as consistently, native populations would progressively make the game their own. The sweeping chaos of revolution slowed, then advanced this evolution in Mexico. The Civil War (1910–20) rendered *priméra* or "first" division futbol largely impractical, especially across the country's populous midsection where most of the clubs were then based (where a majority of today's *Liga MX* clubs are still based).

Outbreak of the Great War in August of 1914 returned many Brits to Britain. Just three teams from the original *Priméra*, including Pachuca A.C., survived into 1915. By then, nearly all league players *were* Mexican born.[6]

Not until 1943 would club soccer in Mexico professionalize or consolidate on a national scale. In the meantime, amateur outfits coalesced into several more regional leagues, the largest of which, the *Priméra Fuerza*, served Greater Mexico City. A.C. Pachuca held itself together throughout the Teens, winning a pair of trophies between 1917 and 1920—only to disband in 1921. The club would not reconstitute as C.F. Pachuca until 1966. Almost sixty years later, *Los Tuzos* (The Gophers, or Moles) are champions of North America.

Several of the country's most famous clubs did form during this turbulent, hyper-patriotic period. Club América announced itself on October 12, 1916, the date countries across the Americas had once recognized as Columbus Day.[7] The club name and formation date are unmistakable in their symbolism: namely, in opposition to the absurd colonial idea that some late fifteenth-century Italian dude (who may have been a Sephardic Jew, according to DNA evidence reported by Reuters in 2024) sailing under a Spanish flag had actually "discovered" anything.

Club América would gather its national following on account of its location in the country's dominant metropolitan area and media market, and because it won. A lot. Under the guidance of co-founder Raphael Garza Gutiérrez, *Las Aguilas* ("The Eagles") claimed four consecutive *Fuerza* titles during the mid-1920s. New York's Ruth & Gehrig Era Yankees are a pretty good comp. When Televisa bought the club in 1959, the comp got that much better.

Today, Club América remains the biggest, richest club in the country, with the broadest base of support, in part because of money and television exposure. But history and symbolism still play a role.[8] For many decades, The Eagles fielded Mexican players exclusively (their rival in the early years of this century was Club Espana, which represented the nation's Spanish expat community). The club's popularity transcends the regional and commercial for yet another reason: that hemispheric name. In choosing Club "América," Garza Gutiérrez himself and his co-founder Germán Nuñez Cortina were purposely making a larger, geopolitical point about the United States. By 1917, the United States had not yet grown into a global superpower. But it had come to dominate the Western Hemisphere, along with the words "America" and "American." The club's chosen identity, then and now, defiantly reclaims a portion of this regional branding.

Most US citizens don't recognize or appreciate how loudly South, Central, and fellow North Americans condemn *gringo* appropriation of the "American" designation—first conferred on the Brazilian coast by a German mapmaker circa 1507, in the name of another Italian (Amerigo Vespucci). Mexican futbol fans may not fully understand that history either. In supporting Club América, however, they do savor the opportunity to redeem the word for Mexican futbol, and themselves.

•••

While FIFA first formed in Paris in 1903, the international soccer movement evolved more quickly and consequentially across the Atlantic. Like Mexicans, the Uruguayans, Brazilians, and Argentinians had all picked up the game from UK expatriates, whose clubs in Montevideo, Rio de Janeiro, and Buenos Aires had also been organized strictly for Brits. All the same, those sporty Sons of Albion had gone abroad to South America mainly to build railway networks. Thus, the game spread to native populations in Argentina and Brazil far faster than in Mexico, perhaps due to the expansive nature of this industry. Let us agree that railway development workers tend to get around a country quite a lot, while mining concerns tend to keep their employees underground, in one place.

By 1907, more than 300 clubs had taken shape across Argentina. The futbol leagues there remained amateur and regionalized, but that didn't stop those in

Buenos Aires, Rosario, and nearby Montevideo from staging, in 1900, the first international club competition: The Tie Cup, a tournament based on the English F.A. Cup and won by Rosario Central (boyhood club of Mauricio Pochettino). Argentina and Uruguay also played the continent's first international match in 1902, before FIFA was even a thing. The initial *Copa América* would be staged in 1916, forty years ahead of the first European Championships.[9]

In nearly every respect, futbol's evolution in Mexico followed these templates, only a bit later and more slowly. Mexico would not contest any international fixtures whatsoever until 1923, when it played a three-match series against Guatemala—all of them in Mexico City, under the leadership of player/coach Raphael Garza Gutiérrez. [Mexican naming conventions follow the Spanish style: the father's surname followed by the mother's family name. On further reference, the father's surname is often used alone.]

When the Mexican Football Federation (FMF) launched in 1927, it formally placed Garza in charge. He coached and captained the Mexican national team at its first international competition, the 1928 Olympic Football Tournament in Amsterdam, though there was little to brag about. Spain dismantled the Mexicans, 7–1, in the opening knockout round (there was no group play). The United States fared no better, giving up eleven goals and scoring just two in its only match, a dispiriting loss to eventual finalist Argentina.

> Three important things to keep in mind about international competitions in the pre-World Cup era:

First, prior to 1930, the Olympic soccer competition represented the sport's *de facto* world championship. Participation at each of the three Olympic tournaments staged during the 1920s dwarfed that of the inaugural FIFA World Cup in 1930 and the second edition in 1934. In actual fact, FIFA was the body that administered those Olympic tournaments on behalf of the far better established and credible International Olympic Committee (IOC).

Second, the IOC's insistence on amateur purity, more than anything else, duly necessitated a World Cup organized by FIFA alone. Futbol was everywhere on the march during the 1920s, rapidly developing and professionalizing. Even the United States had a professional league operating from 1921–33, the American Soccer League (first of *four* enterprises that would go by that specific name). The IOC got around this troublesome lack of amateurism by outsourcing the matter to FIFA, which, in administering the Olympic tournaments, had concocted an "understanding" whereby irregular payments could be made to players—by national futbol associations—to cover their "expenses" and time away from clubs. This practice proved a dodgy, short-term solution; the English Football Association (FA) objected and opted out ahead of the Amsterdam games. It was FIFA's meddling in association affairs that most offended British sensibilities, more than any injury to amateur ideals. And so, England and the Home Nations—Scotland, Wales, and Northern Ireland—all withdrew from FIFA in protest prior to the 1928 Olympic tournament.[10]

Third, Uruguay was clearly the finest international squad in the world during this era, British boycotts be damned. *La Celeste* (The Sky Blue) won the Olympic competitions in both 1924 and 1928, while also dominating the *Copa América*—frequently at the expense and mounting chagrin of continental cousin Argentina. In 1930, when FIFA finally did resolve to hold its own world championship inclusive of *all* players, professional and otherwise, Uruguay was the clear and obvious choice to host. You'll notice the Uruguayan Football Association (AUF) crest features four stars: One each for World Cups claimed in 1930 and 1950, plus the two Olympic crowns in 1924 and 1928, which FIFA designated to be star-worthy in 1992.

•••

We paint this broader historical picture because this early in the World Cup movement—ahead of the inaugural North American Derby in 1934—few of the reputations and hierarchies we recognize today held much water. Prior to the first *Mundial* in 1930, the professional American Soccer League was nine years old, while the Mexican *Priméra* wouldn't form until 1943. In Uruguay, the top four seeds included the hosts, Argentina, Brazil, and (*wait for it . . .*) the

United States. These were the presumed heavyweights that FIFA kept apart in the draw. Also from the "I'll be Damned" Dept: The United States went on to win its group, besting Belgium in the opener and dispatching Paraguay behind Bert Patenaude's hat trick, the first ever recorded at a World Cup. The Yanks went all the way to the semifinal, where they fared better against Argentina but still got shelled, 6–1.

Some have alleged this American squad had been largely assembled with players born or raised abroad—how else to explain their remarkable showing? Well, our friends at the Society for American Soccer History have debunked this slight: There were a few English- and Scottish-born blokes on the roster, but their combined professional experience prior to this competition totaled two games, each in the English Third Division. As a Masshole born, bred, and proud, I'm obliged to point out that the potent Patenaude also hailed from Massachusetts. This guy had a dependable nose for goal. In four years running up front for his hometown Fall River Marksmen, the striker scored 112 times in 114 ASL appearances.[11]

The first World Cup was essentially an invitational event. Many European countries failed to participate, citing the very long journey and/or the tournament's naked professionalism. Playing under Garza, Mexico did make the trip south but failed to impress, losing 4–1 to France in the opener. Juan Carreño Lara, who played his club soccer with Mexico City's Atlante F.C., claimed the honor of scoring his country's first-ever World Cup goal, but it was slim pickin's in the highlight department thereafter. A 3–0 loss to Chile preceded a 6–3 drubbing from eventual finalist Argentina, whereupon the Mexicans slipped quietly out of town.

Here's the take-away: In the early 1930s, any understanding that Mexico was a proper footballing nation, and the United States was not, defies the historical record. In fact, the opposite was true. It took a World Cup play-in to drive this point home and get *El Clásico Norteamericano* underway.

The two nations hadn't exactly avoided one another. The whole idea of friendly matches—of playing internationals outside of Olympic or World Cup competition—remained rare. Mexico had played a grand total of fourteen internationals by the spring of 1934, while the United States had contested just fifteen. The Americans' commendable fourth-place finish in Uruguay changed nothing. They celebrated the showing by playing precisely zero matches in all of 1931, 1932, and 1933.

The Italian World Cup of 1934 was not an invitational event, but qualification did prove rather casual. The tournament organized by the North American Football Union attracted just two entrants: The Mexicans thrashed Cuba in three matches held in Mexico City during March 1934. The US Football Association did not send a team—it had been late in submitting its application. FIFA ultimately green-lit the Yanks, but they were obliged to play a single North American qualifier in Rome, against Mexico, three days ahead of the tournament finals.[12] Winner take all.

The Mexicans spent fifteen days crossing the Atlantic. Luigi Ruggieri, Rome correspondent for *La Afición*, dropped in on their training session a day before that arbitrary playoff: "I was surprised that the Mexicans play much better soccer than I had thought. They are fast and small and have adopted the best kind of game they could have: that of short and quick passes. They are not great shooters, but they shoot quickly and with aim, which is quite valuable. They had a practice that was not strenuous nor rough, but rather scientific, to improve their game . . . They play good soccer but do not seem to be worried about physical conditioning, despite its importance.

"After I went to see the Americans' last practice. They have a team completely different from the Mexicans. They are all strong, well-built, in magnificent physical condition. From what I could see from their practice, they worry more about being in good physical condition than practicing plays. Their game is almost completely in the air, and I noted that they are a group of stars, each one playing for his own saint, without much coordination."[13]

The US squad featured only four holdovers from Uruguay: midfielders Bill Fielder, Jimmy Gallagher, and Billy Gonsalves, along with defender George Moorhouse. The remaining roster had been assembled via tryouts and invitations two months before departure. This new squad played no warm-up matches. Ten days after their arrival in Italy, inside Rome's *Stadio Nazionale del Partito Nazionale Fascista*, the Americans faced Mexico for the very first time—on May 24, 1934. One day after visiting with Pope Pius XI.

Neither side could possibly have scouted the other in any meaningful way, but the United States was clearly the better side on the day. Aldo "Buff"

Donelli scored all the American goals in the 4–2 walkover. Mexico played the last half hour a man down. The prolific Donelli might have made it five, but the Pittsburgher missed a penalty late in the match.

According to Tony Cirino's *US Soccer vs. The World*, Donelli played his club soccer for the Curry Silver Tops when he wasn't coaching Duquesne University's American football team. He potted another goal in the Round of 16, where host Italy boned and gutted the Americans, 7–1. These were the only two games Buff ever played for the national team, though he did appear for the NFL's Pittsburgh Steelers in 1941 and once more for the Cleveland Rams in 1944.

"Mexico had a team that was pretty equal to ours," Donelli later told Cirino,

> but they were not very quick. They had a very, very deliberate style of attack. There was not a whole lot of imagination; it was a predictable attack. And if you did anything, if you moved a wee bit, it would put them off balance. I was just able to go around the man very easily, and once I was around him.[14]

•••

The day after this first installment of US vs. Mexico, *The New York Times* reported: "The Mexican players appeared to be technically superior to the Americans, but they were all of much slighter build and were obliged to yield to the more vigorous game of their heavier opponents."[15]

On the same date, in the May 25, 1934 edition of *La Afición*, Ruggieri wrote:

> The only ones responsible for losing the game are the Mexicans. The U.S. team beat them, but it is my opinion that it was not a game won by the Americans, but lost by the Mexicans. The one that played the game descended to a lower level. It forgot its science, its teamwork and did the worst possible... They forgot speed and technique.[16]

Here's what's remarkable about these ninety-year-old press reports: Sportswriters from the 1990s could have written them. *The Mexicans are small and technical... The Americans "athletic" and direct.* We recognize these descriptions as enduring North American soccer tropes. Ruggieri's post-game analysis, which attributes all on-field agency to the Mexicans, could have been posted on any of a dozen Mexican websites last week.

Even so, we must thank our lucky stars for these reports from *La Afición*. Past issues of the newspaper are available via the Periodicals Archive at the National Autonomous University of Mexico, in Mexico City. Established in 1930 and based in the capital, *La Afición* ("The Fans") served throughout the twentieth century as the country's only daily dedicated solely to sports.

Of course, the tone and scope of *La Afición* articles in particular, and Mexican futbol *reportage* generally, aren't solely about tactics, results, or objectivity. Not hardly. They also reveal what the reporter and his fellow Mexicans felt in their heart of hearts, in the quiet of their own continental anxieties. Sports writing as a discipline is notorious for this allowance of emotion and subjectivity. Rooting interests are often laid bare, or between the lines. This is why excerpts from so many match previews and summaries are included here: They add considerable texture to our understanding of US vs. Mexico—especially as viewed from the south.

"The journalists have a tendency to expect Mexican superiority on the pitch. When it is achieved, all is well in the world: Mexico and its progress can be celebrated and the U.S. dismissed, along with its powerful dollar," wrote Roger Magazine, Sergio Varela Hernández and Aldo Bravo, three more contributors to the *Perspectives* anthology. "However, Mexican wins by a small margin or ties are seen as warning signals of Mexican weakness or regression, and U.S. victories are perceived as tragedies, not just for the soccer team but for the nation and its collective psyche.

"For the Mexican sports journalists, the matches against the U.S. are important because they offer the opportunity to reinforce an *a priori* belief in Mexico's superiority over its northern neighbor on the soccer field. But this kind of interest in the matchup represents a dilemma because the outcome on the pitch may spoil this opportunity and threaten the journalists' fragile faith. Thus, they end up in the contradictory position of depending on the matchup, but resisting the treatment of the U.S. as a competitive rival." [17]

Three cheers to the authors for this bang-on analysis. It superbly summarizes the whipsaw, psychological swings that Mexican media coverage enabled throughout the twentieth century. We should point out that Ruggieri's reporting, issued in 1934, exhibits all the qualities Magazine, Veral, and Bravo (MVB) described more than eighty years later.

These early reports also reflect that Mexican attitudes toward the United States go far deeper than soccer. Evidently, the country's futbol-supporting population undertook this *clásico* pre-programmed to overvalue and overthink the larger context. They wasted little time in mapping onto this brand-new competition the gamut of cross-border relations.

"It is impossible to read Mexican reactions to the U.S.-Mexico soccer matchup in terms of soccer alone," MVB observed. "The U.S.'s geographical proximity and its political and economic influence permeate nearly all contexts of Mexican society. This presents a predicament similar to that faced by the sports journalists. Mexican national pride and the related desire for national autonomy contradict a reality of Mexican political and economic dependence on the U.S., which has increased over past decades. Only by eclipsing this 'special relationship' to the U.S. can Mexico imagine itself as internationally competitive and as autonomous.

"Soccer appears to offer an opportunity to accomplish this eclipsing of the U.S., since it is one set on the world stage, where Mexico is supposedly superior. However, the U.S.'s improvement on the soccer field in recent years has complicated this view of Mexican superiority. In any case, a game known for the arbitrariness of its outcomes is a risky, although perhaps titillating, forum for staking something as delicate as national pride." [18]

•••

By the summer of 1937, Raphael Garza Gutiérrez had pieced together for himself a solid toehold in the Mexican futbol establishment: managing *Las Aguilas* most of the time while periodically training the Mexican national team on behalf of the FMF. Mexico's regional leagues typically played matches each weekend during the season. But once that list of fixtures had concluded? The idea of international friendlies occupying the off-season did not exist. Other than World Cups and Olympic tournaments, the active scheduling of national team matches was not much considered—not in Mexico, nor the United States, which had organized just two friendlies since the 1934 World Cup.

This impoverished futbol-calendar situation changed during the summer of 1936. Once FIFA had awarded the 1938 World Cup to France, most futbol communities in the Western Hemisphere cried foul. All parties had assumed the tournament would ping back and forth between the two primary regions of excellence and popularity, South America and Europe. This unilateral breach resulted in a broad boycott from the Americas. Only Brazil turned up in France for the 1938 competition. The United States and Mexico also stayed home.

Garza and the *Federación* had a newfangled problem: How to fill this troublesome scheduling void? Post-1934, the Mexicans were itching for another shot at their continental neighbor, so the FMF proposed the first US-Mexico matches since the playoff in Rome, a three-game friendly series contested in Mexico City during the fall of 1937. For its part, the schedule-shy US Football Association accepted. [19]

Because neither party had anything better to do with its respective national teams.

And because football always presents the chance for revenge.

"The Americans are very wrong if they think that they are going to find the same team we brought to Rome three years ago," Garza told *La Afición* in advance of the opening match, scheduled for September 12, 1937. "They will see in our squad recognizable faces, but they are going to face something that possibly they do not even suspect: a new technique." [20]

This trio of grudge matches, all contested on consecutive weekends in September 1937, proved surprising and conclusive indeed. The Mexicans prevailed in each one, by lopsided scores, before packed houses across the capital region. It takes two points to make a line. Three points represent a verdict, and the scores left little room for interpretation: 7–2, at the *Estadio Parque Asturias*; 7–3 at *Estadio Parque Necaxa*, where the tour's largest crowd (22,000) showed up; and 5–1 at *Estadio Parque España*. [21]

Taken together, these blowouts immediately transformed Mexico's footballing self-image. It was frankly a lightbulb moment for the Mexican soccer establishment, which couldn't help but notice how eagerly fans supported the national team against the United States—and spent their pesos.

Prior to 1937, the conceit that Mexican soccer was in any way superior to the Yankee version had no purchase at all. The Americans' top-four finish in 1930 and the preliminary World Cup result in Rome, while a vanishingly small sample size, were the only evidence anyone had.

September 1937 supplied conclusive new data. These matches birthed the rivalry—south of the border anyway. For Mexican partisans, the series blotted out the unwanted memories of 1934, cemented Garza's prominence in the national team context, and created a *clásico* wherein Mexico held a commanding 3–1 advantage.

La Selección would not lose another match to the Americans until November 1980.

•••

Boycott of the 1938 World Cup proved the leading edge of an oncoming sporting vacuum, as the Second World War canceled dozens of international events including two World Cups. The United States and Mexico would not meet again until 1947. The war years saw American soccer fade even further from domestic relevance, while the Mexican federation went the other way: It kicked things into high gear.

In the near term, over the winter of 1937–38, the FMF scheduled and hosted *seven* unofficial friendlies against a team representing the Basque Country. Longer term, the FMF laid a foundation for the Mexican *Priméra*, which debuted in 1943 as *La Liga Mayor*, or "The Major League." This reorganization professionalized the game south of the Rio Grande—an advance that did nothing but widen the freshly established gap between Mexico and its archrival to the north. The new first division also consolidated the game under *Federación* leadership. Only the strongest clubs from the three largest regional leagues were invited to join the *Liga Mayor*: Asturias, Atlante, Club América, Marte, Necaxa, and Veracruz, all from the *Priméra Fuerza* in Mexico City; Atlas and Guadalajara from *La Liga Occidental de Jalisco*; Albinegros de Orizaba and Moctezuma from *La Liga Amateur de Veracruz*. Several of these clubs remain familiar to twenty-first-century readers, others less so. Club León and Puebla joined the following season. Monterrey came aboard in 1945.[22]

The first division rebranded as *La Priméra División de México* in 1949. A second division, along with promotion/relegation—the system where, at the close of each season, top finishers from the second division are promoted to the first, while bottom feeders from the top division go down—were added during the 1950s. In 2012, the richest clubs in Mexico created a new first division called *Liga MX*, an enterprise owned and administered by the clubs, not the FMF, a structure similar to that of the English Premier League.[23]

El Priméra was never perfect, but very quickly the league showed itself to be indisputably the finest in North America. It primed the sport for growth in postwar Mexico, a period when US soccer—which did not replace the defunct American Soccer League with another "first" division until 1967—was clearly regressing.

History shows the Second World War to have been a grim point of departure for US soccer, on field and off. In 1945, the national federation changed its name to the US Soccer Football Federation to distinguish itself from the "homegrown" sport that was beginning to take the country by storm. The organization would rebrand once more to the current "U.S. Soccer Federation" in 1974.

Those lopsided results from 1937: not a fluke. When the North American Football Confederation staged its first-ever continental championship in 1947, Mexico dominated the United States on neutral ground in Havana, 5–0.

For the next forty years, the Stars & Stripes were no match for the Mexican national team, now further bolstered by an up-and-running professional league and a broad cultural enthusiasm for the game. As Little League Baseball proliferated in postwar America, piggybacking on the widespread expansion of US suburbs, no soccer equivalent developed. Not until the 1970s. Once those American soccer natives came of age as senior players, early in the 1990s? *Presto!* The USMNT and USWNT were nobody's pushovers.[24]

But that development was a long time in coming. During those intervening decades, the string of Mexican victories kept playing out, to the unmitigated delight of the Mexican public. After more than a century of being bullied by the United States economically, geopolitically, and culturally, *el pueblo mexicano* had identified an arena where they could effectively fight back—thereby asserting a welcome measure of national autonomy.

Those forty-six years without a loss persuaded a predominant portion of the Mexican sporting population that theirs was a preeminent footballing nation. No small thing in this tale of siblings. At the very least, here was a soccer culture preparing to take its place in hemispheric high society. Come the 1960s, Mexico began to act on these feelings of self-belief in concrete ways, batting its eyelashes at FIFA and the International Olympic Committee, while building the richest domestic league outside of Europe.

•••

By the time CONCACAF replaced the North American Football Union in 1961, Mexico was indisputably the confederation giant. Additionally, as Calderón Cardozo makes clear: "In the 1960s soccer became a prosperous entertainment industry in Mexico, with significant support of and participation by the broadcasting television network *Telesistema Mexicano*, in close partnership with the Mexican government and various corporations in the soft drink and beer industries." [25]

Together with the FMF, these institutions, both public and private, all saw fit to double down on futbol, to great and lasting effect. When the 1960s began, sports programming in Mexico featured more or less equal portions of soccer, baseball, boxing, and bull fighting. By the time the global soccer community arrived for World Cup 1970, futbol dominated the airwaves.

See here a handy-dandy timeline that details Mexico's rapid progression to futbol's first world, a standing it achieved—in terms of liquidity, infrastructure, and continental rank—at the direct expense of the United States and its national team.

- September 1961: Headquartered in Mexico City, a new confederation representing not just North and Central America but also the Caribbean replaces the old North American Football Union. Until the early 1990s, Mexico and its broadcast partners would run CONCACAF according to priorities shaped around Mexico, its first division, and *El Tri*.

- October 1964: Mexico is awarded the 1970 World Cup, outbidding (*wait for it . . .*) Argentina for the privilege. FIFA understood what it was doing, as Mexico represented a bigger market for futbol and a more stable political climate. The future host nation also committed to building three new stadiums: *Estadio Cuauhtémoc* in Puebla, *Estadio Nou Camp* in León, and . . .

- May 1966: *Estadio Azteca*, cosmic cradle of Mexican futbol and fated centerpiece of two World Cups, opens for play with an exhibition match between Club América and the Italian club Torino F.C. The Azteca was conceived in 1961, when Mexico City was chasing the 1968 Olympic Games. But the World Cup of 1970, the first ever to be televised in color, instantly transformed the hulking, half-sunken edifice into an iconic futbol venue of global esteem, the original theater of dreams. It also quickly built a reputation as the national team's fortress. The United States has never won an official match at the Azteca—just a single friendly, in 2012. Reportedly, the FMF agreed to play a secondary role in hosting 2026 World Cup matches *only* if the tournament opener were held in the stadium. And so it will come to pass: the capital will host the tournament curtain-raiser on June 11, 2026.[26]

- September 1968: The Summer Olympics visit Mexico City, the nation's capital having outbid Detroit, Lyon and (*wait for it . . .*) Buenos Aires for the privilege. Mexico's self-image as a first-world sporting nation was further bolstered by this undertaking, though Mexicans recognized that this Olympiad and the attendant visibility were secured at significant cultural cost. In the moment, large portions of the population, especially labor unions, objected to the spending of public funds on the endeavor. Five hundred thousand rallied in August 1968, chanting *¡No queremos olimpiadas, queremos revolución!*—"We don't want Olympics, we want revolution!" Ten days ahead of the flame-lighting at *Estadio Azteca*, President Gustavo Díaz Ordaz directed federal armed forces to open fire on a protest gathering in the *Plaza de las Tres Culturas*. Hundreds of Mexicans were killed in the so-called Tlatelolco Massacre, with more than 1,000 citizens arrested.[27]

- June 1970: The ninth FIFA World Cup goes off without a hitch. When it came to hosting a tournament that showcased the arrival of Mexican futbol on the world stage, as opposed to a multi-sport spectacle like the Olympic Games, money was no object. Even public money.

While broadcasters normally exhibit voracious appetites for killer live-sports content, the US media fraternity essentially ignored the *Mundial* contested just across its southern border. Clive Toye, the Cosmos GM who lured Pelé to NASL, tells a great story about that period. In 1970, he and NASL commissioner Phil Woosnam had personally secured American TV rights to the Mexican World Cup. They paid a whopping $1,500 ($13,000 in 2026 dollars) for the privilege.

"We couldn't find anybody to televise a single game," Toye told *The Guardian* newspaper in 2015. "We had to put it on closed circuit at Madison Square Garden, a place in Chicago, and a place in Los Angeles—the only places in the United States where you could watch it live. Now you can't even *say* 'World Cup' without paying $1,500 to somebody, for God's sake." [28]

Televisa—formed by the January 1973 merger of *Telesistema Mexicano* and *Televisión Independiente de México*—went the other way. It doubled down on futbol, again. No longer content to broadcast domestic futbol to Mexicans, the network started beaming Mexican-league content around the Americas. As a result, the *Priméra* entered its first period of true glory, thanks to jacked-up television exposure and enormous post-World Cup interest in all things Mexican futbol. [29]

Starting in the 1970s, for the first time, *Priméra* clubs were generating enough money to invest in foreign players. Go Google "South American footballers in the Mexican *Priméra*". The number of Argentinians who ventured north during the 1970s, compared to those from other CONMEBOL nations, will stun you. Mexican first-division futbol grew rich enough during the 1970s to attract players from Europe as well, including the inimitable Bora Milutinovic (Pumas, 1972-77), Italy's Francesco Gallina (Atlante, 1971-74) and Dutchman Theo van der Heyden (Atlas, 1974-75).

By contrast, the North American Soccer League—which enjoyed precious little broadcast support throughout its 17-year existence—invested in far more European talent, to far less effect.

Still, some of those players did dip their toes in Mexican domestic futbol on account of NASL stints. Scotland's Ronnie Sharp, for example, sandwiched a season with San Luis F.C. (1973–74) between NASL spells with the Miami Toros and Ft. Lauderdale Strikers. The great Portuguese star Eusebio joined Monterrey between NASL stopovers in Boston and Toronto.

The point is, the *Priméra* grew into an economic force to be reckoned with during the 1970s, on account of Mexico's garden-fresh standing as a futbol nation of World Cup-hosting caliber. The NASL was founded in 1968, but the enterprise engaged largely in sound and fury, signifying nothing. By 1984, it was dead and buried.

•••

The Mexican futbol establishment naturally watched the tepid rise and fall of NASL with great interest. In the end, the *Priméra*'s obvious superiority proved one more source of Mexico's growing identification as a global player on the footballing stage. *El Tri*'s serial pummeling of the US Men's National Team did nothing but underscore that identity. What's remarkable, however, in looking back over the decades, before and since 1961, is how much Mexico's futbol reputation was forged not via victories or positive performances outside of CONCACAF, but rather on the evidence of *La Selección*'s unrelenting, almost giddy domination of Team USA.

Between the 3-match series of friendlies in September 1937 and World Cup qualification in 1949, the Mexican national team beat Team USA five straight times. It's relevant to point out that during roughly the same period, 1934 through 1950, the Americans didn't beat anyone other than Cuba and the brand-new state of Israel. Then, somehow, the United States managed to steal a game vs. England, 1–0, at the Brazilian World Cup of 1950. This result, perhaps the biggest upset in world soccer history, effectively obscures just how hopeless the US soccer program had become by mid-century.

Starting in January 1954, FIFA insisted upon a new, more formal system of World Cup qualification administered by the various regional confederations. (The first two such tournaments were organized by the North American Football Union. CONCACAF would take over prior to the 1962 World Cup in Chile.) Mexico won each of these competitions, directly qualifying for World

Cups in 1950, 1954, 1958, 1962 and 1966—beating the Yanks eight more times in the process. The USMNT did manage a pair of draws, each in Los Angeles, in 1962 and 1966.

The *Priméra* had clearly upgraded the standard of play across the country. The Mexicans largely beat up on their fellow Central American and Caribbean opponents during these qualification efforts as well.

But one must ask: To what end? North America's footballing Big Brother did not win an actual World Cup match until 1962. In point of fact, they were outscored at those World Cups, 24–3. Come the Chilean World Cup of 1962, that first victory did turn heads: *El Tri* dispatched eventual finalist Czechoslovakia, 2–0, during the group stage. On the other hand, Mexico had barely qualified for Chile, losing to Costa Rica and drawing with (*wait for it . . .*) the Netherlands Antilles during a final qualification stage. *Nada bueno.*

Inside and outside the region, the song remained the same: *Jugamos como nunca y perdimos como siempre . . .* "We played like never before and we lost like always."

Here's a fun, telling fact: *El Tricolor* did not play a single international friendly outside of Mexico until 1961.[30] Not one! Only when Mexico would mobilize to land the *Mundial* of 1970 did the national team start barnstorming outside its own borders—in much the same way Qatar made the rounds prior to hosting the 2022 World Cup. Still, when the Mexicans did visit Wembley Stadium in 1961, they surrendered eight goals to their English hosts and scored just one. *Ouch.*

Few Mexicans realize their own national team wore Spanish colors until 1955. The country's tri-color flag has been in use, in one form or another, since independence in 1821. However, those colors and the associated nickname, *El Tri*, were not deployed for more than thirty years after the national team debuted—because the team did not wear Green, White, and Red. It was Guillermo Cañedo, then an assistant to FMF President Salvador Guarneros, who dreamed up this seemingly obvious sartorial initiative ahead of the 1956 Pan American Games, held in Mexico City.[31] The green jerseys were a hit, to no one's surprise.

But why are they so hesitant to test themselves against better regional and global competition? And why not play in the country's own colors? For the record, the FMF didn't add the red socks until 1984.

The truth is, in almost every respect, aside from beating up on Punk Brother USA, mid-century Mexican soccer was decidedly underwhelming and plagued by a curious self-doubt. All through the 1950s and well into the 1960s, *Priméra* clubs remained so poorly capitalized that few league champions could scrape together the means to participate in important club competitions like the *Copa Libertadores*. Paraguay and Peru aren't rich nations by any standard, yet their league champions routinely took part in the South American club championship. For reasons perhaps best understood by sports psychologists, Mexico's involvement with the *Copa* did not begin until 1998 and lasted only through 2016.

•••

As an American soccer partisan researching much of this information for the first time, the mediocrity and insularity of Mexico's national team, even within the low-rent context and confines of CONCACAF, surprised me. US soccer fans had long understood it was nearly impossible for the Stars & Stripes to qualify for World Cups: The Yanks could not beat Mexico, and for many years just one side advanced from this region to FIFA's Big Dance.

Less obvious was this consequence: The same system effectively stamped Mexico as a big fish in a very small pond.

"There is this thing about Mexico where there's always this pessimistic sense around the national team. Like we tend to think that everything used to be better before. But, you know, what are they nostalgic for?" asks Marion Reimers. "When do they think that Mexico and *El Tri* were at their best? I mean, there are so many Round-of-16 exits. So many non-qualifications. They run together, for me."

What also jumps out in our examination of this continental derby is the extent to which Mexico's footballing self-image was built specifically on this decades-long domination of the United States.

In 1970 and 1986, the Mexicans hosted the World Cup and qualified automatically. Two quarterfinal exits ensued, the first in Toluca, the next in San Nicolás de los Garza. Nothing to sneeze at, reaching the last eight. However, four years after their first stint as host, *La Selección* couldn't beat Haiti (pop. in 1974, 4.6 million; Mexico, 57 million) and failed to qualify for West Germany.

In 1978, the national team did claim the lone berth out of CONCACAF—only to finish dead last in a field of 16 at the Argentinian World Cup. Honduras and El Salvador both qualified for the next *Mundial*, in Spain, at Mexico's direct expense. To put a black bow of mourning on this period, FIFA banned *El Tri* from *Italia* '90 for fielding overage players in a 1988 youth tournament.

Recall that when the United States finally did beat Mexico in 1980, our media friends at *La Afición* appeared to freak out over its failure to progress as a soccer nation: "We are mired in total deception . . . Because the team does not advance, because it does not have international prestige, because it does not know how to play when not at home." Maybe the writer here had a point, a historically informed point, especially after that last-place, cringe-inducing finish at Argentina '78. One can also view this journalistic analysis as damned prescient. After all, the Fort Lauderdale match report was filed *before* Mexico watched Honduras and El Salvador advance to *Espana* '82 in its accustomed place.

As ever, however, the history of Mexico vs. United States is one of greater and greater interdependence. Team Mexico—the fans, the *Federación* and its corporate sponsors—clearly required a doormat like the United States to project itself as a meaningful soccer nation. Domestically, its dominance of the continental bully served this purpose for more than half a century. To the extent that Mexicans believed this convenient self-deception, their footballing self-image was largely based on and preserved by beating up on the *americanos* over and over again.

Ironically enough, the US soccer community explained away its own ineptitude using the same insular argument and self-deception: *Clearly, Mexico is an elite soccer nation. They beat us every time!*

That's the less-flattering take on these mutually reliant futbol fortunes. Here's the more affirming flip side: In the 1990s, when Mexico most critically required a capable regional rival—one that actually tested its national team; one whose stars went to Europe to better themselves, thereby encouraging Mexican stars to follow suit; one that produced dozens of quality dual-national prospects who had the viable choice of playing for Mexico or the United States—the North American Derby has served it very well.

By the same token, post 1991, when the new-and-improved *Yanquis* sought a foil to raise *their* game and functionally mainstream the sport north of the border, *El Tri* provided the ideal cultural and competitive adversary.

One could not dream up or artificially construct a more codependent relationship in the history of international sport.

•••

The 1990s did change everything. They didn't just reinvigorate the *clásico*. The matches played throughout the decade created a *superclásico* while also allowing each sibling to move forward independently of one another, in many important ways. Mexico's finest national team may have been the 1993 edition, according to Reimers and others. A Brazilian scalp at the 1999 Confederations Cup? Massive accomplishment, even if the high-water mark again occurred in the country.

North of the border, the Stars & Stripes made World Cup qualification routine, while the women's national team felt nearly the same way about World Cup *titles*. Together, they created an unapologetic American appetite for soccer's magnificent international dynamics. It's impossible to imagine that hunger taking permanent hold without the men's national team doing battle with Mexico fifty times since 1991.

Still, post-millennium, the two nations have redoubled efforts to transcend this Sibling Rivalry. Both desperately seek to better compete, as wannabe equals, with top-shelf nations in South America and Europe, and it's fair to ask whether *Der Nordamerikanische Klassiker* aids and abets these ambitions. Yet posing such questions is a bit like wondering aloud whether one should cut off or limit contact with a sister or brother—in order to get ahead at work or better court a spouse from a higher socio-economic station. Families are complicated. They're hard to simply detach from. Weirdness is a given.

For example, it remains paradoxical and, to many Mexicans, mildly hilarious that the United States took so long in coming around to soccer's charms. (Cue Carlo Ancelotti, European Cup winner, Champions League manager extraordinaire, now the man in charge of Brazil ahead of World Cup 2026: "Of all the unimportant things in life, futbol is the most important.") Followers of *El Tri* find it all the more rich that such extraordinary revisions—to the rivalry, to the footballing identities of both countries—have been co-authored by a soccer nation that plays its first-division soccer in the summertime. On fields outfitted with artificial turf and measured in yards. Reimer continues:

> It's really cute, no? Watching that development. It's adorable because it's like, Oh my God: You realized there are other countries in the world? That's *so sweet* . . . I'm saying this really from a loving perspective, no? Like I'm talking to a cousin who we really like a lot and you're over for Christmas dinner, okay? But why, why, why is everything measured in feet? There's always something different, no? Ounces or gallons instead of liters? Why?
>
> I know people in other countries make fun about this as well: Why is it called the World Series? You guys are playing amongst yourselves! It doesn't make any sense. Someone wins the NBA title and it says *World Champions*. In a world of whom?
>
> The whole world plays with a calendar that begins in August or September and ends in May. The U.S. does not, and it will always be a problem.

The American professional futbol calendar does wreak havoc with the transfer of players to and from Major League Soccer. In November 2024, MLS officials finally engaged with team owners to explore the idea of joining the traditional world schedule—beginning the season in August, not February. In April 2025, the league Board of Governors authorized a second phase of exploration, adding that nothing would happen before the 2027 season. Translation? The 2026 World Cup will indeed interrupt the MLS season for a month.[32]

On further reflection, though, we might wonder if this scheduling business is such a big obstacle for MLS, the NWSL or US Soccer. For thirty-five years, American futbol has gone its own way and grown the game like nowhere else. As Reimers herself points out, Leo Messi might never have come to Miami if the MLS schedule were "normal." Neither did non-traditional futbol calendars prove problematic for the Qataris, who convinced FIFA to hold a winter World Cup in 2022 that interrupted every league schedule on Earth—except that of Major League Soccer.

"*Uh-huh*, sure. Absolutely," Reimers responded with mock contemplation. "And what connects the US and Qatar? What connects those two countries? Let me think . . ."

5

Envy and Scorn in the Borderlands

Sometime late in the group stage of the World Cup 2014, I allowed myself to express the unspeakable bits out loud: *I can't help myself, but it's exhilarating to watch the Mexicans win World Cup matches,* I admitted to readers at halphillips .net. *They are so into it—the team, the coaches, the fans. Though it does bother me that they almost certainly do not reciprocate in this regard, even after our completely unnecessary late-game goals vs. Panama in the final Hexagonal qualifier, which delivered them to the final pre-World Cup playoff and saved their entire country from a mass sporting psychosis. They were all full of love and kisses that night, but methinks they'd love to see us crash out on Thursday. Doesn't seem right.*

This admission was published two days before the US Men's National Team played Belgium in the Round of 16 (*we did crash out, though valiantly*), less than a year after the briefly celebrated canonization of San Zusi, and a full decade before I launched into the writing of this book, the research for which has helped me better understand my own feelings of twelve years ago. Why was I quietly rooting for my country's archrival when, without a doubt, their fans would never return the favor? Back in 2014, I reasoned it this way: First of all, Mexican futbol is superb when it comes to pure pageantry. Full stop. Secondly, if Mexico does well at the World Cup, those results reflect well on the qualities and capabilities of its sworn enemy and its home region writ large. The same emotional process no doubt applied to Costa Rica, which so bravely and impressively advanced to the last eight in Brazil.

Psychologists better understand these types of feelings than sports writers because they observe and study them in the context of envy and scorn. We revisit these impulses here to better recognize why these two opponents feel the way they do about each other.

The basic idea: When two distinct groups stand in opposition—such as rival fan bases or national populations—humans cannot effectively *humanize* so many people at once. When generalizing about these "others," we broadly compare and contrast ourselves with them through the lenses of several critical base instincts, including envy and scorn. As a rule, behavioral eggheads agree: *Homo sapiens* envy up and scorn down. Envy is expressed loudly and often. Scorn is mostly silent. These elemental urges shape the way groups affiliate and interact going forward. In short, these psychic goalposts guide how and why groups root against each other,[1] or not.

Our friend Dr. Andrei Markovits has written a great deal about these dynamics in the context of US college football. Dr. Joe Cobbs, in his work, has used envy-and-scorn framing to better understand the fundamental nature of all sporting rivalries. Both scholars lean heavily on Dr. Susan Fiske, whose 2010 work laid the groundwork for sociological study in this area.

Generally, all three scholars would agree that Mexico envies the United States and its place in the world—its money, its power, its influence, some would say its dominant, pervasive culture. When it comes to this border relationship, Mexicans envy up in every regard *but* soccer.

In the futbol space, however, Mexican fans effectively scorned down for the entirety of the twentieth century. They reveled in United States failures; they built their self-image in large part on beating the futile *gringos* repeatedly. But Fiske is right: They did so very quietly because US soccer was beneath their contempt. When they did speak of worthy foes, they envied up by pointed and aspiring to Argentina, Brazil, and Colombia.

When they do verbalize or make public their feelings, Mexican media, fans, and academics are uniformly galled by the idea that not only are these *americanos* lousy at futbol, they don't love the game enough or care enough about being so bad! These are sentiments Mexicans have held for decades and remain eager to voice.

"Every time the Mexicans beat the U.S., it wasn't just winning on the field—they were basically *Sticking it to The Man*," Markovits told me. "But then the scorn becomes problematic. Because when they stop beating the United States consistently, in the 1990s, it became muddled. It's not just failing to achieve results against the entity you envy. It's being beaten by an entity that doesn't even scorn you, that doesn't care, which makes it far worse. Mexicans truly believe the United States just doesn't care that much about soccer. That's why, in the modern context, when they do lose, it's triply hurtful.

"It's like losing to the Washington Generals."

•••

Let's flip it around, up close and personal. In acknowledging that Mexico would never root for the United States, and in recognizing that Mexicans would never place regional solidarity above their own scorn, I found myself envying up. Writing in 2014, I *wished* that US soccer culture was more like Mexico's—its victories, of course, but also its flair and communal obsession with the game. They truly love this sport in ways we Americans still seek to match. A dozen years on, I still fancy all that for my country and our soccer culture. I personally don't feel any real scorn for the Mexican nation, its culture, or people—on the contrary. But there are, *ahem*, plenty of my fellow US citizens who do.

A bit magically, with this helpful framework to work from, many of the puzzling emotional responses we now associate with US-Mexico are rendered far more understandable. They make human sense, especially when we think of these two groups as familiars, which, in the story of North America since 1492, we most certainly are.

"Oh, yeah. Definitely. And big brother invariably wants to keep little brother down," Cobbs told me. "I'm not saying there's no rivalry here, but this explains why Mexico is less prone to admit that little brother has ever been a soccer rival. Right? Because that would legitimize little brother."

Because Mexico is the older brother in soccer, but the younger brother everywhere else, *El Tri* supporters and media have almost no incentive to ease up on the down-scoring. As a matter of fact, this posture brings home why Mexican fans and media, especially those residing in Mexico, are more interested in cultivating a rivalry elsewhere, with another big-brother peer like Argentina or Brazil. "Andy Markovits introduced me to this framework," Cobbs continues. "You're not ignoring little brother necessarily, but you want to pretend like you're ignoring them. The little brother is kind of an annoyance—not important enough to represent a true rival."

As a big brother myself, here was another *Aha!* moment. I'm not at all proud of the way I often treated my younger brother growing up. I also remember it was doubly exasperating to verbalize my issues with him. I didn't want to explain to my parents *why* he was bothering me, or *why* I didn't want to include him in this activity or that. I just wanted him to GO AWAY. I didn't want him hanging around me and my friends. I sure as hell didn't want to discuss him with third parties or treat him as a peer.

Markovits points out that, in this specialized field of study, "There's so much more research on envy. Lots of researchers. There's virtually zero work being done on scorn, though, for one important reason: Scorn is, ultimately, silence."

I am reminded of a great scene from the feted television series *Mad Men*. It's Season 5, and the show's star and antihero, Don Draper, has again behaved very badly in the office: He has presented a colleague's idea as his own. Draper gets on the elevator with this drone whose work he's just appropriated. The underling attempts a scornful stance, one of mock pity: "I feel bad for you," he says to his boss.

Draper responds like the prototype Big Brother: "I don't think about you at all."

According to Cobbs, this interpersonal practice describes the US vs. Mexico rivalry throughout its long asymmetrical phase. "As Mexicans, their stance was: We'll compete when we have to, and we'll beat you, and then we'll forget about you . . . That started to change, of course, during the 1990s when the United States won a few important matches. That's when you started to see our ingredients, from our research: We finally see the conspicuous moments you need to create a rivalry narrative, a new narrative entirely."

If Mexico didn't envy the United States in so many other respects, if it shared an alternative history with this neighboring country, or no history at all, it might have welcomed this new North American rival—in the way first-rate athletes often do. *This competition will make us a better side. It will lift all boats here in Mexico*. But there was way too much baggage being lugged around to enable that sort of practical grace.

What's more, negative baggage rarely dissipates between groups of humans locked in vicious cycles of envy and scorn. Fiske makes this equally clear:

> Downward scorn contaminates interactions, but envy is often far more damaging, because it's often public, and it strikes at individual insecurity that produced the emotion: Envy humiliates and angers people . . . Feeling below someone makes people feel ashamed at their own inadequacy. If a peer can succeed, then people feel inadequate for not doing equally well. Envy also makes people angry at the injustice of their low-status positions. Those who succeeded must have had unfair advantages. Envy correlates with depression, unhappiness, and low self-esteem.[2]

We've quoted several Mexican nationals and media commentators who've cited and/or bemoaned their country's historical lack of autonomy, which spills over into soccer in very real, very upsetting ways—many of them directly affected by the nation's physical proximity to the United States. Take the playing of national team friendlies in Arizona and Texas, not Guadalajara or Morelia. Mexican futbol fans feel slighted by this.

In the Leagues Cup, founded in 2023, MLS and *Liga MX* clubs have undertaken a pretty compelling competition. Yet *all* the matches are held north of the border. Not surprisingly, Mexican clubs and their fans don't cotton to the idea of a tournament where they're always playing road games.

There's a famous saying—attributed to so many people, it too has become apocryphal—that speaks to Mexico's peculiar geography: *So near to God, but so close to the United States.* To better understand this truism and how it affects the *El Clásico Norteamericano,* a quick historical review is required.

•••

After his notorious duel with Alexander Hamilton in July 1804, Aaron Burr became an infamous rogue and outcast. He traveled west, where he publicly schemed the formation of a hulking southern empire centered in New Orleans and inclusive of Mexico, which still belonged to Imperial Spain. Burr wasn't some yahoo with delusions of grandeur. He was a hero of the Revolutionary

War, a former senator from New Jersey whose term as US vice president (under Thomas Jefferson) had just ended. His designs on Mexican territory went nowhere, but his attitudes would prove telling.

As Greg Grandin wrote in *The End of the Myth*, "It's a wonder Mexico survived the nineteenth century at all." Mexican autonomy was acutely disrespected, if not outright ignored, before the country was a "country."[3]

After their founding in 1821, the United Mexican States had a much harder time fending off the territorial appetites of southern planters, though "planters" is a rather polite word for those Americans who would plague Mexico and other parts of Central America through the 1870s. These were slavers who had, in fact, colonized the Mexican province of Texas in the early 1830s, to pursue a plantation economy and culture unfettered by US federal power. Mexico had quickly banned slavery upon separating itself from Imperial Spain. This remarkable disagreement over human bondage precipitated, in 1836, what Anglo-Texans called their War of Independence. Texas would repel the forces of General Antonio de Padua María Severino López de Santa Anna y Pérez de Lebrón (better known as Santa Anna) and enter the Union in 1845 as a slave state.[4]

At no point in its history did Mexico have the stomach for military conflict with the Americans. It was a series of trumped-up "border disputes" in 1846 that allowed Congress and President James K. Polk to declare war and invade Veracruz. After winning the decisive Battle of Churubusco in August of 1847, US forces occupied Mexico City. In the halls of Congress, legislators and lobbyists debated whether they should simply absorb the whole of Mexico— an idea eventually abandoned. This was only because taking on so many non-Anglo, Spanish-speaking Catholics as citizens was deemed impractical.[5]

"I don't think that many Americans know that the U.S. Army came all the way to Mexico City and was here for two years," says Amy Glover, the Michigan-born dual national who has lived in Mexico since the 1990s and also writes a monthly column for the business periodical *El Economista*. "I would say all Mexicans, even taxi drivers, know that—and that the United States took half of Mexico's territory as a result. But honestly: How many Americans know that? I would guess, 10 percent?

"I don't know if you've heard of the *niños héroes*, the child heroes, but the people here know. There are streets named after these young men who were defending the castle. When it was obvious that the Americans were going to take it, they wrapped themselves in the flag and leapt to their death . . . All Mexican school children are taught this. This is something everybody knows. So, this history has had a huge impact on the Mexican psyche. Mexico has suffered for a long time from an inferiority complex vis-a-vis the U.S. I think that is what feeds into this rivalry still today—why it's such a terrible thing to think that now *los pinches gringos* can beat Mexico in soccer. Because that was the one area where the U.S. always kind of sucked. And now, there's not even that . . ."

When it comes to respecting Mexican sovereignty and its physical integrity, the United States has treated Mexicans as it treated indigenous peoples across the North American continent. In the 1850s, Tennessee physician-turned-mercenary William Walker twice led invasions of Central America, an activity common enough to earn these pirates a particular nineteenth-century label: "filibusters." Walker first showed up at the head of an army in Baja California, then moved on to Sonora before being repulsed by Mexican forces. Then, in 1855, he was invited by the Nicaraguan Democratic Party to assist in its civil war against the country's so-called Legitimist faction. Walker instead took control of the entire government, declared himself president (1856), and made clear his plans to re-establish Nicaragua as a slave "state". US president Franklin Pierce wasted no time in recognizing Walker's regime as the country's lawful government.[6]

I share the tale of William Walker for two reasons. First, to emphasize that Mexicans and Central Americans aren't just whistling Dixie when they complain about US imperialism. Mexican autonomy, like that of indigenous North American peoples, has never been respected by the United States.

Second, this sort of behavior from *El Norte* is difficult to move past. To this day, it informs Mexico's broader Little Brother attitudes toward the United States, and not merely in the futbol realm.

"Much more than soccer fuels many Mexican fans' animus toward the U.S. team," Columbia University professor Rodolfo de la Garza told *Sports Illustrated* in 2015.

> There are very few instances in the history of the two countries where Mexico has either been dealt with fairly or has won when there were differences... Central to Mexican nationalism is anti-Americanism. The U.S. invaded Mexico on various occasions, and by their judgment the Mexicans lost half their land. There's a built-in structure of resentment, a built-in rivalry.[7]

This legacy of US military and paramilitary adventurism survives into the twenty-first century in more peculiar, soccer-centric ways—if we look hard enough. Walker's incursion was eventually blunted by the combined military forces of Nicaragua, Costa Rica, El Salvador, Belize, and Honduras. The Honduran forces were led by General Florencio Xatruch. Today, the Honduran national soccer team is known as *Los Contrachos*—a term coined by Nicaraguans, who referred to these anti-Walker Honduran troops as the *Xatruches*. Nicaraguans had trouble pronouncing the word, apparently, landed on *Catrachos*, and it stuck.[8]

Walker was ultimately run out of Nicaragua but evaded capture. The villain published a book in 1860, recounting his misadventures and arguing for the geographical expansion of slavery. He returned to Central America that same year, only to be arrested by the British Royal Navy. The incorrigible filibuster was turned over to the Honduran government, which wasted little time in executing him by firing squad on September 12, 1860.

•••

The entirety of Mexico's chaotic nineteenth century cannot be left at the door of US imperialism. Shortly after winning its own independence, Mexico claimed—then quickly lost control of—all the territories that today comprise Nicaragua, Honduras, Belize, Guatemala, Costa Rica, and El Salvador. From its conception, the weak central government in Mexico City grew increasingly indebted to foreign creditors, a reality further exacerbated by a succession of early *coups d'etats*, civil wars and regional conflicts. The United Mexican States nearly lost the Yucatan to a Mayan peasant revolt in 1847. Fifteen years later, French monarch Napoleon III used Mexico's mountain of debt to invade the country, occupy the capital, and install Austrian archduke Maximilian as emperor.

Little of this activity had anything directly to do with the United States of America, but Mexico's lack of autonomy across the region is plain to see. Then and now.

US bankers, primarily those in northern states, backed the five-year guerrilla war that Mexican republicans fought and won against Maximilian. *He* was executed in 1867, also by firing squad. According to Grandin, the victorious faction in Mexico City saw itself as an extension of Abraham Lincoln's Republican ideals. Its American creditors wanted only to be repaid.

"In the end, though, it wasn't annexation or war but the leverage provided by debt, along with the promise of more loans and investments to build railroads, that brought Mexico to heel," Grandin writes. "With no other options, Mexico's leaders practically handed over the national economy to foreign investors. Led by some of the most storied names in US corporate history—including J.P. Morgan, John Rockefeller and Standard Oil, Edward Harriman, the Astors, the Guggenheims, Joseph Headly Dulles . . . William Randolph Hearst, Phelps Dodge, Union Pacific, and Cargill—US capital radically transformed Mexico.

"Within half a century, the United States' interests would come to control, nearly absolutely, oil productions, railroads, utilities, livestock, agriculture, and ports." [9]

That sort of economic incursion, following on the twenty-four-month military occupation just two decades prior, is difficult to forgive or forget in the long term. Yet scholars generally believe this Gilded Age hijacking of the Mexican economy led directly to the Mexican Revolution of 1910, what historian John Mason Hart called "the first great third-world uprising against American economic, cultural and military expansion." [10] Many US corporate holdings, including most of the oil infrastructure, were seized and nationalized post-revolution. Other American "interests" remain and wield extraordinary economic power on both sides of the border to this day.

As the First World War and the Revolution drew to a close, few North Americans on either side of the Rio Grande would have argued that the United States and Mexico maintained a "special relationship," one that recognized any economic or cultural interdependence. If pressed, citizens of both countries would have correctly described the relationship as top-down exploitative.

The early twentieth century, though, did usher in a more symbiotic cross-border understanding, which, ironically, began with immigration legislation—the hottest of political hot buttons today. According to Carrie Gibson, author of *El Norte: The Epic and Forgotten History of Hispanic North America*, the US Immigration Act of 1917 demonstrated the societal shifts then in motion. American railroad, mining, and agricultural interests lobbied Congress hard to exempt Mexicans from this influential piece of legislation, which instead targeted and greatly restricted Asian and Eastern European immigration. Then, as now, these industries had grown highly reliant on Mexican labor.[11]

The John Reid Act of 1924 codified strict quotas on a still-broader range of immigrant groups (a legal apparatus that stayed in place until the Immigration and Nationality Act of 1965), but Mexican nationals were again exempted. Nineteen twenty-four also witnessed the formation of the US Border Patrol. According to the American Immigration Council, "Many officers came from organizations with a history of racial violence and brutality, including the Ku Klux Klan and the Texas Rangers, carrying over the culture of a racist 'brotherhood' into the new agency." [12]

During the Great Depression, northward migration from Mexico slowed to a trickle, as it always does in times of economic downturn. In 1931, according to Gibson, the repatriation of Mexicans greatly exceeded those emigrating north into the United States.

"My grandfather, Salvador Flores, and his brothers all came to St. Louis in the early 1920s—to work on the railroads," explains Ty Keough, son of American soccer luminary Harry Keough and a national team stalwart in his own right. "Their father was a railroad engineer on the Manzanillo-Guadalajara line. Eventually his sons took the train to Guadalajara, then to the Texas border, where they walked 3-4 days to Galveston, before they landed here in St. Louis. My mom was born in St. Louis, in 1930, but when the Depression hit, they all moved back to Guadalajara after my grandfather lost his job with the railroad. That was 1933. She was raised there—she's 96 and still spends her winters down there."

An identical scenario produced St. Louis native and fellow USMNTer Ruben Mendoza. He was born to Mexican nationals in the Gateway City but lived out the Depression era in his parents' ancestral home in the State of Durango, followed by a second northward migration after the Second World War. Good thing, too. Mendoza was perhaps the finest US national team player of the 1950s—*and* he effectively introduced Ty Keough's father Harry to his mother, the former Alma Flores (!).

While more than 400,000 Mexican Americans were reportedly repatriated during the 1930s, rampant unemployment north of the border resulted in the increased scapegoating of those who remained—as job-stealers and/or "radical" union sympathizers. These inhabitants were largely Catholic, too, subject to a culture, government, and economy still dominated by White Anglo-Saxon Protestants.

The crises of the Second World War renewed and redoubled any and all tensions and co-dependencies. Mexican American labor, particularly in Southern California, proved vital to the war effort. The federal Bracero Program, launched in 1942, would legally invite and effectively *import* more than 5 million Mexican workers to twenty-four states, including California, whose coastline was rife with military installations and shipbuilding facilities. In June 1943, hundreds of US servicemen chased down and brutalized dozens of urban *pachucos*—a young Hispanic cohort identifiable by their broad-shouldered jackets and wide-brimmed hats. This scandalous urban pogrom came to be known as the Zoot Suit Riots.[13]

Half a million US residents of Latino heritage ultimately fought beside those servicemen for the United States. Those Mexican Americans who joined up became naturalized, but only if they could document that they had entered the country legally. This regulatory distinction led directly to 1954's infamous "Operation Wetback," whereby an estimated 1 million Hispanics were rounded up and deported to Mexico from Southern California. The American GI Forum, an organization of Mexican American Second World War veterans, backed this anti-immigrant measure. Its leader, Hector García, argued that illegal immigration threatened the well-being and livelihood of those who had crossed legally. Sound familiar? Meanwhile, *bracero* arrivals doubled between 1953 and 1959.[14]

Then, as now, in times of economic prosperity and depression, immigration from the south pissed off a lot of US citizens, including those of Mexican heritage. Then, as now, however, all parties recognized that the increasingly robust US economic machine could not function without this indispensable pool of labor.

• • •

Most of Markovits' soccer scholarship does not touch directly upon US-Mexican relations. His influential 2001 book, *Offside: Soccer and American Exceptionalism*, spoke directly to the peculiar place futbol occupies in American culture. Mainly, why exactly this global game was so slow in reaching the mainstream here.

When we examine more closely the women's North American Derby (Chapter 10), we'll engage with another soccer-centric interpretation that Markovits introduced: how women's national teams tend to excel in countries where the men's game has demonstrated itself to be culturally weak (the United States, Scandinavia, Japan, and Australia). Whereas in those nations where men's soccer has dominated the sporting culture (Mexico, Europe, and South America), women's soccer has not typically thrived.

Few observers anywhere in the world better understand the sport and how fans respond to it.

Markovits' 2017 paper on envy and scorn,[15] published with Rebecca Shipan and Jillian Victor, concentrated on US college football—though the sport itself hardly matters. Human beings are human beings. Markovits' work confirms what we all understand instinctively: *Homo sapiens* tribalize very quickly and easily in opposition to, or by simple comparison to, other groups of *sapiens*. And we do so according to traits universally held. Which is to say, for deeply rooted biological reasons.

"The other crucial thing in terms of rivalry is that envy and scorn have nothing to do with football, or futbol, or anything that happens on the field *per se*," Markovits told me in January 2025, a year after he retired from his position at the University of Michigan.

I was on the faculty of this university for 25 years. Never ever once—in the three academic departments where I taught—did I ever hear the words "Ohio State" or "Michigan State". Not once. Whereas, when we were discussing whether maybe we should try this or that, I heard Harvard, Yale,

Berkeley, Stanford, Chicago pretty much all time. I never heard Michigan State or Ohio State because they don't exist. Because envy is verbalized, and scorn is not.

This communication framework is held across the University of Michigan community, not just in the faculty lounges. As part of Markovits' college football research, his team scraped Twitter (now the platform X) to gather instances where Ohio State fans trash-talked Michigan, and vice versa. "When you total them up, the amount of scorn generated by Michigan is not even a third of the envy Tweeted by Ohio State fans," he reports.

These examples reveal the distinct ways one tribe thinks about itself, alongside what it must, in turn, think about its despised rival—in order to feel better about its own tribe in comparison!

For decades, *El Tri* played the United States because the two nations shared a border and they qualified out of the same confederation for the World Cup. Well, one of them did... Throughout this period, up until 1991, Mexicans felt better about themselves through scorn: "Technically, the *gringos* are a rival," they reasoned, "but not a great rival, not the stuff of *clásicos*. After all, these *americanos* don't truly understand or care about the game."

This allegation gets at another Envy/Scorn factor relevant to US vs. Mexico, one borrowed from the rise of professional sports.

"Basically," Markovits explains, "authenticity is always defined by noncommercial dimensions, right? You're authentic because you have an old stand, because you are there in a region that used to mine coal, because you're feudal. Capitalism is needed, but it creates the inauthentic. So, the scorn for Bayern Munich, for example, is created out of envy, because they win all the time and that success has been purchased. That's the allegation. The scorn for Manchester United, for Real Madrid, and the New York Yankees: It's all commercial. *Their fans don't care like we do. Their team was purchased!*

"Mexican scorn is all about the fact that we [Americans] are inauthentic, period. End of story. We are what we are—commercial. And this is so interesting: In every context, commercial is bad, even though futbol is so very commercial today. Just look at those shirts worn by *Liga MX* clubs! Every square inch is devoted to capitalism! Even so, to the Mexicans we are newcomers. In fact, it's a double whammy. We are inauthentic because we are commercial. We are inauthentic by virtue of not having futbol at the core of our being."

•••

The most intense international derbies in men's soccer—Argentina vs. Brazil, Iran vs. Iraq, Germany vs. The Netherlands, Cameroon vs. Nigeria—feature remarkably small amounts of envy. This was a hypothesis Markovits had not considered until we workshopped the idea together in January 2025. We agreed there are fewer commercial factors that add texture or nuance to an international *clásico*, as they commonly do in club soccer. As a result, when it's country vs. country, it's all scorn from both sides. Because scorn is silent, less is said or written about these cross-border sporting relationships.

Or rather, the amount of international trash talk pales beside that generated by club competitions like Real Madrid vs. Barcelona, Tottenham vs. Arsenal, or River Plate vs. Boca Juniors—because fans and media in these cases share the country, or often the same city.

"I would say that almost all international rivalries are scorn based," Markovits says.

"The Dutch don't envy the Germans, for example. They just hate them. There's nothing about Dutch futbol or culture envied by Germans. It's all scorn. The larger, more powerful political or economic entity—that can play a role. Think of the dynamic when the Soviets played all the satellite countries during the Cold War. There was nothing but scorn, and also hatred from their opponents. The most intense example"—and an interesting comp for US vs. Mexico—"might be when Algeria plays France. Great intensity on account of the colonial history, as with England playing Ireland. But it's all scorn from both sides, ultimately.

"Croatia and Serbia don't spend time thinking about what they admire about the other's teams or cultures. There's nothing but scorn or hatred for the other."

And here is where the US vs. Mexico rivalry really distinguishes itself. There is more than enough scorn coming from both sides, to be sure. But this *clásico* does feature those rare international elements of envy, those obvious nods toward interdependence—not just in the futbol sense, or in the social sense (those 35 million Mexican Americans living in the United States) but the economic sense, as well.

"While Mexican fans have always preferred to look south, Mexican directors prefer to look north," the journalist and Substacker Jon Arnold explained to me. "The Mexican national team playing friendlies in the U.S.—we all understand how and why that works. We understand the numbers, the dollars. But the Leagues Cup works the same way. *Liga MX* club owners know that no matter where they show up in the States, fans will show up. I mean, that's as simple as it gets. Right?

> It's not cheap to open up the NRG Stadium in Houston or the Cotton Bowl or wherever they're playing, but these matches definitely generate enough revenue, just from the gate. Every international break, there are five or six [*Liga MX*] clubs in the United States playing friendly matches. I think that's kind of the perpetual conflict of the Mexican football business—*How do we monetize these massive groups of fans that we have elsewhere?* It's the only example, the only situation in world futbol, where you have not only a big audience, but also a wealthier audience, paying in dollars. Not in your country, but in the country next door!

To be clear, the footballing powers that be in Spain and Portugal are not exploring the idea of an Iberian-style Leagues Cup. Too much scorn. These two countries don't play friendlies; they don't interact in the competitive futbol sense at all, unless they are required by UEFA to do so. Culturally, as the saying goes, these are two nations that live back to back.

Would a similar, Leagues Cup-type cooperation between top divisions in Argentina and Brazil create economic value, in terms of TV rights sold in South America and Europe? Undoubtedly. But there is far too much scorn from both sides to even consider it.

"There's an incongruence between the soccer world shared by these two countries, the U.S. and Mexico, and the rest of the world," Markovits adds. "It's a very interesting, completely unique story in world futbol."

● ● ●

When I first broached the idea of US-Mexico as a unique international example of envy and scorn, Dr. Markovits resisted. "No, no. Mexico has no profile in the American sporting consciousness." But that's simply not the case.

I myself grew up playing soccer in America, and I actively envied the futbol community in Mexico—not just the national team that kicked our ass through the 1970s, but the country's thriving professional league, its hosting of World Cups, and its widespread, well-traveled, extremely playful fan culture. Having come of age in the 1990s (b. 1964), I watched in peculiar awe each time nearly 100,000 Mexican Americans packed the Rose Bowl or Giants Stadium for North American Derbies. Landon Donovan (b. 1982) reacted the same way: "It's a very bizarre dynamic," he told the producers of *Good Rivals*, "to be playing a home game, in your own country, and having your own federation placing the game in a place where they *know* there's gonna be tens of thousands of Mexican fans." [16]

Perhaps I was part of a niche sporting population, but like Donovan, I definitely wished those things for my own country, for my national team, and for myself. As indicated at the top of this chapter, I struggled with this envy through 2014, when I still found myself rooting for *La Selección* to beat the Netherlands and finally advance beyond the Round of 16.

Jon Arnold is a native Texan, born in 1989, the year Paul Caligiuri's "Shot Heard 'Round the World'" finally delivered Team USA to a modern World Cup. From the moment that volley left Cal's supple left foot, soccer in the United States has surged in domestic popularity. It has grown beyond the mere mainstream. Sometime in the last decade, many have argued, it passed ice hockey to become one of the nation's four major sports.

Nevertheless, Arnold believes that he and millions of US soccer fans—an entire generation of Millennials—continue to be plagued by the same nagging, chronic sense of envy.

"I started paying attention in 1998, and I feel the U.S. soccer fan base is still desperate to be taken seriously, by Mexico fans, by the U.S. fans of football and basketball, and by the European futbol fan," Arnold told me.

Especially today, once you see Mexico play, I'm like, wait—our team is better than this team. Why are we not being taken seriously on this international level? Why are people posting memes about when I sing my songs supporting the U.S.? Because they think it sounds stupid and inauthentic *because I'm American*. Right? But it's a real thing for U.S. soccer fans: There's just always been this desperation to be taken seriously.

While the Mexican American presence in US fan culture has certainly moved the game forward north of the border, that presence has also made it tough on the overall soccer-loving population here. For example, when 90,000 show up to support the de facto archrival, on US soil, what's an NFL- or baseball-loving cynic supposed to think? Perhaps that soccer's popularity here is a creature of the nation's Mexican American population? Starting in the mid-1980s, when futbol had conquered the suburbs and their school systems, many European observers similarly dismissed US soccer as a sport played only in schools, and mainly by girls.

"At some point," Arnold told me,

> at the macro level, we have to say to ourselves, *Yo, we made it. Stop thinking about what other fans and media might think.* In a strange way, I think MLS is the most analyzed soccer league in the world, especially when talking about its business, its TV deals, how many of our fans show up and blah blah blah blah.
>
> If you read *Marca* [the Spanish sports daily], they might put the attendance for a match in there. But are they like, *Oh, La Liga will collapse if more people don't go next week*? Yeah, no. Because it won't. And neither will Major League Soccer. But my generation grew up with US soccer continually facing existential threats. There was this feeling like, if you didn't support MLS hard enough and you didn't post on the Internet and you didn't buy a ticket and you didn't buy a jersey, then it all might collapse. It might go away.
>
> We have this scarcity mindset where we're worried that we will lose soccer if we don't support it. And if the TV ratings aren't good enough, the league will go under. That's where I see this huge reach and grasp—the envy. I think it's absolutely spot on, as an observation. Even though the game here is clearly succeeding.

Overall, I do think the national futbol profile here in the States, the mentality of players and fans, greatly benefits from our completely unique mix of ethnicities and insecurities. In the age of Trump, this melting-pot idea has become politically controversial. In the soccer sense, it's an incontrovertible strength—and there is a specific texture to the national team and the fan base supplied by Mexican Americans. These folks envied this country enough (or their parents or grandparents recognized enough opportunity here) to emigrate, to make their lives and have children—children who may end up playing for, or supporting as fans, MLS clubs, NWSL clubs and the two national teams.

As ever with US vs. Mexico, there is a counter narrative. Consider the Mexican American tailgaters who travel great distances to root for *El Tri*, to cook out with fellow expatriates in the parking lot ahead of a random friendly or a Nations League match. Do they voice sincere scorn for Team USA during derby matches played in Southern California, Phoenix, or Las Vegas? Sure, they may serenade the American keeper with a *puto* chant now and again, but only when *La Selección* has bored or disappointed them. Some may get liquored up enough to boo the US national anthem.

If there is envy from this cohort, it looks south. Across the border. Because *El Tricolor* matches played north of that border represent that rare opportunity to meaningfully recall and reconnect, to express openly their pride in being *Mexican* American, to remember their previous lives in Mexico, to unabashedly miss the family and friends they left behind.

Even if, twenty-four hours later, the same men and women may well root for the US national team against Panama or show up behind the goal of LAFC, waving a black and gold flag.

"With my friends at a Mexico match, we all just want to be Mexicans for the day," says Dante Ramirez, an Arizona resident who followed *El Tri* around Southern California and the southwestern United States for many years, starting in the early 2000s. "This is when I was single. After I got married, I stopped traveling so much to matches. I'm too old for that now. I play pickleball!

Even though I am a U.S. citizen, you don't forget what it's like to be back in Mexico. We had everything there. People open their houses to you, and everyone loves you. That is the feeling they are looking for at Mexican matches here in the United States. That's the reason people drive all those distances. We used to get those experiences at home every Sunday with the family. It's fun. There is food and music and relatives everywhere. Here you can't do that as much because those traditions from home are impossible to recreate.

But that's the reason people drive so far. To visit like this. To celebrate being Mexican again, to be part of the crowd inside the stadium and support the team. It feels important.

•••

Dante Ramirez arrived in the United States twenty-five years ago when he'd had enough of dreaming. Born and raised in Mexico City as a Club América supporter, his futbol apprenticeship began at fifteen in the academy system at Deportivo Toluca F.C. That didn't work out, and in Mexico, "if you're not a pro at 18, the time goes fast. By 23, you're done," he told me. "You have only a certain amount time to make it happen."

After his stint at Toluca, Ramirez came close to latching on with Necaxa, where he played for the senior reserves. By then he was a fully fledged professional trainee, but he kept running into what he calls "corruption," which takes many forms in Mexican futbol. In his case, every time he felt close to breaking into the first team, some foreign-born prospect took his place.

I went to the club president and asked him, *What's going on?* And then I figured it out: The Argentinian they brought into the team, they paid him 20 grand a month, but the first three months' pay, the player's broker gets that money. Brokers are where the corruption is, or one of many, many ways corruption is part of the Mexican system.

This went down in the late 1990s. Ramirez went north shortly thereafter, to Southern California, where he toyed with the idea of US college soccer before latching on with a "Sunday league" team sponsored by a local business.

"They paid me more money on those teams, here, than when I was playing pro in Mexico! I decided I don't need to practice anymore. Maybe I don't need to be professional. Every Sunday they had music, soccer and family time. I missed that. It was great. And the level of play was good, all ex-professionals in their home countries."

This was the period when Ramirez started frequenting *El Tri* friendlies all over the region. But he assimilated, too, on a parallel track. He moved to Greater Phoenix, trained with Ping as a golf club technician, a position he holds to this day. He earned his US citizenship, settled down, and got married. We spoke in early March 2024, the week Mexico's women's national team beat the USWNT for the second time ever, the first time in fourteen years.

"I feel the Mexican women are in the same place the U.S. men were for so long: dominated by their rival, they don't have a league . . . In Mexico, we didn't have a league for women until the last 5–6 years. Now maybe *we* will start to be equals."

Is that the way he views the two men's sides, as equals? Because, as we know, that has been a major sticking point for *El Tri* media and fans through the years.

"I would say there are a lot of people who refuse to believe the U.S. is an equal, on the field, but a lot of those people are media," Dante says, adding that he actively roots for both US national teams—unless they're playing *La Selección*. "If you don't play soccer, maybe you can make yourself believe that, but they don't know what they're talking about. These teams are equals, for sure. Before, these games were 8-nil. Today they are very tight. My opinion: We're equals.

"Mexico needs more players in Europe, where the US has so many. That is one way Mexico can be better. One reason we consider ourselves better. But," and here Dante stops and chuckles a bit, "that is also what we want to believe."

Note the pronouns Dante deploys. Straddling these cultural demarcations, navigating these dual identities, remains a delicate exercise for many expats. Even for Ramirez, a US citizen, a dual national who has lived here for twenty-three years, in a region as culturally Latino as any in the Union.

> It is difficult. My dad is getting older; I try to visit him every year. The expats here do feel as if they are missing that part of life, in Mexico. They understand they need this part of Mexico in their lives, to feel better. My wife, she's a white girl from America. No Spanish, and she's glad that my son

has white skin—so he won't struggle. She's not a racist. She sees that it's not right to think this way, but it's real.

Today when I try to go and support Mexico, I will wear my jersey. I wear it to the stadium but only when I'm there—or when there is a World Cup game to watch somewhere. We can see now a lot of Mexicans supporting a lot of teams in the United States, in California especially. The Galaxy and LAFC. You can see now there are more Mexicans in the MLS crowds, a good mix of Mexicans. Their families are Mexican, but I expect most are born over here... You know, I'm still a Club América fan. When I played at Toluca, I came to love the club. But I still supported América.

I live here and I've become a fan of the U.S. national teams—unless they're playing Mexico.

Such situational support remains controversial in certain quarters. As opinionated Stars & Stripes veteran Alexi Lalas complained to the *LA Times* in 1998,

> You don't get used to it. It stinks every time. I'm all for roots and understanding where you come from and having a respect for your homeland, but tomorrow morning all of those people are going to get up and work in the United States and live in the United States and have all the benefits of living in the United States.[17]

Lalas later apologized for these comments, but maintaining a dual allegiance is more complicated in 2026, not less. "As discrimination and anti-immigrant sentiment rises, so does the desire to apply these terms as they play with the concept of nationality and nation building," professor Erick Calderon points out. "This is especially true with concepts of Americanization, which is the forced assimilation of ethnic groups in the United States through education, language, and other social and cultural factors."[18]

"Days before I graduated with my associate's degree in criminal justice," continues Calderon, a native of Southern California, "my Mexican grandfather began interrogating me, asking if becoming a police officer was really what I wanted to do. After I had nodded affirmatively, he began preaching how good this country had been to us and how the decision I had made to serve this country was an honorable one. He paused for a while, looked at me with a serious face and told me that no matter what I did, or how I decided to serve this country, I should never ever root for the U.S. national soccer team. We both laughed infectiously and when I had a moment to breathe, I replied with an affirmative, *Of course. I would never.*"

USMNT legend Harry Keough and the former Alva Flores, a native of Guadalajara, on their wedding day—August 30, 1952. Their transnational union produced another US national team standout, son Ty Keough. Courtesy of the Keough Family.

Ruben Mendoza, preserved for all time on Niedringhaus Avenue in Granite City, Illinois. The Mexican American was the finest US striker of the 1950s. He also introduced club and national team colleague Harry Keough to his future wife. St. Louis Soccer Hall of Fame.

NASL and national team stalwart Al Trost inside Estadio Azteca, prior to a 1972 Olympic qualification match. Courtesy of Al Trost.

Leonardo Cuéllar, El Tri and NASL alum, ahead of the World Cup qualifier contested in Mexico City, November 1980. In the twenty-first century, he managed El Tri Feminil. Jon van Woerden.

The 25th North American Derby, played before a capacity crowd of 90,000 partisans inside Estadio Azteca on November 9, 1980. Jon van Woerden.

American Perry Vanderbeck rises above the indignity of a 5–1 defeat at the Azteca, November 9, 1980. The loss eliminated the United States from its eighth consecutive World Cup. Jon van Woerden.

November 23, 1980: Teammates mob USMNT striker Steve Moyers (11) at the final whistle. Moyers' brace made the difference, ending a 46-year winless streak vs. Mexico. Jon van Woerden.

Bora Milutinovic managed El Tri twice (1983–86, 1995–97). In between (1991–94), he coached the USMNT—transforming a regional rivalry into a clásico. He remains beloved in both countries. Tony Quinn.

Mexico fans set fire to the US flag during a 1992 Olympic qualifier on March 25, 1992, in Mexico City. Jon van Woerden.

El Tri supporters make their rooting interests clear during a US-Mexico match in Washington, DC, June 18, 1995. Tony Quinn.

The Last Laugh: The broad, goal-producing smile of Thomas Dooley shines through a mass of USMNT humanity during the June 1995 US Cup. The Yanks prevailed 4–0 on this day, June 18, 1995, at RFK Stadium in Washington, DC. Tony Quinn.

Eric Wynalda outduels defender Claudio Suárez at the Rose Bowl in Pasadena, California, June 1996. Tony Quinn.

Rose Bowl crowd, US vs. Mexico, June 1997. No segregated seating at derby matches north of the border. This scene would not be possible or practical at the Azteca. Tony Quinn.

USMNT striker Brian McBride duels El Tri defender Joel Sanchez during a 1999 US Cup match in San Diego. Tony Quinn.

Mia Hamm and Generation 1999 took women's soccer to a new level, in America and abroad. Their rivalry with Mexico, however, was something of a non-starter back then. Today the dynamic has changed. Tony Quinn.

Maribel Domínguez Castelán, the most prolific goal scorer in Mexican national team history, on the ball during a 2010 World Cup qualifier in June 2010. Mexico beat the United States for the first time that day. El Tri feminil would do it again in 2024. Tony Quinn.

Mexican media canonized USMNT player Graham Zusi in October 2013, after his goal—against Panama—enabled El Tri to qualify for and participate in the 2014 World Cup. Sporting KC.

The Flop, from artist Mike Shultis (2014), in oil, acrylic, ink, astroturf, bed sheet, string, wood, photo transparency, found skis and American flag. Mike Shultis.

Pitchside during the anthems at Estadio Azteca in October 2024. Ahead of Donald Trump's second inauguration, no booing of the Star-Spangled Banner could be heard. Hal Phillips.

Moon over Estadio Akron, to be renamed Estadio Guadalajara prior to the 2026 World Cup. Hal Phillips.

La Brigada d'Oro, the Latin fan group supporting MLS club Nashville FC, went underground during the spring of 2025, fearing fan activities would expose members to undue scrutiny from ICE. Christina Moore/cmoorestoryteller.com

6

Soccer Made in America (or "How to Wander in the Footballing Desert for a Century")

US soccer fans and media, in addition to a glut of academic and cultural observers here and abroad, have spent a whole lot of time over the last forty years trying to understand and explain why the game took so very long—all of the twentieth century basically—to become popular here. For decades, the thrust of these inquiries was simple: "When exactly will Americans start to love soccer? When will the game mainstream itself?" Now that this evolution clearly *has* taken place, folks have moved on to, "Why did it take so long?"

Many believe the prior elevation of a different brand of futbol, the *American* kind, doomed its elder cousin to irrelevance—the way rugby has similarly back-seated soccer in places like South Africa and Australia.

Others have argued that the essential foreign nature of the game never sat so well, not in a country that felt so strongly about the elevation of homegrown sports.

Some academic observers argue that once a modern industrialized nation settles on its principal sports—what we in the States call "major" sports—it's very difficult for late-coming contenders to break through.

Dr. Andrei Markovits makes the latter case—that countries have only so much cultural space or *bandwidth* for so-called major sports. Once these are established, there's no room for more. Or rather, supplanting one is extremely difficult. Markovits also argues persuasively that Americans strongly prefer their sports to be homegrown, despite the fact that gridiron and baseball clearly share common ancestors with two very British games, rugby and rounders.[1]

Some of these theories were fleshed out in my 2022 book, *Generation Zero: Founding Fathers, Hidden Histories & The Making of Soccer in America*. It was, after all, a story about why and when the game finally came of age in this country, and how exactly these obstacles were ultimately overcome.

All of these theories help explain the evolution, in part. I tend to place the most emphasis on how futbol was cast, by millions of twentieth-century citizens of the United States, as a foreign sport largely played by and foisted upon Americans by so-called "foreigners." This dynamic was only accentuated by soccer's clear dominance around the world—everywhere but here, basically—and its obvious popularity with this country's primary immigrant groups, including the largest one: Mexican Americans.

Here again in the story of US vs. Mexico, we see what an important influence this ethnic minority has had, and continues to have, on futbol culture north of the border, coast to coast.

For the record, scholars of sport generally don't sit around wondering when and why Mexicans started to love futbol. As we established in Chapter 4, they embraced it from the moment of first exposure. The fact that the game wasn't Mexican *per se* did not bother them, as it bothers very few of the 270 nations and sovereign territories that compete in FIFA events. The relative lack of competitors in the Mexican sport "space" is surely relevant; it allowed soccer there to go from strength to strength.

Nevertheless, despite the very different ways that soccer popularized itself in these neighboring countries, it's striking just how closely their respective histories with the game tracked one another throughout the twentieth century, like distinct strands of the same story.

We *americanos* have this oddly ahistorical notion that Mexico's futbol tradition is ancient compared to our own. But the two national team programs were launched at roughly the same time, and Team USA was organized and played matches seven years ahead of Mexico's. With the formation of the American Soccer League in 1921, professional futbol arrived here first—two full decades before the Mexican *Priméra* debuted.

Futbol north of the border clearly went into a deep societal funk mid-century: from the moment the rivalry with Mexico was first joined, in 1934, through to the arrival of the North American Soccer League in 1967. Thereafter, the two rivals have each grown into hemispheric powers—not on parallel tracks, but on paths that basically moved in the same general direction, through the same general timeframes, arriving at roughly the same place circa 1990. That's when the two national teams began competing as equals, as increasingly co-dependent rivals.

The result is a twenty-first-century sporting battle royale that feeds off more compelling economic, political, and civilizational factors than any international derby on Earth.

However, it must be said: This overlapping historical narrative is not the way Mexican futbol fans and observers have conventionally viewed the history.

And it's not the way Americans have viewed it either.

•••

It's telling that FIFA and the broader soccer world view the parallel footballing fates of Mexico and the United States more accurately than either nation does on its own. "Black hole" is perhaps a bit strong, but North America in the mid-1960s was not looked upon as a modern, lucrative, competitive market for world soccer. The Mexicans were right: The United States didn't care about futbol back then. But the *Priméra* and *El Tri* were nothing special either, not prior to 1970. Here was the largest Spanish-speaking country on earth, with the most powerful economy in that world. Yet it lagged well behind a half-dozen South American nations (and Spain itself) in terms of World Cup performance, the quality of players it produced, and the competitive nature of its domestic competition.

Mexico and the United States came of age as soccer nations in different ways, but not *that* different—and not so very far apart in time.

FIFA had quite a bit to do with the similarity of these timelines.

We poke fun at this organization because it's a big, fat, stuffy, impossibly rich and easy target. It's also a heedless bureaucracy with a shameless track record of sucking up to authoritarian figures. In March of 2025, *The Independent* newspaper of London questioned the "dignity" of FIFA president Gianni Infantino after he and President Trump chatted breezily in the Oval Office about crypto deals, their Super Bowl hobnobbing the month before, the upcoming Club World Cup, and stolen elections.[2] Dignity? This is the man who moved his family to Qatar ahead of the 2022 tournament so as to fawn full time over key sheiks—on the heels of gift-wrapping the 2018 World Cup for Vladimir Putin. *The Guardian* has predicted the "2026 World Cup will be leveraged for the glorification of a leader to a degree not seen since Benito Mussolini dominated the 1934 World Cup in Italy or the Videla regime's stage crafting of the 1978 World Cup in Argentina."[3]

Still, FIFA's bureaucratic inclinations and initiatives *do* matter. They shape the global soccer landscape whether we find Infantino's behavior (or predecessor Sepp Blatter's behavior) distasteful or not. Plainly and simply, by bringing the World Cup to Mexico in 1970 and 1986, then to the United States in 1994, the organization jumpstarted soccer's success in North America, north and south of the Rio Grande. More recently, FIFA leaders have demonstrated the ability to similarly supercharge the fortunes of regional soccer communities in Africa and the Middle East.

Mexicans are more likely to interpret *Mundial* 1970 as FIFA *recognizing* their country as a worthy tournament host. Nevertheless, the decision to bring the world to Mexico was the foremost catalyst in the development of the modern game there. The Lords of Futbol did much the same thing when arranging for the 2010 World Cup in South Africa. When they anointed Qatar as host of the 2022 World Cup—when Infantino handed Saudi Arabia the 2034 tournament—FIFA stimulated soccer development from one end of the Middle East to the other. Does the Arab/African world produce its first major-tournament semifinalist (Morocco, 2022) without that sort of advocacy? No way.

In short, what FIFA wants it generally gets. By 1986, thoroughly fed up that soccer had failed to mature in the United States (despite two World Cups held just over its southern border), the governing body was determined to similarly nourish the game north of that border. FIFA had grown impatient with mere incubation. It didn't care about promising suburban demographics or how well the Cosmos drew crowds. The game's global power broker wanted to know why US-based corporations couldn't play more central, lucrative roles in its showcase event. General Secretary Blatter and his minions wanted to know when NASL, gone belly up in 1984, would be replaced. What had been construed as America's incessant bungling in these areas—specifically, its inability to bring the professional game before its hundreds of millions of well-heeled consumers—was costing FIFA and its corporate partners a fortune.[4]

On July 4, 1988, FIFA damned the torpedoes and simply awarded the 1994 World Cup to the United States, a country with no professional first division, no notable futbol culture to speak of, and a national team that hadn't played a World Cup match since 1950—because said USMNT couldn't come close to beating Mexico and qualifying for one.

The European and South American soccer establishments were more than slightly appalled by this decision. Yet FIFA had done something comparable in 1964, when it handed the 1970 World Cup to a country that showed promise but was hardly a mature futbol nation. Pelé, *La Canarinha* and the advent of color television did the rest.

Come 1988, US soccer needed the same nudge, one that only a World Cup can provide. With the stroke of a pen and a few suitcases full of cash (to lock up the necessary votes),[5] FIFA reversed half a century of American indifference toward the game. In doing so, it laid the groundwork for what quickly became one of the sport's signature rivalries, on the world's richest continent.

•••

Twenty-first-century Americans have developed a soft spot for expertly produced, soccer-centric docuseries. The FX-produced *Welcome to Wrexham*, in particular, has engendered a specific appreciation for futbol clubs that predate internal combustion engines.

As a sporting culture, we Yanks have traditionally failed to give a fig about this concept. Fans of the NFL Chicago Bears, for example, don't make a big deal about the franchise having been established in 1920. Most Cubs supporters can tell you when Wrigley Field opened (1914), but not when this storied organization joined the National League (1876).

Surely it's relevant that Wrexham AFC itself, est. 1864, is owned by two Hollywood celebrities: Rob McIlhenny and Ryan Reynolds. But US viewers do seem genuinely taken by the show's historical sweep. Witness the Red Dragons' foil from Season II, Notts County F.C., which has operated without interruption in the same place by a verifiable chain of ownership since 1862. The English Football Association itself didn't form until 1863.

If you've ever wondered about the oldest professional soccer clubs here in the United States, prepare to swallow hard. That honor goes to the indoor Milwaukee Wave, which celebrated its fortieth anniversary in 2024.[6] Or maybe it's the Baltimore Blast, est. 1980? Either way, this meager heritage speaks to just how incidental *professional* soccer has been to the American futbol ecosystem over the long term. Pro leagues and clubs have come along, but they've all failed and pretty quickly, too. This also explains why the men's and women's national teams here are so popular: Between 1984 and 1996, outdoor, fully professional club soccer did not exist, for men or women.

Be that as it may, when we move the goalposts slightly and change "fully professional" to "semi-professional," our perspective opens up to hundreds of outdoor clubs that date back a century or more. They all played, and many continue to play, in regional, semi-pro circuits like the Cosmopolitan Super League in metropolitan New York (est. 1923, as the German-American Football Association), or the San Francisco Soccer Football League, where urban/ethnic clubs have competed at a very high level since 1946. Bavarian United of Glendale, Wisconsin dates back to 1929. Still going strong today, it fields everything but a "fully professional" team—meaning every variety of men's and women's sides in dozens of youth, semi-professional, and "pre-professional" leagues, including USL League Two.

Unfortunately, until 1990, this surprisingly rich history never produced a broader cultural appreciation for the game, or a professional version that a critical mass of Americans would take to their bosom. Nor were the players produced by this semi-pro system good enough to get results in an international setting. Instead, we got iteration after iteration of semi-pro clubs named after thread companies, furniture stores, and funeral homes. These entities were super cool in their own eccentric ways, but the players they produced weren't good enough to beat minor international rivals, much less Mexico.

These clubs didn't make money, either, and never cohered into a national, professional futbol system. In truth, that didn't happen for real until MLS launched in 1996.

•••

History exists to be understood, so it might then be applied to our current understandings. This brings us back to all those academics theorizing about why a country whose long soccer history never amounted to much until 1990.

The US Open Cup, for example, was born in 1913 and baptized as the National Challenge Cup.[7] Organization of this competition was among the first official acts of the new US Football Association, one of the earliest member organizations of FIFA, the very first from North or Central America. But this century-old competition didn't help soccer grow or professionalize in this country.

US club conventions are older than the federation or the US Open Cup, and maybe that's a good place to begin any forensics. That rich semi-pro history extends from the Scots factory workers who suited up for Clark Thread Co. in the 1870s to the short-lived American League of Professional Football, which lasted just long enough to crown a single champion, the Brooklyn Bridegrooms (1894). The St. Louis Soccer League (est. 1915) and Chicago National Soccer League (1919) were each founded by and for, new arrivals from Eastern Europe. Early in the Roaring Twenties, enough societal soccer steam had been gathered to enable a first concerted stab at truly professional futbol: the American Soccer League, which started up in 1921—only to fold its tent in 1933.[8]

After each league failure, the US futbol community simply snapped back to its established, regional, ethnic, semi-professional model.

As an organizing principle, the ethnic component showed itself to be exceedingly powerful, adaptable, varied, and widespread. Most of these clubs and leagues were founded by different sets of first- and second-generation émigrés. And yes, Mexican expatriates first staked their claim in US futbol circles by following this template.

Club Necaxa materialized on the South Side of Chicago in 1927, as both a futbol team—competing in the Chicago National Soccer League—and a community center. To close this elaborate, cross-border loop: William Frasser, owner of the light and power company in Puebla state, had founded the original Club Necaxa in Aguascalientes, north of Mexico City, in 1923. Though some portion of its fan base clearly moved north to Chicago, Necaxa established itself as a potent force in the pre-*Priméra* period, winning several *Fuerza* and *Copa México* trophies before disappearing completely prior to the Second World War. *Los Electricistas* reorganized postwar in Mexico City, where they rejoined the country's new first division.[9]

Perhaps no team in Mexican futbol has experienced such a roller-coaster ride of competitive form, location, ownership, and solvency. A Spanish group purchased Necaxa in 1982. Grupo Televisa took over in 1988. The club was relegated, moved back to Aguascalientes, and, under yet another new owner, returned to the top flight in 2011.

A decade later, the star-studded American consortium, NX Football USA—shareholders include actress Eva Longoria, MLB pitcher Justin Verlander, and German footballer Mesut Özil—purchased 50 percent of Necaxa. NX also saw fit to buy 5 percent of Wrexham AFC, a move that prompted Rob and Ryan to reciprocate in 2024, prompting noted futbol wag Jon Arnold to dub the Liga MX club *Wrexacaxa*.[10]

•••

So, why did the bellwether American Soccer League (ASL) go under? Primarily, the Great Depression did away with nearly all discretionary consumer spending nationwide. Unlike the English first division or the Mexican *Priméra*, the ASL was not owned or operated by a central authority, i.e. a national federation. As an unaligned collection of emergent clubs, only a few were decently capitalized. Bethlehem Steel FC was perhaps the only one with real money behind it. J&P Coats F.C., the 1922–23 champion, was backed by the Pawtucket, R.I. branch of another Scottish thread company—the sort of outfit we moderns would expect to sponsor a company softball team, not a professional sports franchise.

The ASL was fun and enterprising. It represented the sport's first big swing in this country, but worldwide depressions are no joke. The Dust-Bowl-era National Football League barely survived the 1930s. Nevertheless, this failure underlined two issues that would restrict US soccer development and public acceptance through the 1980s.

First among them was this pesky notion that soccer was a foreign game, played by foreigners. For example, when the American Soccer League had first assembled, clubs threw a lot of money at importing talented Englishmen and Scots (British papers called the upstart ASL an "American Menace"). This strategy didn't sit well with some xenophobic American sports fans either. What's more, in securing their services, clubs ignored UK player-transfer rules. FIFA intervened to hash out a workaround provision in 1927, but domestic soccer supporters had no experience with foreign bodies playing such a role.[11] They didn't like it much.

A year later, no such diplomacy prevailed. The USFA conducted its National Challenge Cup during the ASL season. Cash-strapped clubs had long bridled at the cost of these fixtures, especially the travel, and come 1928, the league resolved to opt out of the event entirely. When three clubs entered the Cup anyway, the US Football Association, backed by FIFA, declared the ASL an outlaw league—and immediately launched a rival competition! The new Eastern Professional Soccer League (EPSL) promptly poached several ASL franchises.

This so-called "Soccer War" did nothing but further strain the finances of all concerned, but the American Soccer League broke first. In 1929, the EPSL merged with the ASL to form a new Atlantic Coast League that operated in lockstep with both the USFA and FIFA.[12] It started the 1930 season as the Atlantic Coast League, only to finish the campaign having returned to the ASL moniker—a textbook example of how *not* to brand a league product.

By this time, alas, the power struggle had significantly crippled the ASL. The Depression finished it off, and FIFA's stateside reputation as a nefarious overseas meddler was set in stone.

A replacement American Soccer League—let's call it ASL II—took amorphous shape almost immediately. Not as a business venture but rather as a confederation of leagues, all of them regional, semiprofessional, and urban. After the Second World War, these clubs grew demonstrably more ethnic, not less. Go Google the list of US Open Cup and National Amateur Cup finalists from mid-century forward: Ukrainians, Maccabees, Greeks, Pancyprians,

Germans, Croatians, German-Hungarians, Portuguese, Danes . . . The list remains an impressive testimony to America's melting-pot cred. Twentieth-century Europeans who arrived here clung to the game of soccer for the same reasons twenty-first-century Mexican Americans do today—to stay connected with their respective customs and traditions.[13]

Totally understandable. Just not the sort of club ethos that ably countered the sport's broader reputation as a foreign game, played by foreigners.

Branding is important, but competence matters more, and ASL II's stubbornly semi-professional template simply did not produce enough US players who met the international standard. Some stars were paid in this system, others were not, and everyone had jobs outside of soccer to make ends meet. I don't think it's presumptuous to make this generalization: Day jobs don't help athletes reach their professional potential.

While the rest of the futbol world was professionalizing (see the Mexican *Priméra*, est. 1943), clubs operating during the ASL II Era never got there. Never even tried really.

• • •

Harry Keough played on the 1950 national team that upset England in Brazil. He starred in defense for the finest club team of the 1950s, St. Louis Kutis F.C.—a collection of talent so impressive, by American measures, the Federation deployed the club as a de facto national team for a pair of World Cup qualifiers in 1957.[14] A quite incredible moment, but not a productive one for US soccer. The makeshift national team lost both matches, including a 7–2 drubbing at the hands of Mexico.

Here's the dispiriting kicker. Once the Yanks were eliminated from that World Cup, Keough went back to working at the US Post Office, a gig he held down for thirty-six years, all through his athletic prime.

Ruben Mendoza played alongside Keough, for club and country. His parents were Mexican nationals, but Ruben was born in St. Louis in 1931. After a 20-goal season with Zenhoefer's Furs in the St. Louis Major Soccer League, Mendoza moved over to Keough's club, the Raiders, which soon took the name of a local funeral home, St. Louis Kutis F.C.[15] Mendoza was almost certainly the finest American striker of the decade. Keough spoke Spanish, having grown up in the ethnically Spanish, soccer-savvy Carondolet Park neighborhood of St. Louis. He and Mendoza hit it off immediately.

"My dad's future father-in-law, Salvador Flores, used to come out to watch the great Kutis teams—to watch Ruben Mendoza specifically," says Harry's son, Ty Keough. "Apparently, Ruben was invited back to Salvador's home at some point. They were having a party—for my grandmother, I believe. Ruben brought my dad along and that's where my parents met."

Great story. But when Mendoza wasn't scoring goals for Kutis, the USMNT, and the US Olympic Team, the man was a barber. That's what paid the bills.

These two pioneers led extraordinary, unmistakably productive lives. In his "spare time," Harry also led St. Louis University to five NCAA championships. Once Ruben moved his own brood to the St. Louis suburb of Granite City, Illinois, he put down his shears and operated Mendoza Sporting Goods there for twenty years.

The launch of NASL in 1967 is often presented as a turning point for US soccer, and in some ways, it was. By the mid-1970s, the league had grown into a national, nominally professional first division with a sprinkling of American stars. With Pelé on board, soccer matches were finally broadcast on network television. But the North American Soccer League also leaned disproportionately on foreign players, coaches, and general managers. The finest US players in NASL weren't paid like the imports. Many held down day jobs. And when it came to qualifying for World Cups, NASL-era national teams still couldn't beat Mexico.

And oh, *by the way*, NASL went out of business in 1984.

•••

In the end, it was suburbia that rescued US soccer. Boys and girls in their thousands sucking on orange slices at halftime . . . Soccer Moms and Dads schlepping kids to and from practice in gargantuan, wood-paneled station wagons . . . Soccer camp, white picket fences, The Black Pearl & his Cosmos, the emerging high school chic of Adidas and Puma.

Most US soccer fans today recognize that American kids started playing the game in outsized numbers during the 1970s. We refer to this phenomenon as the Youth Soccer Revolution, but that phrase sounds almost quaint. As in, *What impact can a recreational youth sport honestly have on a nation's athletic culture?*

For starters, our own perceptions of suburbia solved a big hunk of soccer's cultural issues. Founded in 1964, the American Youth Soccer Organization (AYSO) first delivered futbol to the suburbs, these familiar and indisputably "American" communities, where the sport finally adopted a framework that fellow citizens recognized.

In his 2015 dissertation, *Fútbol Americano: Immigration, Social Capital, and Youth Soccer in Southern California*, David Keyes asserts that AYSO purposely decoupled futbol from ethnicity—by fostering clubs in the suburbs, by effectively banning foreign club names, and by insisting that only English be spoken on the field. Keyes calls this "triple domestication," and it worked. Hewing to these rituals helped to mitigate the sport's "foreign" and "immigrant" labels.[16]

By packaging and presenting the game to households in those wholesome, healthy environments, soccer was quickly recast as an activity *obviously* suited to red-blooded American boys and girls.

Critically, 1970s suburbia also produced the first glut of home-grown American talent. When Generation X—born in the 1960s, raised on the game during the 1970s—came of age, it immediately stocked national team rosters that qualified for World Cups, won World Cups (thanks, USWNT), and beat Mexico.[17]

FIFA played its role with carrots and sticks, but we don't call it the Youth Soccer *Revolution* for nothing. Across all the fifty states, this mass movement created the nation's first stock of American soccer natives. In doing so, it retrofitted the sport of soccer according to a format Americans understood. For example, the way Little League baseball ultimately seeds the field for high school, minor league, and Major League Baseball. We recognize this system, as we recognize this bit of gospel: "Train up a child in the way he should go: and when he is old, he will not depart from it" (Prov. 22:6).

US soccer today takes a lot of shit for being a sport of white, suburban privilege. Our blind faith in capitalism is partly to blame. The travel teams, the pay-to-play paradigms, the *premier* camps, and *select* designations—all these factors underline this fairly rendered observation. Most everywhere else in the world, futbol talent is developed in the street, among the urban underprivileged.

Love it or hate it, this distinctly American working model took hold in the 1970s, and it worked where many other frameworks had failed. As part of an unfolding process, the alleged alien nature of this game—always a flimsy, casually xenophobic attitude—faded away under a hail of carpools and grandparents watching from the sidelines in lawn chairs. The suburbanization of soccer during the Youth Soccer Revolution represented an immense cultural shift, a reboot. This new presentation and social location of the game completely undermined decades of reflexive nativism.

Steve Trittschuh competed on the national team for ten years, starting in 1986. A Generation Xer, he had grown up playing youth soccer on the outskirts of St. Louis starting in 1971. He was born in the 1960s and learned the game in the suburb of Granite City, Illinois, all through the 1970s. Tritt could well have served as a YSR poster child.

But here's the thing: Trittschuh played with twenty different guys on the famous 1989 national team—the one that beat Trinidad & Tobago on November 19 to qualify for *Italia '90*, the nation's first World Cup in forty years. Every single one of his teammates was born in the 1960s and raised on the game, in the suburbs, during the 1970s. Ditto for the entire US Women's National Team that won the first of its four World Cups in 1991.

In short, when that first cohort of native players came of age as senior players, in the early 1990s, *Presto*! American soccer was no longer a footballing doormat. Lo and behold, after a century of relying on players raised on the game in faraway elsewhere, the United States was finally producing indigenous soccer players who could really play.

● ● ●

So, who coached all these kids? Mainly a bunch of clueless soccer dads who had never played the game themselves. "I was fortunate in that I had a lot of good coaching," says Trittschuh. "When I got to be about 12, I had an ex-professional who knew the game, and he was my coach. His name was Ruben Mendoza. He kinda brought proper soccer to Granite City, Illinois." [18]

We're already familiar with Mendoza, and we already know this story of urban-to-suburban movement. In oversized numbers and diversity, immigrants arrived in this country after the Second World War. After a generation or two in citified America, economic success and the lure of a two-car garage shifted these families to the 'burbs. The US Census reports that suburban populations grew by 30 percent during the 1960s, or 15 million people in a country of 200 million.[19]

Voila. That's how the urban/ethnic game proliferated across a previously lily-white, suburban landscape during the 1970s. And heaps of Youth Soccer Revolution coaches came from this influx of ethnic, soccer-savvy dads.

Mendoza's impact as a youth coach was not exactly typical. When Trittschuh got to high school, his head coach at Granite City North was NASL veteran Bob Kehoe, who had played for the hometown St. Louis Stars. When Mendoza joined Kehoe's staff, the two ex-pros quickly established a high school soccer dynasty.

This was overkill, to be honest. All it took in 1970s American suburbia was *one* dad, one energetic individual who knew what he or she was doing. Guys like Scots-born Jim Harkes, who trained up son John, Tony Meola, and Tab Ramos in the New York City suburb of Kearny, New Jersey. First-generation immigrants like John Kerr, another Scot, or Hungarian-born Michael Vermes, who tutored future stars Peter Vermes, Bruce Murray, and Desmond Armstrong in the suburbs of southern New Jersey and Washington, D.C.

It's tempting to be overly impressed by The Mendoza Effect: Trittschuh grew up to be the first American ever to play in the European Cup, what we today we call the Champions League.

Think instead of *all* the Granite City kids who played on youth and high school teams coached by Mendoza and Kehoe, Kerr and Vermes—the less remarkable talents, whom they also put through the paces. In their thousands, those boys and girls also grew up with the sporting sensibilities of futbol natives.

By 1990, these young Americans hadn't just grown up into sporting consumers. They had emerged as home-grown, soccer-literate citizens whose dollars and eyeballs made successes of the 1994 World Cup, the 1999 FIFA Women's World Cup, and Major League Soccer, which launched in 1996. Many coached succeeding generations of American soccer natives. They were also ripely positioned to appreciate and loudly back a bona fide *clásico*, which US vs. Mexico provided at exactly the same moment in time.

When the 1970 World Cup concluded, Mexico had clearly raced well past the United States in terms of soccer development—on the national team level, on the professional-league level, on the youth development level. American soccer had gone next to nowhere on all three fronts since the Derby was first joined in 1934. As the 1970s began, *El Tri* had made the most of what amounted to a thirty-six-year head start.

In twenty years' time, a single generation of suburban players and enthusiasts didn't just close the gap. They vaporized it.

•••

In the fall of 1973, looking for a post-World Cup bump and more premium broadcast content, an emboldened Mexican Federation proposed a series of exhibitions with its Sibling to the north, against whom *El Tri* had not played a friendly since 1937. It seemed a match made in heaven for two futbol nations in growth mode. From a viewership standpoint, it's surprising the *Federación* and Televisa had not suggested it earlier, as the Mexican public leapt at any opportunity to embarrass the Americans at futbol.

It's worth another timeline here to understand what happened next. To begin with, the two nations faced each other as part of the 1974 World Cup qualification out of CONCACAF. The Mexicans won both matches, held three days apart in September 1972: 3–1 at *Estadio Azteca*, and 2–1 at the Los Angeles Coliseum. Thereafter, as part of this new series of *amistosos*, *El Tri* prevailed four more times—running its overall record against Team USA to eighteen wins, one loss, and two draws. See here those four results: 2–0 at *Estadio Azteca* on October 16, 1973, 3–1 in Monterrey on September 5, 1974, 1–0 in Dallas on September 8, 1974, and 2–0 at the Azteca on August 24, 1975.

Despite their longstanding rivalry, despite the obligations of World Cup qualification and simple geography, these two national teams had never played each other so frequently, over such a short period of time. Yet these were not 1950s-style blowouts. The match scores prove as much. The two sides played twice more during the ensuing round of World Cup qualifying: a scoreless draw in L.A. on October 3, 1976, and a 3–0 US loss in Puebla two weeks later.[20]

U.S. midfielder Al Trost played in four of these matches. The St. Louis native also points out that the 1972 US Olympic Team faced the Mexicans twice more, ahead of the 1972 Munich Games. "We had some battles with them. I think we tied them twice and we both went through," he recalls. "Considering how often we played back then, we could measure the progress we were making as a national team against the Mexicans. We were already confident that we could get points from other CONCACAF nations. But if you were ever going to advance in a Cup competition, you'd need to come up with points against Mexico. And playing Mexico always presented a test of our self-control.

"It's hard to recall every detail of these games, but we had our chances. The skill level wasn't there yet. But in terms of how we defended, Walt [Chyzowych, USMNT coach] believed in as much man-to-man marking as possible. Don't give them any room. Now, it's difficult to turn that around and get into offensive mode when you play that way, but it kept us in the games. Obviously, the technical capability of the Mexicans was greater, but these were competitive matches. We made them that way. We had our chances."

For almost forty years, no national team alumnus could credibly make that claim. The tenor of the rivalry had quietly grown into something different during the 1970s.

Trost told me the following story in December 2024:

I remember 1974, in Monterrey. We were really competitive in that game. That was a period when the U.S. brought in Dettmar Cramer to help with the national team program. I really admired his work. But more than that: We're at the hotel the night before and we're supposed to go train—at the same time the match is scheduled the next night. First the bus is late. On the way to the stadium, it takes forever to get there—not the direct route, if you know what I mean. When we finally arrive, I'm sitting there talking to Dettmar, in front of the bus, and we see the stadium lights are turned off.

When Cramer sees that, he goes and talks to the stadium folks, who tell him they can't turn the lights on. So Dettmar tells them, "If you're not gonna let us train, we're going back to the hotel, getting on the plane, and we're not coming back." So they turned on the lights.

A statement was made. You deal with all sorts of things when you play on the road in CONCACAF, but that was the first time U.S. made it clear:

We're gonna stand our ground. Even when I played on the Olympic team, it seemed like we were always so obliging. One time I remember we even took the visitor's locker room and gave the good one to Mexico! The idea being, "Oh, they're bringing in the crowd." We stopped being so obliging in Monterrey. That felt like a turning point to me. I just wish we could've done better in that game. We had our chances.

Yes, they did. The 1974 friendly in Monterrey went to halftime nil-nil. Three minutes after the break, Danny Vaninger converted one of those chances, giving Team USA a 1–0 lead. Did the niche US soccer community take notice? Did anyone north of the border realize the national soccer team had momentarily put the fear of God into *El Tri*? Unlikely, unless they happened to be a *Soccer America* subscriber.

Did the Mexican futbol community notice that *El Tri* scrambled to tie the match, only to escape embarrassment—via a Horacio López Salgado winner—with ten minutes to play? Undoubtedly. Televisa carried the game live on national television.

Three days after this great escape, the two sides traveled up to Dallas for a rematch, the first USA-Mexico friendly ever to be played stateside. The crowd inside the Cotton Bowl numbered 22,000—75 percent of them Mexican Americans, according to our man on the ground that day, Al Trost. "My parents told me that. I remember they came down from St. Louis to see the game."

The earlier friendly in Monterrey had drawn 25,000, according to the Society of American Soccer History (SASH).[21] That sort of attendance surprised no one. The Dallas crowd, by contrast, proved something of a revelation—because all those Mexican American attendees paid for their tickets *in US dollars*. The seeds of hundreds of *El Tricolor* friendlies to come, all of them played on US territory, were planted that September afternoon.

If the FMF and its broadcast partners weren't yet fully clued in to the revenue possibilities, the two sides played a 0–0 qualifier in Los Angeles two years later. That October 1976 match drew a crowd of 33,171, to that point the largest ever for soccer in Coliseum history.[22]

For *El Tri* supporters in Mexico, the novelty and charm of these friendlies had worn off. Close matches with the *gringos* were not what they wanted to see on television. The 1970s had been imagined as a coronation, a post-World

Cup victory lap that celebrated Mexico's arrival into the upper echelons of world futbol. Instead, while the *Priméra* dazzled, the national team fizzled. *La Selección* failed to qualify for the 1974 World Cup and struggled to slap the Americans around as they once had. Then, more embarrassingly, it finished dead last at the 1978 *Mundial* held in Argentina.

Nonetheless, for Televisa and the FMF, a new revenue prototype was born. North of the border.

∙ ∙ ∙

Only eighteen months after Mexico laid that egg in Argentina, another World Cup qualification beckoned. *El Tri* hosted the United States at the Azteca early in November 1980, and Hugo Sanchez opened the floodgates after twenty-four minutes. The match finished 5–1; the crowd of 90,000 went home jubilant. For one more brief shining moment, everything was forgiven. Normalcy had been restored to North America's soccer relations. The United States had shown none of its recent pluck. Rapturous supporters found the old-fashioned blowout particularly sweet because it formally eliminated *Los Yanquis* from another World Cup.

But we should be careful to heed Hilary Mantel's warning: "History is not the past . . . It's the record of what's left on the record."

"You have to a take a closer look at that game," confirms Ty Keough, who turned twenty-four shortly after this match, one of eight he played for Team USA. "We played a man down for a good portion of the second half [Greg Majkowski was sent off in the 75th minute] and you can't do that against Mexico, not with Hugo Sanchez running up front, at altitude, with all the usual challenges.

> We were gaining confidence. A lot of us were getting minutes in NASL. Most of us were playing indoor, as well. The funding level from U.S. Soccer had been boosted a bit by 1980. So, instead of meeting everybody at the airport, then going to play a World Cup qualifier, we were able to get together and train maybe five or six days prior to an international. And we had already posted some very good results against Mexico at the Olympic level.

The 1980 US Olympic soccer team is best known for qualifying and *not* competing in Moscow, following President Carter's shock decision to protest the Soviet invasion of Afghanistan. But that Olympic side, Keough asserts, was coming into its own. The Olympic tournament in 1980 was a U-23 event. In February of 1979, the Yanks beat their Mexican counterparts, 4–0, in a friendly that drew 40,000 to the L.A. Coliseum. A month later, on April Fool's Day, the same American U-23s beat Mexico, 2–1, in a Pan American Games qualifier in Bermuda.

"Mexico panicked," Ty told me. "Now we'd beaten them twice; it was double the panic. That's when the Mexican federation brought in a whole new, professional squad, and *that* became their Olympic team. And they got caught."

According to Keough, those players on the US Olympic squad had signed special "amateur" contracts with their NASL and Major Indoor Soccer League clubs. In lieu of typical salaries, Ty and his teammates were paid "stipends," supplemented with perks such as cars and apartments. This startling bit of administrative savvy preserved their eligibility for the Olympics.

The FMF took no such precautions. When the two teams met for home-and-home Olympic qualifiers in May and June of 1979, Mexico fielded a team comprised almost entirely of the professional Club Unión De Curtidores, a León side then struggling to remain in the first division. "They were mostly under-23 guys," Keough says, "but they had been full-time pros, most of them probably since they were 17, 18, 19 years old."

The Mexican pros dispatched Keough's U-23 side with a pair of *dos a ceros*, one in León, the other at Giants Stadium in New Jersey. When the truth came out, Mexico was obliged to forfeit both matches and the US advanced, qualifying for the Olympic tournament alongside Costa Rica. In the end, no US athletes traveled to Moscow that summer of 1980. Mexican athletes *did* participate—just not the men's soccer team.[23]

As such, *La Selección* had no lack of incentive to thump and perhaps embarrass the senior USMNT when the two rivals next met—at *Estadio Azteca* in November 1980. And *El Tri* did exactly that: 5–1.

A fortnight later in Fort Lauderdale, fielding the same lineup, Mexico lost to the United States, 2–1—its first such defeat since 1934. "I remember being with Coach [Walt] Chyzowych after the game," Yank captain Ricky Davis told *Men in Blazers* in 2016. "I had never seen someone with so much joy in his heart. Being able to look at the Mexican players and say, *Yeah, you haven't beaten us every single time for forever and a day . . .* " [24]

• • •

Keough did not participate in that historic upset. His MISL club, the St. Louis Steamers, needed him back in the squad. Because the United States had been eliminated from World Cup qualification, he dutifully returned to St. Louis. Ty didn't watch the match on television because it wasn't on television. Not in his country.

Once Keough returned home, he quickly heard tell of the shock result, but it didn't stop him in his tracks. "We knew we could play with them. It was a great win—but we were eliminated. And I was playing three games a week, indoors. To tell you the truth, I don't remember studying the lineups thinking, *Who did Mexico bring to Florida?* I just didn't."

Make no mistake: The result gratified Ty Keough no end. He'd grown up alongside Steve Moyers, who accounted for both US goals. While Harry's kid was raised in Carondelet Park, Moyers grew up in the North County community of Florissant.

"That's St. Sabina Parish, and he was one heckuva baseball pitcher, too," Ty reports. "Just a fast, courageous, natural athlete. Moy-Moy (that's what we called him) did just one season at UMSL [University of Missouri-St. Louis]—I think we played them my senior year at St. Louis University—before turning pro with the Stars. I remember watching him later, with the Cosmos. [Georgio] Chinaglia shoulda bought him a steak dinner every night. Steve did a lot of dirty work for him, all the running. He was a scrapper. Steve and Bobby Smith were roommates on the national team. They'd get into a fist-fight almost every day at practice, then later you'd find them playing cards in the room."

Did you ever speak to Steve about his two-goal place in US soccer history?

"I might have seen him 8 months later and said, 'Hey, congratulations.' I honestly don't remember. This was before cell phones. It's not like you're talking or texting the guys directly after the match. I know it sounds strange but back in 1980, that's just not what happened."

A win vs. Mexico is always its own reward, and forty-six years is a very long time. But you don't hear an abundance of triumphalism about the Fort

Lauderdale victory, not from anyone on that 1980 national team. In fact, that attitude didn't even carry the day when Keough went home for Sunday dinner.

"I'll let you in on something: As you know, my dad played for the U.S. national team in Brazil; he played for the U.S. at two Olympic games. Her son played for the Olympic team and the national team—against Mexico, a bunch of times. But my mother is from Guadalajara. If my dad wasn't playing, or I wasn't playing, my mom is rooting for *El Tri*. Even today, if Mexico plays the U.S., she's pulling for Mexico."

Harry's kid doesn't recall how his mom reacted to the Florida result, but readers will remember how it played south of the border, from Chapter 1: "We are mired in total disappointment," *La Afición* howled. "And worse still, in a disorientation . . . the team does not advance . . . does not have international prestige . . . does not know how to play when not at home."

At this point in our story, having just taken in the *clásico*'s curious arc through the 1970s, this reaction feels less berserk and unhinged, no? After all, *El Tricolor* followed up this dubious performance by screwing up even more royally—failing to reach the 1982 World Cup finals in Spain.

Four years would pass before Mexico and Team USA agreed to face each other again. Their October 1984 friendly was held at *Estadio Neza*, on the Mexico City campus of the *Universidad Tecnológica de Nezahualcóyotl*. *El Tri* needed games prior to the next World Cup; its automatic bid meant Bora Milutinovic could not rely on the qualification process to prepare his side.

Team USA needed the match, too—mainly the players. The North American Soccer League, their meal ticket, teetered on the brink of collapse that October. Come June of 1985, NASL had died on the table and the national team had crashed out of another World Cup, leaving the American professional game in tatters. Most US professionals drifted into the Major Indoor Soccer League, various regional backwaters, or retirement. In February 1986, the US Soccer Federation started over, handing the senior men's national team program to a remarkably green group of Youth Soccer Revolutionaries.

Amid this widespread upheaval, the friendly at *Estadio Nez*—the 27th renewal of the North American Derby—created little stir. The YouTube highlights reveal Mexico curiously decked out in red jerseys and blue shorts, playing in a half-empty stadium. Courtesy of two long-range bombs, *El Tri* eked out another razor-thin result, 2–1, against a US squad that, seventy-two hours earlier, had dropped a 4–0 decision to mighty Guatemala (pop. 7.8 million in 1984).

The two sides would not meet again until 1991. When they did, Bora stood on the opposite sideline, wearing stars and stripes.

7

The 1990s Changed Everything

The Potent Politics of Identity and Myth

It was Michael Orozco Fiscal's goal on August 15, 2012, that lifted the United States to its first—and, to date, only—win over *El Tri* in Mexico: a friendly 1–0 result before 56,000 at *Estadio Azteca*. At the time, the center back played for San Luis FC, in the *Priméra* (which would rebrand as *Liga MX* a year later). Was that club affiliation relevant to the man's identity, or to the USMNT's identity, now or then? What about the fact that he was born in Southern California to Mexican nationals, then settled in Orange County upon retiring from the game?

Because Americans so prize the power and primacy of the individual, posing such questions seems only natural. At the same time, understanding the elemental importance of family heritage in a nation of immigrants, such inquiries feel almost *too* personal. But in actuality, Orozco's choice to play for Team USA, and to identify as an American citizen footballer, certainly did matter back in 2012. And it matters today. Because national teams do represent *us*. They always have, for better and worse. National teams embody the population and act on our behalf, as physical representations of our shared identities, as avatars of our tribe.

Correspondingly, identity doesn't just inform international futbol. It enables it, full stop. Identity and tribe are the life forces that course through the arteries of World Cups and international competitions of all kinds. Their peculiar powers made possible the US-Mexico rivalry from its Depression-era beginnings straight through to its full and magnificent flowering during the 1990s.

Identity is the primary ingredient in every meaningful and sustained competition, regardless of the sport. Without it, the contest might as well be shirts vs. skins in the park. Without it, our support for—our identification with—preferred clubs or national sides would boil down to rooting for mere laundry (as Jerry Seinfeld keenly observed[1]).

Orozco's historic goal and his maze-like path through the professional club cultures on either side of the border also underline identity when it comes to tribal mythmaking: what we tell ourselves about ourselves, what we tell ourselves about an archenemy. Such narratives can extend to what we tell ourselves about the trolling power of a chant (*Dos a Cero!*), or the invincibility of an opponent's home fortress (the cosmic confines of *Estadio Azteca*). They are the stories certain populations repeat often enough to believe. In time, these portrayals can grow so potent that adversarial populations might just buy into them, too.

However, mythmaking does not amount to a hill of beans without identity, which is both the purpose and manifestation of tribe.

And here is where Orozco's example gets postmodern: The man *chose* his tribe.

So did his parents. They emigrated and raised Orozco in Anaheim beside that most American of attractions, Disneyland. Their son played his club soccer for Irvine Strikers, the outfit that produced fellow USMNTers Benny Feilhaber, Bobby Wood, Matthew Hoppe, and Jonathan Bornstein, another dual national. In 2002, when Major League Soccer sort of sucked, Orozco signed on with San Luis, south of the border, though he also did a season in MLS with the Philadelphia Union.[2]

Many Mexican Americans with that resume, especially those with parents born in Mexico, might have elected to play for *El Tri*. But not Orozco. He never doubted that he'd represent the United States. The centerback came up through the Federation youth system and, in Beijing at the 2008 Summer Olympics, started all three games for the Yank U-23s. He debuted for the senior national team later that same year.

To answer the questions at the head of this chapter: These bottom-line, passport assertions of identity mattered far more compared to where Orozco played his club futbol in 2012. When his career in the Mexican first division—with San Luis, Tijuana, and Puebla—did come to an end, Orozco went home to Anaheim, where he spent his final professional seasons playing the elder statesman with Orange County SC in the USL Championship.

Orozco is proof that tribes are not, as authoritarians would argue, a strict matter of blood and soil. Rather, and in the twenty-first century especially, we *sapiens* buy into the power of national identity of our own free will. And here again, the exceptional attributes of US vs. Mexico—these bitter on-field adversaries who live side by side, competing across "borders," while at the same time growing closer in a shared North American futbol community—ring through the noise.

•••

World futbol is an immense, sprawling enterprise undertaken literally in every corner of this earth. Still, there are no direct comparisons for the particular competitive and cultural dance undertaken by Mexico and the United States.

It's rare enough that mere fans can sally back and forth across these borders of identity, physical and metaphysical. The same June 2024 *New York Times* story cited in Chapter 3 makes plain the fluidity of these varying movements among ethnic Turks in Germany:

> Zeynep Bakan, twenty-five, who works in the German soccer museum in Dortmund, was wearing German team apparel, but only as a professional necessity: She is from Istanbul. "They go to German schools, they go out to German clubs, they watch German soccer, they're so focused on German things," she said of Germans with Turkish heritage. "And then at the end of the day, they are saying they are Turkish."[3]

This transnational exercise is delicate but manageable for fans. The consequences aren't so lasting. Soccer players with professional aspirations don't have the same luxury. "I am German when we win, but I am an immigrant when we lose," wrote the German-born, ethnic Turk midfielder Mesut Özil on Instagram when formally announcing his retirement from the German national team in 2018.[4]

Every year without fail, hundreds of young Mexican American dual nationals make the same choices Orozco and Özil made. Before we pick through that thicket of agonies and uncertainties, we must parse how and why identity operates the way it does, in this sport that lays bare tribal realities more than any other. Why *do* we care so much about tribe in futbol? What symbols do we attach to these identities, and how exactly do rivalries between national teams push so many emotional buttons?

To be clear: For US soccer fans, more so than our Mexican siblings, these examinations remain relatively new areas of inquiry. Until the 1990s, none of the sports we've traditionally obsessed over asked from athletes or fans such big, broad questions and commitments. For a century, American soccer in particular had no identity at all. The sport and its national teams commanded and required no tribal pledges from what remained a tiny, domestic fan base.

That situation has changed, of course, and the transformation took maybe two decades.

"For so long, we were so focused in the U.S. on our own sports, on our own very insular sports culture, which was so unique," says Dr. Joe Cobbs.

> Only in this age of digital revolution, where we can now watch sports from all over the world, did we see soccer really take off in the U.S.—from a spectator standpoint. If you wanted to follow Tottenham 20 years ago, for example, it was a lot harder to do. Whereas now, it's so simple and cheap. That evolution enables identity.

In this respect, Mexicans are much further along. They've cared far longer about international futbol and their country's reputational place in it. They've also demonstrated a specific brilliance for using this "digital mirror"—the act of projecting Mexican personality to millions of fans watching on TV—to strengthen their tribal brand and change the way their country is viewed around the world. With a North American *Mundial* close on the horizon, US fans seeking to influence or impress the larger futbol community would do well to pay attention to their example.

"World Cups do provide genuine windows on a country," Marion Reimers points out, adding that Mexico is happy to share the spotlight in 2026. "It's probably just as well that Mexico will get that exposure—but not have to build any stadiums!"

•••

Without national identity, international sport doesn't really work. As a compelling spectacle, it's the tribe vs. tribe component that makes such a confrontation so tasty, so distinct from a domestic club match.

Like the sport of soccer itself, international competition is a product of the Victorian Age, when nineteenth-century Englishmen proved no longer content to play amongst themselves at games they invented. The first futbol international took place in 1872 (England vs. Scotland), though the America's Cup sailing regattas (England vs. the United States) came first, in 1851. It's no coincidence that the modern Olympic movement organized its first games in 1896, and FIFA was formed in 1903. If we substitute *Industrial* Age for *Victorian* Age, we perhaps better understand that such athletic competition and modernity go together.

Those who study sport and society tell us that these newly industrialized societies created modern sport, not merely international competition. This is one major theme in Dr. Markovits's 2001 book, *Offside: Soccer and American Exceptionalism*. He also points out that domestic sport came first, in England, laying very British ground rules for how international futbol would later be conducted and supported.[5]

"The status of each soccer tribe is measured in the short term by the results of the last match and, more importantly, in the long term by the League tables," observed Desmond Morris in his 1981 book, *The Soccer Tribe*.

These tables are scrutinized eagerly each week by all the Tribal Followers and discussed at length. In England, there are four "divisions," presented as a parody of the social class system. The First Division is the upper class; the Second Division the upper middle class . . . This does not mean that tribesman come from these social classes. It means simply that the official, player or follower of one particular club will look UP to [those] from a higher division and DOWN upon those from a lower division, regardless of their social positions outside the clubs. Outwardly they will often deny this . . . But secretly they will envy the higher-placed clubs and will long for the day when their own club will gain promotion.[6]

Note the way Morris effortlessly substitutes class for identity while reaffirming the powers of envy and scorn. A very English, Anglo-centric take—but the broader world required little convincing. This concept of pitting one tribe against another, each one eager to represent and compete on behalf of its own God, Country, and Flag (read: national identity), spread so quickly and effortlessly because it felt so elementally human.

Given this overarching context, it's easier to understand why Mexicans feel so strongly about their matches with blue-blood adversaries such as Argentina and Brazil. And why Americans, who have so little experience thinking about international sport, have leaned disproportionately on US vs. Mexico to learn what much of the world already knows. One more thing to which American futbol fans are increasingly wise: National tribe, gathered over and over in support of a national team, doesn't so much choose supporters as *produce* them—not just individual fans but the collective.

Very little has changed about this culturally manufactured consent since it was first hit upon in 1872. Because there truly is something biological going on here. The desire to beat an opposing country at futbol, or basketball, or the development of superior A.I. technology—to prove that *our* capabilities are superior to those of another—feels built into the genome.

Sport psychologist Robert Cialdini describes this social tie to success as BIRG, for "Basking in Reflected Glory." In his 1976 study, Cialdini describes BIRG or BIRGing as an act of "publicly announcing one's associations" with anything or anyone deemed to be flourishing.[7] Cynics may call that "frontrunning," but it's more benign than all that. When futbol supporters deploy terms like *us* and *we,* when they indulge in things like pitch invasions, they become imaginary extensions of the team itself—a practice that likely goes back to 1872.

What *has* changed through the years are the props that national teams, federations, and supporters use to express and engage with these national identities. For example, the way soccer spectators dress today in fashions symbolic of national character. Let's call it situational BIRG-infused cosplay. More often, identity or tribe is conveyed verbally, by simple wordplay, in the form of nicknames, or in the context of chants and songs.

•••

Starting in the 1970s, the medium of television supercharged these fan habits, because "being on TV" encouraged supporters to perform not solely for their fellow in-stadium fans—or the team playing before them—but for a broadcast audience exponentially larger. Remember the Mexican Wave? What about those over-the-top mustaches and sombreros similarly unveiled at the 1986 World Cup? Mexicans have a special gift for this sort of interaction with the global futbol audience—even if Mexican Americans assert their identity quite differently from those *mexicanos* in Guadalajara or Veracruz.

"Images of Mexican masks on giant global HD screens intertwine with most of the fans in the stadium to determine the best representation of a *fanático mexicano*," wrote Juan Javier Pescador in his *Red, White, Blue & Green* essay (warning: long-but-informative title approaching), *Global Futbol, the Masked Fan, and Flat Screen Arenas: Mexican Soccer Communities in the USA and the Genesis of the Tricolor Brand in Global Landscapes, 1970–2012.* "They are also a testimony of the resilience and agency by U.S.-Mexican sports communities to participate in global networks—to generate and disseminate images of themselves as protagonists, as heroes, successful *enmascaradas y enmascarados* [masked women and men] fighting evil like *El Santo*, but now in the global ring." [8]

Here Pescador cites the symbol most in vogue today when it comes to asserting US-based Mexican identity in futbol crowds: the wrestling mask. *Lucha libre*, or freestyle wrestling, and masked men like *El Santo* have evolved into important emblems of Latino cred. US soccer fans—as members of a younger futbol culture still experimenting with such theatricality—would do well to explore these tribal tactics. After all, these are the traditions of *El Tri* fans who live here in the United States, not in Mexico.

"In the USA, Mexican fans have embraced the use of masks, borrowed originally from popular Mexican wrestlers and now evolving into sophisticated visual symbols of 'Mexican-ness' in the twenty-first century," Pescador explained.

> The current wide use of wrestling masks by soccer communities in the USA is definitely linked to one of the most popular icons in U.S.-Mexican communities: *Santo, El Enmascarado de Plata*. Rodolfo Guzmán... started wrestling out of the Tepito barrio in Mexico City in the 1930s under different names. In the 1940s he became *"El Santo"* wearing a silver mask that became a signature. While *El Santo*'s popularity increased significantly in urban areas, in 1952 José G. Cruz, an editor-artist, launched a comic book (actually a photomontage) centered on the *Enmascarado de Plata's* adventures.[9]

That comic book, or photomontage, has taken on a life of its own thanks in large part to the *El Santo* character subsequently starring in no less than fifty-three feature films (!).[10] The masks that made him famous are everywhere during US vs. Mexico matches, especially on this side of the millennium. Yes, US fans have rolled out a few models in stars and stripes—an enigmatic bit of in-stadium dress-up that resonates even with *gringos*. And yes, Jack Black did star in a 2006 Hollywood film, *Nacho Libre,* that riffs on these cultural tropes.

In spite of all that, the leather facemask is no shared symbol but a badge of Mexican cred through and through. It's also a creature of broadcast television, just another example of self-conscious, performative conduct in the service of identity-building. As our American Outlaw friends observe in Chapter 3, fans on both sides of US-Mexico relations understand there is a right time for costume dramatics: World Cup games or WC qualifiers, where the stakes and the audience are largest. In Guadalajara, during that October 2024 friendly, the occasion had limited need for wrestling garb, sombreros, or Elvis pantsuits. The locals wore their green *La Selección* jerseys out of habit and respect, in solidarity with the team, with their fellow spectators. But that is all.

●●●

The business and culture of soccer have grown up alongside these increasingly sophisticated, influential assertions of identity and tribe. The World Cup itself isn't merely a useful lens through which to view these evolutions. It's by far the best one.

Prior to 1966, host countries did not create and attach mascots to tournaments, for example. True to form, the English pioneered this practice, too, with "Willie," a congenial lion wearing a Union Jack jersey. Not coincidentally, the English national soccer team is known as The Three Lions, which symbolizes the English kingdom and harkens back to a royal crest first deployed during the reign of Richard I (1189 to 1199). A pretty sound collection of brand elements here—history, authenticity, ferocity, legit royal majesty—especially for the feudal era.

Two points are needed to make a line. Organizers of the first Mexican World Cup liked the Pommies' mascot idea well enough to follow suit. They firmly established the practice with the introduction of "Juanito," a young boy wearing the *El Tri* uniform (minus the red socks) and a sombrero.

A fine line separates the assertion of identity and stereotype, depending largely on who's doing the asserting. In 1986, Mexico followed on Spain's 1982 mascot—"Naranjito," a doe-eyed, childlike orange—with the unveiling of "Pique," an animated jalapeno pepper. In a sombrero. Organizers also saw fit to graft a whopping big, turn-of-the-century mustache on "Pique." This was an affectation the Mexicans could assert about themselves, in fun. Had FIFA suggested it (or worse still, some US marketeer), the decision might have bordered on caricature.

Then again, maybe not.

"Mexico might depend on the U.S. economically, but the U.S. depends on Mexico because of its flavor," Marion Reimers told me. "And I think that also transcends futbol. I think that transcends many, many areas, even the important area of cuisine—and it helps to build a *North American* identity. We tend to think of North America as something that only includes the U.S. and Canada. And that is not true. It's a party of three."

As a major-league fan of poutine, I heartily agree. As a North American writing in the early wake of Trump's tariff war, however, I fear some of these warm fuzzy sensations may strike 2026 readers as a bit dated.

Back in the 1970s, futbol culture was changing on several relevant fronts. In 1966 and 1970, no one attending World Cup matches showed up wearing game jerseys. Well, no adults indulged in such behavior. Check the historical match films. You rarely see it. At Mexico's first *Mundial*, attendees generally dressed to the nines—formally, the same way folks from that era got dolled up to fly on airplanes. By 1986, broadcast and satellite television, those ever-more pervasive digital mirrors, had altered behaviors.

English club Leeds United is generally credited with first selling replica jerseys to fans during the club's 1970s heyday. Across the pond, the North American Soccer League pioneered a boatload of terrible, ultimately ill-fated ideas: cheerleaders, a 35-yard offside line, artificial turf. But it *was* the NASL that started experimenting with players' names on the back of jerseys. When the starting XI for Italy's Club Monza appeared in a 1979 *Coppa Italia* match with surnames across their backs, the shirts were derided for hewing to *all'Americana,* or "the American style."[11] The national federation fined Monza—but soon enough the practice was commonplace across Europe.

Why exactly? Because compared to generic versions, team jerseys featuring the names of star players sold like hotcakes. Thanks, Captain Capitalism.

Many wardrobe trends converged in Mexico during the 1986 World Cup finals, where thousands of supporters at each match gussied up in order to inhabit national tropes/stereotypes. They eagerly participated in The Wave and generally played to the cameras in ways that were very different, say, compared to West German fans in 1974. By the mid-1980s, run-of-the-mill adult fans dressed more informally and increasingly clad in national team jerseys.

That more casual, commercial era of enhanced fan identity wasn't all sweetness and light. Once the unerring free market got its filthy mitts into these outward expressions of tribe, federations and clubs doubled down on the Leeds example. Merch revenues exploded. Now supporter groups had uniforms, too—and marching orders. The 1980s represented futbol's low point when it came to fan violence, especially in Europe where the English once again led by grim example. No one's about to defend this thuggish practice, certainly not this author. But here was a bright, not-so-shining, loudly colored expression of cultural identity through futbol fandom.

Starting in 1990, every US-Mexico skirmish has featured an all-you-can-eat buffet of these flourishes, most of them playful: banners, national team jerseys, outfits befitting the national "character." But all of them were undertaken to plant a flag, to express solidarity with the tribe, to assert identity, and often, scorn.

Sometimes the assertion is grammatical. Every time "America" is used to refer to the United States—in an anthem, on a placard, in a chant, here in this book (written by a US citizen, in American English)—our neighbors roll their eyes.

Note the way Pescador refers above to "U.S.-Mexicans," not "Mexican Americans." The word remains freighted with identitarian baggage. Many across the Americas feel as though the US has embezzled the term and, to no small extent, hogged the associated identity. To set the record completely straight: "America" was first coined in reference to an Italian, Amerigo Vespucci. The term was first used to describe the northeast coast of Brazil—a reality set in stone, come 1507, by German mapmaker Martin Waldseemüller.[12] At the beginning, the word had nothing to do with North America, much less the United States.

"Absolutely. And not only Mexicans complain about this. I can assure you Chileans, Argentinians, and Brazilians feel the same way," Reimers chimes in. "It's this way in which the U.S. tends to look at its navel and not understand anything that is going on around them. I mean, I'd say this very respectfully, but it's this tunnel vision that is characteristic of the U.S. And it's also this very colonialistic way of looking at the world. And no, unfortunately, you're not the whole continent. You're just a country. A big country, an important country. But just one of many."

Glover, an expat based in Mexico City for going on thirty years, agrees:

> It's interesting to think about this in the reverse sense. Mexico really is a country of North America, by geography, and certainly now, over the last 25 years, by virtue of economic integration . . . But the U.S.-Mexico War in the 19th century has had big impact on the psyche of Mexico—in many ways, certainly the futbol but very much in terms of *America*, the word. The British use it a lot, referring to the United States. I read *The Economist* frequently. They always refer to the country as *America*, and *the Americans*, and it's super annoying. Mexicans find that annoying. I don't say I'm from America, for example. I usually say I'm from the United States.

●●●

While the 1980s proved norm-shatteringly busy on the futbol identity front, the decade was very quiet on the US vs. Mexico front. The Siblings met but twice: the startling US victory in 1980, and *El Tri*'s 2-1 friendly decision in the capital, four years later. That's it. They did not play any further World Cup qualifiers during this period because *La Selección* qualified automatically as host in 1986, and Mexico was banned from *Italia* '90 for using over-age players while qualifying for the 1989 U-20 World Cup.

During this lull in the action, an important thing happened: All those Yankee Doodle Revolutionaries from the 1970s came of age as senior internationals. This single cohort did more to change the course of US soccer and *Der Klassiker* than any other—and the effect was immediate. In 1989, the USMNT qualified for that World Cup in Italy, its first finals appearance in the modern era. Then the US Women's National Team wasted no time in claiming the inaugural Women's World Cup in 1991.

This sudden rise produced several curious phenomena, the downstream effects of which we still feel today.

U.S. sporting culture in the 1990s was entirely unprepared to support a national team of any kind, outside the Olympic context—the country's underdeveloped soccer culture being a big reason why. USA Basketball's formation of the NBA Dream Team, which competed at the '92 Barcelona Olympiad, helped matters a great deal, as did the 1994 World Cup. But our century-old sporting universe has remained strongly domestic and insular in scope.

Accordingly and to this day, the United States lags behind on the national sporting identity front. Readers can appreciate that, by now, we've spent nearly 150 pages referring to the Mexican national soccer team by its beloved, established nicknames: *El Tri* and *La Selección*. Thirty-five years into the Modern American Soccer Movement, the men's national team still does not have one, and neither does the world-beating, four-times-crowned USWNT. Team USA and these unwieldy acronyms have been in place since the early 1990s, but they seem to me very ordinary, largely inadequate generics.

Meantime, the current mascot representing the Mexican national team is *Kin*, an animated Mayan magician wearing a cool red-white-and-green mask festooned with colorful plumage. Does the US Federation even have a mascot?

Did it ever? I'm not aware of one. I searched the USSF website for the word *mascot*. No results.

History is always good for a dose of relevant irony. Just when the United States got clued into world futbol, African nations—who've exhibited a true genius for national team nicknames—first started making outsized impressions on World Cups and the global game. The French played a significant role in these shifting demographics. Arsene Wenger brought Liberian George Weah to club Monaco in 1988; by the early 1990s, many considered him the best player on the planet. Several years earlier, Mali-born Amadou Jean Tigana had teamed with Michel Platini and Marius Trésor, born in Guadeloupe, to transform the French national team (*Les Bleus*) into a major-championship contender. Another former French colony then made a stupendous impression at *Italia '90*. Cameroon's splendid run to the quarterfinals, led by aged striker Roger Milla, is widely credited with increasing African World Cup berths from two in 1990, to three in 1994, to five by 1998.

More to the point, all of these national sides arrived with killer, next-gen team names in tow: Nigeria's Super Eagles, the Pharaohs of Egypt, the Black Stars of Ghana, and best of all, the Indomitable Lions of Cameroon. Here were teams and nations that, in their struggles to achieve self-governance, understood the value and substance of identity. Many of these nations were not formed until the early 1960s, when they shook off the burden of colonial rule. Perhaps that is one reason they undertook the branding of national teams in such earnest.

We use Stars & Stripes in this book, and Yanks, but mainly to avoid deploying USMNT and USWNT over and over again. They don't feel like honest-to-goodness nicknames, not yet, not to this author and fan. It's baffling that the US Soccer Federation has so far resisted the solicitation of comparable, identity-promoting national team nicknames. How is it that the Federation has not hired keen American marketing minds to right this tribal wrong? In 2014, ahead of the second Brazilian World Cup, I recommended in print the adoption of "Roughriders"—in homage to President Teddy Roosevelt, whose swashbuckling Spanish-American War battalion went by that name, and whose adventures exploring the Amazon River basin in Brazil nearly killed him. Alas, my one-man campaign went precisely nowhere.

Perhaps this reality is not so bewildering. Maybe our national team nickname void is an indication of just how much we *americanos* still have to learn about ourselves in the futbol-identity department. Does this country even *have* a soccer identity? Or do we have so many sporting identities—all of them domestic, regional, and insular—that we don't know where to begin?

By contrast, witness Mexico's deft use of cultural iconography on behalf of *El Tri*. In 1996, ABA Sport rolled out a green national team uniform overlaid with a zoomed-in stencil of the Aztec calendar, with the sun god, Tonatiuh, dead center—eyes popping and tongue fully extended. "Clearly a statement of identity," Erick Calderon points out, adding that eight of the last eighteen national team uniforms have featured similar pre-Hispanic markers. Consumers went wild in acquiring them. As early as 2015, Adidas reported that *El Tricolor* kit sales in the US matched those in Mexico itself.[13]

Ahead of the 2022 World Cup, the new *Selección* away shirt was off-white with several more pre-Columbian icons—conch shell, spiral staff, fire—stamped in a deep burgundy. "These items represented display the history, roots, and culture of our country, carrying knowledge and power to the playing fields of Qatar, revealing not only a uniform, but armor filled with magic, power and poetry," Adidas and the Mexican Soccer Federation asserted, rather extravagantly, in a joint statement.

The American federation does not issue statements like this. Not a single US team jersey since 1996, men's or women's, has generated anywhere near the buzz—or the sales. Team USA outfitting is mainly met with yawns. The only visceral response was negative when Nike and the USSF trotted out their infamous 1994 kits. Yeah, the ones with faux denim shorts.

In looking back to that specific era, we'd be remiss to ignore the fact that USA '94, the first World Cup hosted north of the Mexican border, *did* have a mascot. "Striker" was a floppy-eared canine kitted out in red, white, and blue. He looked a lot like Huckleberry Hound, despite being a product of the Warner Bros. animation department, not Hannah-Barbera's.[14]

Not every World Cup mascot that preceded "Striker" pointedly sought to embody the host country's national character or identity. Some didn't bother to try. "Ciao," a mascot chosen from some 50,000 entries prior to *Italia '90*, was an angular, tri-colored, gender-neutral Tinker Toy that remains highly esteemed despite displaying or revealing very little about the Italian people themselves. I like "Ciao" because it's one of the few mascots that possesses neither doe eyes nor an insipid cartoon grin. Still, it's never been clear what "Striker" was supposed to represent in the US futbol character, except perhaps the outsized influence of Hollywood's adolescent essence on every nook and cranny of American life.

•••

In the 1990s, all of these identitarian factors combined to elevate an already culturally rich, politically charged *El Clásico Norteamericano*. FIFA could not have drawn it up any better. In July 1988, when it awarded the 1994 World Cup, there was no professional US first division, precious little soccer culture, and no national team culture whatsoever. By 1991, the Team USA had smacked *El Tri* upside the head, the USWNT was world champs, a World Cup loomed, and MLS was slated to start up by mid-decade (FIFA stipulated this new first division be up and running by 1994; it missed the deadline by two years.[15])

In a backhanded way, the generic quality of "Striker" turned out to be a rather perfect straw man/dog for a soccer culture and a national team that, after a century in the wilderness, appeared to have emerged fully formed from the brow of Federation president and '94 World Cup chairman Alan Rothenburg.

That's certainly the way the Mexicans viewed it. For *El Tri*, its fans, and the futbol establishment south of the border, the United States had landed this World Cup because FIFA wanted access to American corporate cash—a true and accurate statement. These suddenly competitive Yank national teams? Much harder to explain or understand. Thus, the 1990s produced a complex confluence of cross-border events, nearly all of them shaped or made doubly fraught by persistent matters of identity and rivalry, spurred on by good old-fashioned capitalism.

Let's take a methodical, capsule look at critical 1990s milestones, lest we miss something material to our story:

The Breakthrough: Legendary Mexican striker Hugo Sanchez well remembers the loss in 1980; he went the full 90 in Fort Lauderdale. When the fateful SoCal Gold Cup semifinal was contested eleven years later, Sanchez witnessed something different. "Winning that game and winning the Gold Cup was a way for them to say, *We are here*," said Sanchez, speaking to journalist Grant Wahl in 2021. "And from that moment on, the U.S. started gaining more positive attention, sort of saying, *We are going to be a serious rival now*." [16]

Sanchez projects no shame in making this observation. This is what separates players and coaches from excitable media folk who bend game stories to fit preconceived narratives or cast blame in place of analysis—from behind expansive studio desks. The Mexican manager that night in Los Angeles, Manuel Lapuenta, spoke post-match to *La Afición* with equal candor and humility: "Mexico is no longer the giant of CONCACAF," he said flatly. [17]

For the record, that unmistakable sentiment from *El Mister*—a direct quote, for heaven's sake—was not what *La Afición* conveyed in the resulting story. Instead, the same press account downplayed the US performance, at remarkable length, while mainly finding detailed fault with Lapuenta and his team's performance. According to Martín Vásquez, who played for both national teams in this era, "Mexico took it as just one day, one bad game and the U.S. getting lucky. For a while, that mentality didn't help," he told ESPN in 2015.[18]

By now, the reader understands why *La Afición* took this gaslighting tack: From a Mexican tribal standpoint, that pill was judged too bitter to swallow. As was the case in 1934, the United States had very little to do with winning this Gold Cup semifinal—according to the popular Mexican press. Lapuenta, on duty in a caretaking role and perhaps anticipating a sea change, smartly stepped down.

Such a landmark result warrants a few more meaty details. The USMNT also played host to Mexico on March 12, 1991, three months before the inaugural Gold Cup. The two nations met at the L.A. Coliseum as part of a four-team exhibition tournament—what national team players call a "made-for event"—named the North American Nations Cup. Bora wouldn't be hired until March 28 (indoor national team coach John Kowalski led the United States), but the Americans had been consistently barnstorming the world since the months prior to *Italia '90*. It had grown into a capable side before the Serb showed up. They proved as much in March 1991 when Bruce Murray's late goal earned the Yanks a 2–2 draw before a paltry crowd of 5,261. To be fair, the Mexican federation had sent its B Team to SoCal. The A Team was in Buenos Aires, where it scrabbled out a nil-nil draw with the vaunted Argentinians.[19]

The July 1991 Gold Cup semifinal—the first time *Dos a Cero!* ever got attached to a US win over Mexico—showed itself to be an uptick in every respect. The FMF sent *El Tri*'s first-choice squad, from which great things were expected come World Cup 1994. The spectacle drew 41,000 fans to the Coliseum, a majority of them Mexican Americans, who went home stunned and disillusioned after goals from John Doyle and Peter Vermes. With Bora calling the shots, this match represented something new for both combatants: a battle of well-matched sides playing for a newly minted confederation championship, not a mere friendly, before a big crowd overwhelmingly supporting the "visitors."

The young Americans didn't merely vanquish Mexico. They had previously taken down a very good Costa Rican side in group play and would go on to squeak by Honduras in the final on penalties. A crowd of 39,000 showed up for that match, which delighted CONCACAF all the more. Though not so much as both federations and their respective TV partners. This was clearly the clearly stuff of broadcasting gold.

This reborn *clásico* would never go seven years between fixtures again. From 1934 to 1991, the two teams had played twenty-seven times in fifty-seven years. Mexico went 22–2–3 over that stretch. The next twenty-seven encounters were contested in less than fifteen years. El Tri's record over the course of Chapter 2: 7 wins, 8 losses, and 8 draws.[20]

• • •

The Clap-Back: In the summer of 1993, both national teams were back at *Estadio Azteca* for the second Gold Cup—this time in the final, before 120,000 delirious-but-demanding Mexican partisans. They didn't leave disappointed. *El Tri* eviscerated the Americans, 4–0. Order, as *La Afición* made clear, had been restored: *The anguish and anger have been left behind. Exactly two years ago, Mexican soccer was shaken by having finished in a dishonorable third place in the Gold Cup. Today we enjoy an absolute and total triumph of the Tricolor which yesterday finished its activity by blowing out the United States 4–0 and* *confirming that Mexico is once again the giant of CONCACAF, or to be more accurate to the competition, it is a complete Gold Champion. That is what really matters because it was not logical that having everything to be a power, Mexican soccer was falling in an absurd manner.*[21]

In Mexican media, US victories were invariably punctuated by condemnation and charges of "dishonor"—only to be followed by triumphalist restoration of a divine right to rule the region. These wild swings in emotion continued throughout the first Clinton Administration and into the second. North of the border, reactions were way more muted. The relatively puny US soccer media and fan communities (each constituency helmed by still more former Youth Soccer Revolutionaries) showed themselves to be far more grateful, win or lose. We couldn't quite believe such a thing was finally happening in the land of our birth: a World Cup spanning the country, the return of first-division club futbol, and a ready-made border nemesis that *really* wanted a piece of Uncle Sam.

On June 4, 1994, in the final World Cup tune-up, the two national sides played for the first time at the Rose Bowl, where 91,000 showed up to watch the US claim victory, 1–0, behind Roy Wegerle's goal just after halftime. Here was the magic TV formula—US vs. Mexico, inside colossal American stadia, filled to bursting with pro-Mexican crowds—to light entire marquees above the noggins of federation and broadcast bigwigs, on both sides of the border. Televisa had fantasized about this scenario during the 1970s, but the USMNT was green, unready. The *gringos* couldn't truly compete. In 1994, they bloody well could. For its part, the Mexican American fan base could be counted upon to supply numbers and atmosphere to burn.

The strategic driver? Same as always: identity.

"The effort by both nations' federations to play friendlies in front of Mexico supporters living in the U.S. is clearly a strategy for building a rivalry," wrote Roger Magazine, Sergio Varela Hernández, and Aldo Bravo in the *Perspectives* anthology.

If Mexicans were somewhat indifferent to the U.S. as a serious rival, the federations were correct in predicting that the rivalry would be taken much more seriously by Mexicans and Mexican-Americans in the U.S. Whereas Mexicans in Mexico were and still are, to a large extent, more interested in Mexico's soccer success in relation to the world powers of South America and Europe, Mexicans and Mexican-Americans in the U.S. are in many cases as interested in measuring themselves as Mexicans against their American neighbors.[22]

The two North American light heavyweights didn't face each other at World Cup 1994. Each advanced from the group stage but went out in the Round of 16. A year later, however, The Hatfield & McCoy Thing was renewed on a rare bit of neutral ground: Uruguay, host to the 1995 *Copa América*. Ahead of their quarterfinal date with the United States, *La Selección* had not forgotten about the original wake-up call from four years prior. Mexican newspapers and television would not allow it. *El Tri* captain Alberto García Aspe, as filtered through a *La Afición* reporter, was respectful but resolute: "This permits us to aspire to a precious revenge for the defeat they dealt us in the [1991] U.S. Cup." [23] In truth, García Aspe didn't have to go back that far: A month before the *Copa*, in June 1995, the Stars & Stripes had pummeled *El Tricolor* at RFK Stadium in Washington, D.C., 4–0.

What followed in the western river city of Paysandu? A blood bath— and a watershed. García Aspe himself was sent off for the last of multiple indiscretions. "Every tackle, every loose ball, every ball that was not loose, every ball in the air: We fought for everything and they fought for everything," USMNT midfielder Tab Ramos told the producers of *Good Rivals*. "I felt like, before [this match], we couldn't fight them. We started to fight here. That's when we got through that hurdle. It was likely the first time where, for Mexico, it hurt." [24]

After the Americans bounced *El Tri* out of Uruguay, on penalties, the account in *La Afición* was predictably dire: "The United States' national team is becoming our 'bogeyman.'" The writer then proceeded to blame this "failure" on the entire economic and political structure of the national team program.[25] The FMF sacked manager Miguel Mejía Barón the next day.

•••

The Politics: On the field, it's no coincidence that US vs. Mexico matured during the 1990s. The Youth Soccer Revolution, after a fifteen-year gestation period, had delivered a homegrown cohort of competent players. Suddenly, the two national sides were quite well matched. However, such a fervent, intense competition would not have taken shape so quickly without several key geopolitical developments all bubbling to the surface early in the decade.

The Derby was renewed only twice during all of the 1980s, a period when Ronald Reagan and his "Just Say No" anti-narcotics campaign permanently changed the relationship between these neighboring cultures. The president's leadership on drug issues had remained largely rhetorical until 1982, when citizens of Miami lobbied the US federal government to take action against the Colombian cocaine trade. The resulting South Florida Drug Task Force mobilized a coordinated response—from the DEA, Customs, FBI, ATF, IRS, Army and Navy—targeting those traffickers serving US drug consumers through the port of Miami.[26] This successful action prompted a critical reaction: Cocaine smugglers shifted transport to Mexico, where policing a 2,000-mile land border proved far more difficult.

The United States remains the most populous country in North America by a factor of three. It is the richest nation on Earth. When recreational drug habits exploded here during the 1980s, supply met this demand over land, from the south. The shift in delivery routes led to the development of rich, powerful drug cartels whose business interests destroyed local communities in Mexico. Many of the affected natives fled north to the United States. Where the Mexican government successfully confronted drug lords, the cartels moved to other Central American countries, where similar cultural disruptions sent more refugees north.

This isn't news to most readers; the bedeviled situation persists to this day. Still, the late 1980s and early 1990s represent the moment in time when southern migration first pierced the larger American consciousness. This was the era when Mexican migration went from a fact of North American life—a regional reality that, for the better part of a century, had been specifically carved out to accommodate US business interests—to a national political platform ripe for opportunism.

U.S. Senator Pete Wilson ran successfully for governor of California in 1991 on a so-called immigration "containment strategy." Conservative Pat Buchanan went further, challenging President George H.W. Bush's re-election in 1992 under an "America First" banner.[27] The xenophobia inherent in these campaigns was no longer unspoken. Though neither strategy brought electoral success, Bill Clinton's victory in November 1992 enabled the new president to make good on his promise to pass the North American Free Trade Agreement (1993), an economic treaty designed, among many other things, to employ more Mexicans in Mexico, at the expense of employing US citizens in the Rust Belt manufacturing sector.

The backlash to NAFTA, up for renewal in 2026, has been nothing if not controversial and sustained. The economic arguments, for and against, have shown themselves to be multi-layered in the extreme. The Trump Administration renegotiated the agreement in 2018, renaming it the USMCA, but eight years down the road that acronym is largely ignored. In starting his 2025 Tariff War, Trump II wasted little time ignoring the measures he negotiated. Amy Glover, whose corporate clients do cross-border business as a matter of course, believes NAFTA has been a net economic positive.

"It's a very, very complicated economic equation," she told me in 2024, "but no Mexican politician questions NAFTA. No one says, *Oh, maybe we should tell these Americans where to go and do our own thing.* Nobody says that. Nobody. Not even [then-President Andrés Manuel] López Obrador, a man of the left. Mexicans are pragmatic people. These are honest, hard-working people. They don't give a damn about ideology. They recognize, I think, that it was important to shake things up. They also respect Americans, even if Americans can be annoying partners—if they can't win at every single aspect, they're upset. They're like, *I don't play on anybody's team, I am the team.* Whereas, the fact of the matter is, they do depend on Mexico and Canada for a lot . . . In my opinion, if you look at all of the economic indicators, people are better off now than they were before [NAFTA]. Mexicans now eat more animal protein than before, whereas beans were the main source of protein before. As a result of NAFTA, what happens? Prices go down."

Historian Gregg Grandin, writing in *The End of the Myth: From the Frontier to the Border Wall in the Mind of America*, is more dubious, and Trump's re-election in November 2024 underlines his cultural critique:

> In particular, commentators argued that the North American Free Trade Agreement—a flashpoint in today's politics—would bring the xenophobes and extremists to heel. "This new global economy is our new frontier," Bill Clinton said, making the case that liberalized trade with Mexico would bring about civic renewal . . . NAFTA, though, didn't help the country rise

above the border but rather hardened the border, transforming the line—and all the hatreds and obsessions that go with it—into a permanent fixture in domestic politics and a perennial source of nationalist grievance.[28]

If NAFTA has produced cultural backlash, Reimers sees only continental irony. "For Mexico, there is a big, big rivalry with Honduras. There is a big rivalry with El Salvador, with Costa Rica. In sportive terms, they tend to hate Mexico. And the reason why is obvious: because it's the Spanish-speaking giant. It's like the big brother who's always bullying the younger brothers."

There's no escaping the fact that, in these cases, Costa Ricans perceive Mexico in much the same way that Mexicans perceive the United States: as a domineering, capitalistic behemoth.

"Yes. In those terms, absolutely," Reimers says, "and it goes deeper. Mexico is a country that doesn't allow immigrants to cross as easily. It has very difficult policies in terms of migration. There is a disrespect or disregard for human rights when it comes to migration. It's a paradox. We tend to think of Mexicans going to the U.S. as also being bullied, especially at the border where their rights are not being respected. And yet, Mexico does this to others at our own southern border."

This paradox extends to a piece of Central American bar etiquette offered up by Paul Theroux in his beautifully reported 2019 travel book, *On the Plain of the Snakes: A Mexican Journey*. When drinking in the bars and *tavernas* of Tegucigalpa or San Salvador, he warns, be cautious when wading into conversations about the money-hungry, self-righteous colossus from *El Norte*. In other words, be sure to first confirm which one they're talking about.[29]

•••

From the moment the 1995 *Copa América* concluded, the tournament schedule produced North American Derby collisions at least twice a year, thanks to three Gold Cups, a manufactured event called the US Cup (1995, 1996, 1997, 1999), two 1998 World Cup qualifiers, and the Confederations Cup in 1999. We can thank market economics for this development. The glut of games generated big money, as designed, but neither did it diminish the product. The *clásico* never disappointed when the ball was in play. The cavalcade of competitive thrills and spills—to say nothing of all the cultural, economic, and political sideshows—never let up.

Demonstrations of Mexican American identity before, during, and after these Clinton-era matches were more than cultural. Match attendance became a kind of political expression, a community badge of honor that *la afición*, the fans, could share and communicate inside the stadium, but also outside it. This performative instinct has carried forth into the twenty-first century, fueled by the awesome, portable power of the hibachi.

No one can say precisely when Mexican Americans started tailgating en masse outside these grudge matches, as contemporary press reports concentrated on in-stadium matters. Still, the 1994 Rose Bowl friendly lurks as the likely candidate. In the forward to this book, Seamus Malin, the broadcast "Voice of U.S. Soccer" throughout the 1990s, refers to having waded through a sprawling "pre-game" frolic on his way into the stadium on June 4, 1994. In thirty years, the US-Mexico Tailgate has grown into a flamboyant staple of The Derby. For *chicanos* attending *El Tri* matches, however, parking-lot feasting has grown into something specific: a transnational, hybrid tradition that remains oddly apolitical.

"With soccer being central to the Mexican culture, these behaviors carry symbolic and political significance; yet, they do not suggest any particular sympathy toward the country of Mexico politically or economically. The Mexicans proudly wear green, white and red to assert their identity," wrote Oscar Coche and Roxane Guerra in *Perspectives*. "They merely reveal a pride and love for the country that goes beyond one's American upbringing. By supporting Mexico in a match against the U.S., Mexican Americans rally to reaffirm their cultural heritage and a collective identity. Eating *tacos de carne asada* in a tailgate party can only help toward that endeavor." [30]

Mexican intellectuals across the ideological spectrum agree: If soccer did not historically contribute to the formation and construction of the Mexican nation, politically, today the decades-long futbol confrontation with the United States provides an expansive, fertile field for establishing a distinct *tribal* identity—especially for Mexican nationals and dual citizens living north of the border.

For those wearing red, white, and *blue* in Pasadena, back in 1994, the identity politics weren't so pointed. They have *never* been so pointed, not in the Team USA context.

Still, for Yank supporters, these derby matches were an opportunity to express American love for a sport that had been ignored and/or skewered by the larger culture their entire lives. The international spice of this Sibling Rivalry was also something exciting and new. Rumbles with Mexico (and other strong sides) allowed the United States to play an unfamiliar, welcome role: that of plucky underdog. To the larger culture, the atmosphere inside and outside the stadium distinguished US vs. Mexico from everything else in the insular, overstuffed US sporting universe.

Be that as it may, for USMNT players and coaches specifically, these mammoth match-day crowds came with significant strings attached.

"For guys of my generation," remembers Alexi Lalas, "playing against Mexico, whether we were in Mexico City or Guadalajara or Los Angeles or Foxborough, Massachusetts . . . It was always an away game. And we came to grips with that reality very quickly." [31]

The US camp put up with this perpetual away-game handicap because, in every other respect, the Federation couldn't believe its luck. Here was an outfit that had operated anonymously for eighty years, in a soccer-indifferent culture, on a shoestring. Post-1991, it couldn't resist the revenue and media attention these *superclásicos* were generating at the Rose Bowl, the L.A. Coliseum, RFK in D.C., the Meadowlands outside NYC, or Soldier Field in Chicago. Soccer had never grabbed the American public in this way. Even the broadcast networks could see the potential for a never-ending pageant of nationalist athletics and emotions, punctuated every four years by a World Cup.

The only problem for Team USA specifically was the prospect of ceding home-field advantage in big match after big match. The Yanks more than held their own throughout the 1990s, regardless of location. But the larger the home venue, the more the adversary benefited. In a battle of identities, Mexican Americans too often tipped the scales toward *El Tri*.

Someday soon, the Federation recognized, gate-receipt greed might just cost the national team a World Cup qualification. No one wanted that, especially the broadcast partners. A World Cup without Yanks would never deliver TV ratings high enough to justify what FIFA charged for broadcasting rights.

There appeared to be no solving this puzzle. Not until US soccer went markedly anti-NAFTA and solved its problems. In the Rust Belt.

8
Veni. Vici. Venue. Where Tribe, Home Ground, and Hashtags Collide

Christopher Columbus is not the villain of this story. But neither does the Renaissance-era explorer come off particularly well. When I was a kid, growing up in suburban Boston and playing soccer during the 1970s, he was the hero who bravely sailed the ocean blue. The intrepid captain of not one transatlantic vessel, but three. By the fourth grade, we fledgling Massholes knew the Santa Maria was the biggest of these, a vessel known as a carrack, while the Nina and Pinta were smaller caravels. Columbus was no mere figure from history, but rather the flag-flying fellow for whom national holidays, sixty different US cities and countless streets were named.

Today? Increasingly, the navigator-governor-admiral is seen as a cultural supremacist, the Western European who pioneered our modern understanding of colonialism and genocide (a specific and grave term blithely substituted for war crimes these days). Across the Americas, where he blazed the trail for a raft of contemptible historical contemporaries, Columbus remains the face and standard-bearer of a cruel and exploitative past.

I don't believe that many US nationals lie awake at night reckoning the Genoan ship captain's factual place in history. He's been discredited surely, probably fairly. But *El Clásico* can hardly be examined without invoking *Señor Colón*. It was he who begat Hernán Cortés, who destroyed the wondrous, bloodthirsty empire for which *Estadio Azteca* was dedicated. According to Jeffrey Kassing, writing in the *Red, White, Blue and Green* anthology he edited, the stadium was named and designed to actively recall the great pyramid of Tenochtitlan, where ancient enemies were sacrificed to please the gods. Are these pre-Columbian associations a stretch? Unlikely. Kassing believes "they do tap into an ethos that the stadium's name produces. That is, a place where hostile locals intend to figuratively slaughter interlopers."[1]

El Tricolor has, without doubt, marshaled the powers of history, myth, and identity to slay an extraordinary succession of opponents inside the Azteca. And consider this: For every national-team victim, the stadium experience unnerved countless fans watching on TV. Sometimes, when the futbol gods were feeling particularly sadistic, *Estadio Azteca* ripped out their beating hearts. Kassing has it right: "The stadium has become a significant character in the US-Mexico rivalry." This realization hits home every time we see the *circus maximus* packed with 100,000 partisans, every time the camera shows opponents hooked up to oxygen tanks at halftime, every time we hear a US national team alum testify to the fact that playing there is *worse* than we imagined.

"It's everything. Not just one thing," Marcelo Balboa told me in 2020.

> You walk out there and it's hot: 12 noon on a Saturday or a Sunday. The field is huge, the grass is long, the smog starts kicking in and you're coughing all the time. The feeling of playing in such a huge stadium filled with *so* many people—just a sea of green. The sound of the place, the crowd, is unlike anything I've experienced—a loud buzz that never stops.

"All the stories about Azteca are true," Balboa's teammate Alexi Lalas told ESPN in 2015. "The coins, the batteries, and bags of urine, all the different stuff. It's not an urban myth." [2]

• • •

Cut to Mapfre Stadium, the other reason our *superclásico* just cannot get away from Mr. Columbus. Opened in 1996 and sandwiched between two sets of railroad tracks and Interstate 71—behind a shopping center anchored by Lowe's and a supermarket—the Mapfre was not created with mystical iconography in mind. That's a tough sell when, prior to kickoff, supporters leaving bars on 4th Street and Summit must illegally cross two sets of tracks, snake their way through a campground, then negotiate gravel parking lots and a concrete stormwater drain to reach the stadium. Yes, those parking lots take up residence on the north side of the Ohio State Fairgrounds, and yes, the tailgating there can be darned lively. But the arena itself holds just 20,000 people. There are high school football facilities across the American Midwest that are twice as ambitious in scale and scope.

That this mundane place, of all places, would emerge in 2001 as the birthplace of American Soccer Cred, as an effective kryptonite to the time-honored and magisterial Azteca narrative, is one of our soccer family's most unlikely, tide-turning realities. And yes, the fact that it's located in Columbus, Ohio adds yet another delicious layer of symbolism—for US supporters.

"The key site for both symbolic importance and grounded experience of collective identity is the stadium," wrote Hunter Shobe and Geoff Gibson in *Red, White, Blue and Green*. "For some supporters, the home stadium is a sacred place. Ritual behavior in the stadium serves to ground the amorphous notion of identity by providing a venue for both individuals and groups to viscerally experience that identity." [3]

We all recognize that venue matters, that rivalries, as Kassing spells out, do transform brick, mortar, and corrugated steel into characters as prominent as any player or coach. Camp Nou and the Bernabéu. Lambeau and Candlestick. The Boston Garden and The Forum (one in L.A., another in Montreal). Their lasting notorieties confirm that it doesn't much matter how large the stadium is, how beautiful the walk-up might be. Only that the home team rallies the tribe, over and over, by winning there.

Estadio Azteca exemplifies this practical and exalted conception of Home Field as Fortress, with a healthy dose of the paranormal thrown in.

"Estadio Azteca is the most beautiful stadium in the world and like all of Mexico, it is a mythical place," Marion Reimers attests. "It's the place that saw the triumph of Maradona, the triumph of Pelé, where the most beautiful stories in futbol have been told. So Azteca stadium is undoubtedly the epicenter of that tradition. The first time I really fell in love with futbol, it was a Mexico friendly against Germany, which had just won the World Cup, 1990. I was five or six years old and when I entered the Azteca, it was packed. That is an experience I will never, ever forget. It's a magic land."

The ancient gods of Azteca, who still preside there, were surely puzzled by the Mapfre, by *El Tri's* inability to win inside a stadium whose cosmic rise first stemmed from sterile-if-strategic administrative decisions like ticket allocations and seasonal weather reports.

Soccer federations don't typically conjure critical results by hosting World Cup qualifiers in the dead of winter, far from a country's largest population centers, in purposely pint-sized stadiums located in curiously exurban fairgrounds. But that's what happened in Columbus, starting in 2001. In all these respects, *Dos a Cero!* created a brand-new template for how to hold serve, at home, against an international futbol nemesis—a template specifically developed for and by US soccer, its futbol culture and the North American Derby.

And it could easily have gone for naught, all that planning. Had Brian McBride not cracked heads with Rafa Marquez early in the match on February 28, 2001, had the striker's unheralded replacement (Josh Wolff!) not nicked a goal just after halftime, had Earnie Stewart not scored on the counter forty minutes later, US soccer fans wouldn't know the phrase *dos a cero* from the latest promotion at Taco Bell. Had temperatures not dipped into the 20s at kickoff, maybe the Mexicans would have scored first, and the hand-picked American crowd would have gone limp. Then silent.

As it happened, though, everything went as the US Federation and coach Bruce Arena had intended, and a system to match the unearthly powers of Azteca was born. And here's the thing: The power of *Estadio Azteca*, formidable though it may be, is confined to a single square kilometer on the south side of Mexico City. In contrast, *Dos a Cero!*—the match-siting antidote that became a chant, then an identity-soaked branding strategy—is portable.

●●●

Joe Cobbs witnessed this mobile mojo for himself on November 12, 2021, 100 miles to the south. The good doctor lives just over the Ohio River from Cincinnati, another Midwestern river town whose cozy stadium houses a Major League Soccer club. That afternoon of the scheduled World Cup qualifier, Cobbs and a colleague crossed the Brent Spence Bridge to check out the Continental *Clásico* in person.

By this time, the US Soccer Federation had taken *Dos a Cero!* on the road half a dozen times, always in winter, to midwestern communities far from the more multicultural coasts, to small stadia where MLS clubs could ensure tickets were mainly distributed to American fans. These executive decisions had become part of a twenty-first-century soccer ritual. What started as a brass-tacks, near-formulaic effort to win home qualifiers soon grew into a thoroughly American, feel-good roadshow.

Cobbs and his wingman wanted to luxuriate in that sacrament, in Cincy, so they found a Mexican restaurant down the street from TQL Stadium and wandered inside for some pre-game worship.

"I know it sounds crazy, but we didn't even think, *Oh, this is a Mexican restaurant and we're about to see a USA-Mexico match*. It was just where we got off the bus!" Cobbs recalls. "It was only when we got inside and our server came over—wearing a Mexican kit—that it dawned on us. We were like, *Are you excited for the match?* I was struck by what he said, "Oh, there's no way Mexico is gonna win this match." *No way.* Those were the words he used.

"I mean, we knew the history. So did he, of course, and we thought maybe he'd have been skeptical. But then he went on to say that he hoped the U.S. 'wouldn't beat us too badly.' Kind of anecdotal, but I thought, Wow: This *Dos a Cero!* narrative is clearly in this guy's head."

Naturally, inside the TQL, the United States won the match 2–0 on second-half goals from Weston McKennie and Christian Pulisic.

Hoodoo hype can be fun, but it can also obscure the competitive realities. The confidence and skill and cold-blooded savoir-faire of the Mexican national team are surely more relevant, over the course of sixty years, than smog levels. In November of 2021, the United States were clearly the better side; the victory was Gregg Berhalter's third straight win over *El Tri*. There is nothing obviously mystical about the happenings at TQL, Mapfre Stadium, or Allianz Field in St. Paul, Minnesota—only a string of World Cup qualifier results that, between 2001 and 2016, clearly got into the heads of Mexican players, supporters, media, and at least one restaurant server in Cincinnati.

In 2026, Mexico and the United States will each qualify automatically for the World Cup as hosts, the same as Canada. With the tournament expanding to forty-eight teams (and likely never going back to thirty-two, the numbers game since 1994; the women's tournament will undertake a similar expansion in 2031), it's nearly a lock that CONCACAF will receive 6–8 berths in future World Cup finals. I can't imagine the confederation won't create two qualification groups that keep these two continental supremos apart.

Upshot: That 2021 World Cup qualifier in Cincinnati may be the last of a dying breed. We may have already witnessed our last *Dos a Cero!* opportunity in a World Cup qualifier.

What happens to the Derby if we cannot count on two home qualifiers, two truly meaningful matches, every four years? Because it travels so well, *Dos a Cero!* has established itself as viable anywhere on the continent. We even heard a few facetious versions echoing around *Estadio Akron* late in Mexico's October 2024 victory in Guadalajara. *El Tri* will surely host the United States again at *Estadio Azteca*—for friendlies, perhaps future Nations League competitions. But Columbus, Ohio? It might never see another derby encounter in any form. That's sad. Even the Crew's fancy new stadium (est. 2022) is too small for a friendly, for Nations League or Gold Cup duty.

It's sadder still to think *Der Klassiker* may never again be renewed in any World Cup context.

F.C. Cincinnati maintains its own intrastate dogfight with the Columbus Crew. The so-called "Hell is Real Derby"—named for an evangelical billboard along Interstate 69, the main highway connecting the two cities—does not stretch back a terribly long way. Their first meeting was a US Open Cup date in 2017. Still, with the primordial and mature stages of the *Dos a Cero!* era now concluded, and with the bummer prospect of no more qualifiers at either venue, what a fabulous bragging right F.C. Cincinnati fans now maintain over their MLS nemesis from *El Norte*: "Yeah, the chant and the legend was born there in Columbus. But *we* fuckin' nailed it—so well, in fact, they retired the whole idea of U.S. v. Mexico qualifiers."

●●●

Bruce Arena is generally credited with hatching the plan to play World Cup qualifiers against Mexico at Mapfre Stadium, information which ought to surprise no one. Few US figures understand the administrative, tactical, and identity politics of American soccer better than Arena. The man's bona fides are without peer. When NASL was throwing money at European playboys and cast-offs during the 1970s, the Long Islander was scrabbling out a career playing goalie in the semi-pro American Soccer League—let's call it ASL III, the incarnation that effectively served as a national second division from 1967 to 1983. Hired by the University of Virginia in 1986 to coach both soccer and lacrosse, Arena won five national championships in ten years, grooming the likes of John Harkes, Tony Meola, Jeff Agoos, Ben Olsen, and Claudio Reyna.

Arena is a simple coaching figure to assess. His personal charm is apparently an acquired taste, but wherever he lands, he wins. When Major League Soccer launched in 1996, he got the D.C. United gig and won the inaugural MLS Cup. In the fall of 1998, after two more finals appearances (and one more Cup), the Federation tapped him to manage the US Men's National Team. Arena went 7–4–2 against the Mexicans in that role. No American skipper has fared better. Again, the man understood the American soccer condition, how to motivate and deploy the American player, better than anyone.

In the nation's capital, United had played its home matches at RFK Stadium, the closest thing to a USMNT fortress leading up to and including Arena's tenure in the District. The national team went 15–3–5 there from 1977–2015. Not too shabby. But Arena was in the house, as a fan and observer, on October 3, 1997, when the Americans hosted a World Cup qualifier vs. Jamaica. Fifty thousand showed up with tickets, more than half of them to support the Reggae Boyz.

Once Arena had control of the men's national team, he started looking for alternatives. He recognized this crowd thing wasn't really a Mexico problem or a Jamaica problem. It was a national team problem, a broader home-field advantage problem, a Federation problem, potentially a World Cup qualification problem.

Also, a *longstanding* problem. According to the Society of American Soccer History, the US national team played matches in no fewer than seventy-two different "home" stadia prior to 2011.[4] That's a lot—and yet another state of affairs peculiar to American soccer. England played national team matches in just eighteen different stadia between 1945 and 2011.[5] Even so, the Football Association always scheduled matches of import at the sanctified Wembley, in North London. To state the obvious, at none of those eighteen venues did the F.A. ever worry about a majority of foreign fans diminishing the national team's home-field advantage.

In America, starting in the 1990s, filling specific facilities with a clear majority of US fans proved a structural, competitive stumbling block for the national team—not just against Mexico, but against a half-dozen different CONCACAF opponents. From the Federation standpoint, not addressing this issue could make the difference between playing in a World Cup or staying home.

In the spring of 2000, the US hosted Costa Rica for a World Cup qualifier in Columbus. The nil-nil result that night was nothing to write home about. Arena, though, came away impressed with the partisan atmosphere in a sold-out Mapfre Stadium.

"Bruce probably deserves some credit for saying, 'I think this is the way we can get a competitive advantage against Mexico, by playing in a smaller stadium, a Midwest market and a passionate crowd,'" Columbus Crew general manager Mark McCullers told SI in 2013. "And oh yeah, *by the way*: Why don't we play . . . in February when it's going to be freezing cold, and provide ourselves even a further competitive advantage—and get into the heads of the Mexicans?"[6]

Federation president Sunil Gulati, another architect behind the Columbus strategy, admits, "The weather wasn't the primary issue," he told Wahl in 2021. "That turned out to be a bonus." [7]

Here's how the scheme worked logistically on this maiden voyage. Game tickets for the upcoming home qualifier vs. Mexico—scheduled for February 28, 2001—were sold first to Columbus Crew season ticket holders, and then to members of Sam's Army, the national team fan club formed in 1995. (American Outlaws were founded in 2007, FYI.) Just 4,000 tickets remained; those were made available to the general public on a first-come, first-served basis.

You know the rest. The 2–0 victory that cold winter night in 2001 didn't just launch a sing-song chant. It changed the power structure between the US and

Mexico immediately and forever, according to the players themselves. Striker Earnie Stewart: "The fans were fantastic. I've never experienced that before [against Mexico]," he told ESPN.[8] Winning goalkeeper Brad Friedel, a veteran of two MLS seasons in Columbus: "I think the crowd helped us more than the weather did." Mexican defender Alberto Macías didn't disagree: "The way the people backed them surprised us, and the cold was tremendous. When we went out to warm up, we did so with pants and gloves, and even [keeper] Jorge Campos wore long pants. I think it was the only time in his career that he used them."

Landon Donovan, not yet nineteen years old that February night, felt the earth move beneath the Mapfre: "You could feel it in the game. The whole dynamic had shifted. It was 180 degrees."[9]

•••

The legend and lesson of *Dos a Cero!* isn't that the United States managed to hold serve in a handful of home qualifiers ahead of World Cups. Rather, it's that the recipe and scoreline have shown themselves to be so durable and portable. They fortified the national team fan community with an identity it hadn't enjoyed before. In the new millennium, Team USA has slayed Mexico eight times via *Dos a Cero!* Seven of those victories took place on home soil. Four 2–0 decisions, all World Cup qualifying matches, went down in Columbus.

The chant itself, in point of fact, was not coined in Ohio but sixteen months later at the World Cup, in Jeonju—another reason that fateful Korean match sticks in the craw of so many Mexicans.

"What you start to see with rivalries is a string of those conspicuous moments," Cobbs told me in 2024.

> One after another, and there's usually a few conspicuous characters that come to the forefront. That's what creates a narrative over time. Because that's really what rivalry is, right? It's a narrative that develops and deepens over time. And today it's a completely symmetrical rivalry. From a marketing standpoint we'd call this its "main product life" phase. U.S.-Mexico is moving toward maturity—in a good way, where the rivalry is recognized beyond core soccer fans in America. It's reaching those fans

who maybe don't follow the national soccer team other than every four years. But they know who the rival is.

US sport has conjured and preserved no shortage of fabled narratives: "The Immaculate Reception," "The Music City Miracle," "The Bloody Sock." Some are abstract but remain recognizable: "The Shot," "The Catch," even "The Play," a Cal-Berkeley fairy tale summoned in part by the unwitting Stanford Band. Some even pertain to national teams: "The Miracle on Ice," and Paul Caligiuri's "Shot Heard 'Round the World'" (a callback to the original coinage—Bobby Thomson's epic homer off Brooklyn's Ralph Branca—itself borrowed from the mythic Revolutionary War battles of Lexington and Concord).

Still, there is no ongoing component, no common thread to these one-off marvels. They are meaningful, but they're also preserved in an inert sort of amber. The Pittsburgh Steelers and their fans cannot effectively deploy "The Immaculate Reception" to help them win in 2026.

This is the remarkable alchemy of *Dos a Cero!*, the mundane match-siting gambit that became a kind of transportable psy-ops weapon the national team deploys around the country. On the internet, the sing-along phrase became a hashtag, then a meme.

"*Dos a Cero* has become a living and breathing artifact that is a foundational myth of U.S. soccer cultural identity," argues Stephen P. Andon in his *Red, White, Blue and Green* essay. "To understand this mythological scoreline requires an investigative history of the U.S.-Mexico rivalry—a history that reveals a monumental shift beginning in the twenty-first century—but it also requires an examination of the power of nostalgia as it is linked to sport, place, and rhetorical discourses of memory." [10]

Couldn't agree more, Professor Andon, who teaches at Nova Southeastern University in Florida. Such is the activity we undertake here.

Because Mapfre Stadium is located not in downtown Columbus but 3 miles north, on the State Fairgrounds, the birth of *Dos a Cero!* took place in a "heartland" setting. This detail may seem minor, or a tad contrived, but American sports fans consistently warm to this folkloric type of physical surroundings. Think of Wisconsin's Lambeau Field, where ordinary Packer fans own shares of the team. Recall the film "Field of Dreams." Consider all the "pastoral" qualities attached to baseball for going on 200 years. Scholars agree the game's proverbial founding in rural Cooperstown, N.Y., is entirely fictional. Still, summer after summer, the sport's demigods make the trip there—for Hall of Fame inductions, but for the communal, countryfied pilgrimage, as well.

"The myth of *Dos a Cero* seeks to derive its power from its place in the heart of Middle America," Andon further expounds. "The myth is rooted in its place, forever etched on that now-sacred ground. This language bears a striking resemblance to the depictions of Green Bay's Lambeau Field and the religiosity that is often connected to the ritual qualities of sport."

Apart from all the wins, the extracurriculars that swirl around Fortress Azteca could not be more different. This chasm may explain why, with regard to *Dos a Cero!*, the Mexican futbol establishment took the bait rather clumsily.

After the February 2001 loss, Mexican captain Rafa Marquez was anything but gracious. In fact, he took the opportunity to diss Donovan, claiming not to know who he was. Come 2005, back in Columbus following another *Dos a Cero!* defeat, Mexican manager Ricardo LaVolpe refused to see any significance in the result or the tableau: "This was a 0-0 game. The first team to make a mistake would lose. We were the first to make a mistake. They just found two goals. That's it. It wasn't a game where the opposition was superior to us." [11]

By 2009, after two more World Cup qualifier defeats in Ohio, the magical powers of *Dos a Cero!* could not be downplayed. Ahead of the away qualifier that February—the third in Columbus—the Mexican website *MedioTiempo* may have been the first to dub Mapfre Stadium *"La Casa del Terror para El Tri."* Kudos to the art director: That story ran beside the picture of a lonely ticket booth covered in snow. This piece may also include the first derby-specific reference to *La Guerra Fria*, or the Cold War. [12]

The overall Yank run of form in these twenty-first-century World Cup qualifiers cannot be downplayed either. Between 2000 and 2015, Team USA met Mexico twenty-four times, claiming thirteen wins and five ties against six losses. The romance of *Dos a Cero!* emerged in this dominant context.

Is the scoreline of these games really so important? To the players, to the diehards, to the media? In 2013, leading a World Cup qualifier 2–0 in Columbus, Clint Dempsey stepped up to take a meaningless 95th minute penalty. The crowd buzzed with a weird anticipation: Would Dempsey botch the spot kick to preserve the fated scoreline? Miss he did, and former Stars & Stripes midfielder Cobi Jones immediately tweeted his verdict: "Dempsey missed on purpose. #dosacero"

●●●

If we apply Dr. Cobbs' sequence-of-blockbusters theory to the myth-building around *Estadio Azteca*, one does not know where to start. Four years after its opening, Pelé and Brazil reigned supreme there in living color. Sixteen years later, the stadium served the same historic supporting role in elevating Maradona and Argentina. To recap, these are the two most famous players in futbol history. Each experienced his crowning moment on the south side of Mexico City, 7.2 km from where the Battle of Churubusco took place.

From the moment the Azteca opened in 1966, straight through to the end of the millennium, the Mexican national team won every World Cup qualifier it played there. Not just against the *gringos,* but everyone in CONCACAF. *Estadio Azteca* was where Mexico earned its apex triumph, beating the great and powerful Brazil to claim the 1999 Confederations Cup. The Mexican people clearly attribute a not-insignificant portion of these happenings to the cosmic powers of *their* Aztec forebears. As well they should. These are the divine avatars of conquest (of not being conquered), of artistic and cosmopolitan expression, of ancient Mexican traits and capabilities that shine through to the modern day.

From a Mexican supporter's perspective, the cup of supernatural juice overfloweth—it pours more than enough to share with the futbol world at large.

English fans feel the same way about Wembley—the way Brazilians feel about the Maracana in Rio de Janeiro. There is no US stadium that carries anything like this cultural heft—to say nothing of its implicit traditions of blood, gore, and menace.

"Imagine if America had only one major sport and we built a single stadium for all the games we played against other countries in that sport. Now, imagine we built that stadium on a de facto burial ground, infamously known as a cultural epicenter of grotesque human suffering, and named the stadium after the perpetrators," wrote Buzzfeed's Aaron Gordon, who made the trip to Azteca for the Mexico-US qualifier in 2013.[13]

> As we arrived at our section in the upper deck, the steep grade, never-ending steps, and intensity from the home fans implanted me with an apocalyptic certainty that Azteca was named quite purposefully to remind visitors of the pyramid of Tenochtitlan, the infamous Aztec structure that stood on the same ground as present-day Mexico City. Human sacrificial victims would ascend the massive pyramid before their blood would stain the steps, much to the delight of the Aztecan citizens. As the riot police escorted us up, until we reached the very top, I couldn't resist the vision of my own blood running down the stadium stairs, flowing to field level and pooling in the ancient, dried lakebed sands, pleasing the same gods as the human sacrifices from centuries previous.

Full disclosure to the reader: I have never set foot in *Estadio Azteca*. When the United States last played there, in 2022, I was busy preparing my first soccer book, *Generation Zero*. During 2024–25, when researching this book, Mexico's grand footballing cathedral was closed to *Liga MX* and *El Tri* matches for pre-World Cup primping. Hence my Chapter 3 pilgrimage to the GDL.

Nonetheless, accounts from earlier matches are better than anything I could have reported personally. *Why?* (Warning: Sacred Cow Debunking Zone ahead.) Because *Estadio Azteca* peaked as an effective fortress late in the previous century. Folks who know also agree the late-2013 addition of luxury suites—a move undertaken in part to prepare for hosting NFL games—reduced capacity and blunted the Azteca's infamously blood-curdling vibe. The remodeling work prior to World Cup 2026 is likely to take things further in that dampened direction, further away from any reverence for the gods, as renovations centered on complying with something more boring and mortal: FIFA security mandates.

Which is all to say, *Estadio Azteca* from 1966 to 2013 produced a spectator experience that no longer exists today.

"I have unbelievable memories of going to *Estadio Azteca* and attending U.S.-Mexico matches," MLS Commissioner Don Garber told *Sports Illustrated* in 2011.

> Some of my greatest memories in pro sports. And for somebody who's not been through the experience, it's almost something out of a Hollywood movie . . . One of the things most people don't understand about World Cup qualifying at Azteca: The fan has a relationship with that game that is different, in ways unlike anything in professional sports. You're not just a spectator.

This sentiment from Garber is a common one from those who have journeyed to Azteca for US vs. Mexico. The celebrant does take part in the drama, in the way ancient Roman spectators (fans of *La Selección*) and Christian martyrs (US players and supporters) participated in gladiatorial dramas. American Outlaw Matthew Eison certainly felt the spectacle wash over him in 2009—his first visit to Azteca and, so far as he's concerned, "the best one."

"It was certainly the most intense—the one after which my buddy's wife and my wife swore off going to another one; the last one before they scaled the place down for NFL games," Eison recalls. "Over 110,000 fans. Middle of the day. Extremely rowdy. USA went up 1-nothing with the Charlie Davies goal, just a few days before his tragic accident. We were going nuts and stuff was being thrown at us from across the police barricade."

Eison and the US congregation were seated that afternoon in a corner of the upper deck, what became the routine place to stash *gringos*. "Before that, they put the USA fans closer to the field," Eison explains. "The stories I hear of things being dropped on them: like flaming dirty diapers and Ziploc bags of urine? We saw none of that. The weirdest thing was Ramen noodles. And water bottles. As we were leaving, someone got hit in the forehead with a battery. But we *all* got doused with ramen noodles."

Evidently, Americans who make the trek to Azteca return home with many memories that hinge on projectiles, which makes sense. This particular hazard is a relative rarity in US sports fandom.

"In 2013," reports fellow Outlaw Craig Hanh,

> the police evacuated the U.S. section immediately at the final whistle [0–0]. They blocked off all the ramps at each level leading down to ground level—standard procedure—and then moved us slowly through the crowd, inside a phalanx of riot police. Lots of trash, empty cans, insults being thrown

into the group, over top of the police line. At some point, I see a flash out of the corner of my eye and there's a full, unopened Gatorade bottle coming down. I fling my hand up and miraculously catch it directly in the palm of my hand, no bobble. And then I drank it.

What color, Craig? "Purple. Riptide Rush!"

•••

I would argue that "Peak Azteca" took place late in the all-important 1990s, when the national team came closest to achieving its destiny—to rub shoulders on equal terms with the global futbol elites. In one sense, an emergent USMNT had sorely tested Mexican futbol's self-image and belief during this period. The Americans" newfound competence was first considered an illusion, then an affront. In the end, though, victories over the bully from *El Norte*, at *Estadio Azteca*, grew more meaningful than ever. Looking back, Dr. Cobbs isn't surprised by this serial tension.

> I teach a rivalry class and the term we use is *symbiotic*—the same exact thing we know from biology, But we could call it codependence, right? Think about the Yankees and Red Sox, or Real Madrid and Barcelona: the idea being that the Yankees wouldn't be who they are in terms of national prominence, all those World Series titles, if it weren't for the Red Sox. That rivalry went through an evolution. After years of asymmetry, in the early 2000s, it just blew up.

> But getting back to the symbiotic aspect: The Red Sox also wouldn't have the prominence they have today if they weren't the primary rival of the Yankees. Both clubs have been elevated to a place they wouldn't have achieved on their own. Real Madrid and Barcelona, and now U.S.-Mexico are on the same path.

If there was a single, defining moment representing Peak Azteca, in this shared light, it's hard to argue with the November 1997 World Cup qualifier—the one where Mexican defender Ramón Ramírez famously kicked red-headed US talisman Alexi Lalas in the down-belows, as a nervy nil-nil match hung in the balance.

"If you watch the video, Ramírez waits for the crowd to gather round and then it's just this stealth strike . . . I was not expecting it, to say the least. Given who we were playing, I probably should have," Lalas told ESPN.com in 2015. He claims to have not sought any retribution. "Because I was able to go and recover—I have two beautiful children. I'm a much kinder and gentler version of myself in my ripe old age." [14]

Amazingly, the Mexican left back finished this match. He got booked, as did two more comrades and three Yanks during this fierce encounter. But Ramírez did not get red-carded for his clearly dangerous play. In fact, he was later hailed as a hero, having so expertly and publicly sown *desmadre* against the highest profile *Yanqui*, to such belittling effect.

"With the passing of time, I realized what I did was stupid, silly," Ramírez told ESPN.com, adding that, in Mexican Spanish, the preferred euphemism translates as *noble parts*. "Fortunately, Alexi took it with a dose of humor. I have always publicly apologized to him because cowardly actions don't correspond to being a sportsman. I regret it. It was a wrong, I'll say it again, but maybe it did highlight the passion in those games." [15]

At this specific moment in time, perhaps as Lalas shook it off and rose to his feet, the US Soccer Federation saw clearly what Bruce Arena saw. Continued failure to develop a similar fortress for Team USA might someday cost the national team program a place in the World Cup Finals. Eighteen years later, Grant Wahl revealingly reported in SI that the USSF had "tried to strike a deal with its Mexican counterpart on the sites for their home-and-home World Cup qualifiers. Along this line of thought, if you host your game in some other city—say, low-altitude Monterrey—we'll stage ours in heavily Hispanic Los Angeles, where Mexico's supporters normally outnumber US fans by a factor of 10." [16]

Wahl's source? None other than US Soccer Federation executive vice president Sunil Gulati.

During Peak Azteca, however, the Mexican national team program was in no mood for horse-trading. In 1997–98, *La Selección* occupied a position of perceived strength, one the *Federación* thought it might enjoy forever. Post Confederations Cup, Mexican prospects appeared brighter still. And so, Wahl reported, "The *Tricolores* . . . never accepted, prompting the USSF to schedule two straight qualifiers with Mexico during frigid weather in Columbus, Ohio."

In other words, Peak Azteca led rather directly to *La Guerra Fría*—an inspired Mexican media coinage—and The Cold War was joined. You know the rest.

What is markedly less appreciated, even in retrospect: Mexican dominance at *Estadio Azteca* was already on the wane. That raucous 1997 qualifier was a tipping point. *El Tri* was forced to settle for a nil-nil draw that afternoon— the first points it *ever* dropped to the Americans in a home qualifier. Lalas considers that point more than fair compensation: "Oh my God! That was a *win*. That was a point in Azteca. When we got back into the locker room, we knew we had done something historic." [17]

• • •

The first verifiable crack in the armor of *Estadio Azteca* didn't involve Team USA, in fact. Five months after the first *Dos a Cero!*, the Mexican national team hosted Costa Rica in a June 2001 World Cup qualifier and bowed to the talented *Ticos*, 2-1, on a now-famous goal from Hernán Medford. Prior to this match, no CONCACAF side had beaten *El Tri* at Azteca. Ever. Obviously, the unprecedented result proved a sensation in Central America, particularly in the Costa Rican newspapers. *La Nación* celebrated by coining a new phrase in 60-point type across its front page: AZTECAZO! [18] Mexicans and *Ticos* alike still refer to this match by that name. Another CR outlet, *Diario Extra*, trolled *El Tri* with this inspired, take-the-piss headline: ¡*Quiúbole, manitos!*—"What up, dudes?"

Always remember: While Mexicans may resent the United States for its political, cultural, and economic browbeating, Central American states like Costa Rica resent Mexico just as much for some of the exact same reasons.

Amy Glover spoke with me about this in 2024:

Mexicans don't know anything about Costa Rica, Guatemala, or Central America, nor are they interested—in a way that is comparable and aligned with the way a lot of Americans think about Mexico.

Mexicans, too, are very racist, but not the way Americans are racist. There's no history of slavery here, but they inherited a Spanish version which is very colorist, if you want to put it that way. Very conscious of color, which results in a lot of discrimination against indigenous people. It's amazing to me the amount of skin cream that is sold here, for the purpose of whitening the skin ... I guess there's more political correctness now with Lopez Obrador [who preceded the current president, Claudia Sheinbaum Pardo], which I actually think is a good thing. But people here in general are very aware of color.

Mexico City is a whole different ballgame compared to the rest of the country. The city is pretty progressive. There are areas like *Condesa y Roma*, where now you see foreigners all the time. But until fairly recently you never saw a Black person in Mexico, ever. I mean, it was a bit insane how infrequently—and now you do. There are Haitians, and there are tourists. I think it will be complicated in terms of how we're going to absorb this immigration because a lot of people who can't get to the U.S. are deciding to stay, which I always see as a very good thing. But Mexicans have a very particular way of speaking, a way of eating. They're not that used to different manners from all sorts of different people—especially outside of Mexico City.

Four days post-*Aztecazo*, the Mexican national team traveled to Honduras and blew another WC qualifier, 3–1. Suddenly, the idea of Mexico rubbing elbows with the finest footballing nations on the planet—an argument strongly buttressed by its invincibility at *Estadio Azteca*—seemed awfully far away.

Thus, in July 2001, when the Stars & Stripes showed up in Mexico City for their first meeting post-Columbus, a desperate futbol community lay in wait. A mere 60,000 believers had witnessed the embarrassing defeat to Costa Rica. More than 110,000 showed up to support Mexico against *Los Yanquis*.

Unbeknownst to the faithful, though, something had already shifted in the celestial sphere. The divine protections of Fortress Azteca hadn't evaporated, but they had taken a hit. Mexico got the win it needed, but only just: 1–0, on a goal from the stylish Jared Borgetti. And *El Tri* did manage to qualify for the 2002 World Cup by virtue of its 3–0 home victory vs. Honduras on the final Matchday in November. But this specific *Selección* arrived in South Korea as damaged goods. The second, far more devastating *Dos a Cero!*—punctuated by the new-born chant—confirmed this point rather definitively.

Sporting renown often outlives competitive realities. This is true for individuals. It's true for teams. It's true also for the supernatural juice that squads may gather from their home stadium and fans. Still, US futbol supporters may be late in appreciating what Mexicans have quietly acknowledged since the turn of the century: The ghosts of *Estadio Azteca* have lost a bit off their fastball.

•••

El Tri would best the *gringos* in each of the next two home qualifiers, in 2005 and 2009. Both matches finished 2–1. In August of 2012, the Americans finally broke through. Their famous 1–0 victory has often been dismissed as a meaningless friendly. But here's a fun fact for those who diminish such "exhibitions": Mexico has not beaten the United States at *Estadio Azteca* since Orozco etched his name in the history books.

The context of this *amistoso* helps account for why Fortress Azteca has been diminished since 2012. Michael Orozco, the goal scorer, didn't start the game. He came on in the 77th minute and found the net 3 minutes later. Instant legend. The defender had replaced Edgar Castillo, one of the few senior internationals to appear for both *El Tri* and the USMNT. In total, Jurgen Klinsmann relied upon a half dozen Mexican league veterans that night. Jose Torres and Herculez Gomez started alongside Castillo; Joe Corona and DeMarcus Beasley came off the bench, along with Orozco. All six competed routinely for their *Liga MX* club sides at the Azteca, effectively demystifying the experience.

Klinsmann is not exactly beloved in US soccer circles these days. During his tenure, he was better known for bringing a whole host of German-born players into the national team program. But the Americans had never been better equipped to win at Azteca than they were under him in August 2012. Each of the ensuing World Cup qualifiers there—2013, 2017, and 2022—ended in draws. To further underline the larger point, Mexico dropped *another* home qualifier at the Azteca to Honduras in 2013, a result that set the stage for San Zusi's divine intervention down in Panama. Without that random bit of third-party fortune, Mexico would not have participated in World Cup 2014.

At the same time, the idea that Mexico in 2012 was in the midst of a competitive tailspin is too simple to be true. *El Tri* authored several signature wins during this era of US vs. Mexico. Increasingly, however, those statement performances took place in the United States, where *La Selección* was now playing ever more internationals, friendly and otherwise. They certainly looked very much at home during the 2009 Gold Cup final, a 5–0 Yank-thrashing result before a king-sized, 50–50 crowd at Giants Stadium, across the Hudson River from New York City.

Anxieties ought to have been soothed by *El Tri's* scintillating 4–2 victory at the Rose Bowl in the 2011 Gold Cup final, a result that earned American manager Bob Bradley the sack. There, the crowd was largely pro-Mexico, and *El Tricolor* thrilled those in attendance by prevailing with great gusto and panache after falling behind *dos a cero*. Post-match, Landon Donovan acknowledged that Mexico—by winning another important trophy north of the border—had humbled the Americans.

All the same, neither result inspired widespread joy in Mexico, not from national team supporters, nor the ever-more-surly media gatekeepers based there. Gone was the consistent swagger they demanded. Instead, *El Tri* performances provided still more opportunities for astutely drawn cynicism and disillusion:

"For now the fantasy and the ghost of disgrace are over and gone," wrote essayist Roberto Velázquez Bolio following the 2011 Gold Cup.

> The maximum symbol of the age of fear does not have any choice but to accept it. The evil Landon Donovan, the suckling child of the *migra* and Yankee imperialism, made a statement that tastes of victory because it is true: 'It is important to be realistic and in the last few years, Mexico is very clearly the better team.' A defeat against this *gringo* team would be viewed with contempt, considering the Mexican [players'] long voyage from Europe. A triumph would be seen as a formality. Like this there is no point, like this it is very boring. [19]

Here Velázquez gave new voice to the peculiar-but-familiar dilemma Mexicans had wrestled with since the early 1990s: The stubborn projection of dominance in a match one cannot control, against a rival one would prefer not to have.

The suckling child had a different take. "What I realized after the 2011 Gold Cup final," Donovan told Wahl in 2020, "was that soccer has grown a lot in our country. Bob Bradley, a guy who just succeeded with us, had his job on the line. And that would have never happened in the past with U.S. soccer—because people just didn't care enough. But now they did." [20]

•••

By 2011, Mexican futbol identity had entered a new phase. Epic victories against world futbol's privileged class had not come. Instead, hopes were raised by several important youth championships, including the 2005 and 2011 Under-17 World Cups. *El Tri* would also claim the 2012 men's Olympic gold medal in London, a competition for under-23s. Through this new lens of coming success, partisans began to believe once again that *La Selección* was poised to make the leap, to grow beyond its continental confrontations with the United States.

In the wake of the same Gold Cup final in 2011—a match the Mexicans had won, impressively, before a rapturous crowd in Pasadena—*La Afición* columnist Barak Fever couldn't seem to choose between celebration, remorse, hope, or the idea that promising Mexican youths couldn't possibly rescue the senior national team fast enough:

> Now except for the Texan, Dempsey (who is not ours thanks only to Santa Anna), no American soccer player would have a place on the Mexican national team . . . United States has a crisis of young players. Its league is almost 20 years old and it continues to be a joke and their protagonism in Junior World Cups is null . . . But Mexico is still not a great team. And while on FIFA game day, Brazil gets to dance with Germany, and Italy with Spain, the rival at our level continues to be the United States. [21]

First, allow me to say that I greatly appreciate Fever's allusion to Santa Anna. It might be the biggest compliment any Mexican has ever publicly bestowed on a US soccer player.

Second, these sad-sack assessments of Mexican futbol fortunes were issued almost exactly a year *before* Mr. Orozco netted his famous goal, the one that sapped the Azteca and its gods of so much vigor. Las Vegas native Herculez Gomez, who spent much of his pro career in the old *Priméra*, started that famous *amistoso* in the no. 9 shirt. He also sees 2012 as a significant point of departure, when a generation of Mexican players grew steadily more embittered in ways voiced publicly by the likes of Fever and Velasquéz Bolio.

"When I was at Santos [Laguna], Oswaldo Sánchez bet me $10,000 that Mexico would beat us in the Azteca," Gomez told ESPN in 2015.[22]

> It wasn't something that I turned around and charged him for. In fact, I never broached the subject again . . . Yeah, it was a friendly. And maybe it didn't mean much to people outside of that game. But to everybody that was there—who knows the history, how hard it's been for us to get any type of result there—that was huge. It was one of the most fun times I've had playing a soccer game. I came back to my club team in Mexico, and those veterans who were in the thick of things back in the day, they had long faces. They were quiet.

Rafael Ramos, who covered Mexican national team matters for one of LA's Spanish-language newspapers, *La Opinión*, saw this coming dark age as early as 2005. In his view, the degradation of *El Tri*'s home-field advantage was just one component of a larger problem:

> The Mexican writer Octavio Paz once said, Mexicans have more fear of victory than of defeat. The fans are the same way. Just watch this next game against the U.S. No matter how much confidence they have in their team—in the altitude, in the smog, in the pressure they'll bring against the U.S.—they will grow worried. There will be total euphoria the first 10 to 15 minutes, but if a goal doesn't come, there will be complete silence. The doubt kills you. It's a very Mexican idiosyncrasy.[23]

If FIFA's 48-team World Cup truly does mean the end of US-Mexico qualifiers, the last one—held at the Azteca in March 2022—spoke with great clarity. The crowd that evening was limited to 50,000 on account of ID protocols necessitated by Covid-19, in addition to FIFA-enforced sanctions related to homophobic chanting during previous *El Tri* home dates. The upper deck was mostly empty. US players themselves remarked on the decrease in volume, owing to the small crowd and proliferation of new luxury boxes in the lower bowl. Missed sitters from Christian Pulisic and Jordan Pefok were the only things that kept the Stars & Stripes from a second victory there. The match ended in a 0–0 stalemate.

•••

By the mid-2010s, the old adversaries had spent the previous twenty years delivering and absorbing one competitive haymaker after another. All around them, ironically and inexorably, the two sporting communities had only grown closer together.

In August 2016, the NFL staged its first official game in Mexico City at the newly retrofitted *Estadio Azteca*.

Four months later, back in Columbus and post-election, the two national teams clapped back at the recently elected Donald Trump's nativist campaign rhetoric. In an extraordinary pre-game gesture, both starting XIs stood together—arm in arm, before a phalanx of cameras—in a show of unity, shared purpose and humanity.

By 2016, *Dos a Cero!* no longer packed the same punch, either. Mexico had played too often in the United States—*El Tri's* home away from home! On November 11, 2016, Rafa Marquez officially vaccinated himself and his teammates against the Columbus stadium virus. His late goal delivered a 2–1 victory at the old Mapfre—a result that went a long way toward denying the Yanks a place at World Cup 2018, in Russia. Outside the Gold Cup, it was Mexico's first stateside win since 2001.

"Home" fields and their attendant competitive advantages mean less and less against this sort of distressing political backdrop. The sovereignty of venue is further diminished where one country plays the majority of its friendlies in the other; where competitor leagues shut down for a month in order to play tournaments, one against the other; where national-team prospects, men and women, might choose to play for one country or perhaps the other; where politics in one country so profoundly involve and affect so many lives and livelihoods in the other.

The North American Derby would never again return to Mapfre Stadium, now known as Historic Crew Stadium—the first soccer-specific facility ever built by an MLS team. Today, when not hosting high school matches, it functions as the club's practice facility.

The final showdown there in November 2016 did signal the beginning of another new phase, one where the *superclásico* still dominates the continent, but venue matters less and less. While the invincible era of Azteca, like the mocking heyday of *Dos a Cero!,* may fade, US-Mexican interdependence moves inevitably forward.

After all, in a family—in rivalries between and amongst siblings—the idea of home-field advantage remains elusive at best.

9

The Accidental Confederation

How Soccer's Best, Brightest, and Richest Have Come to Covet CONCACAF

Nowhere do world futbol enthusiasts maintain warm, fuzzy feelings for their home confederations. Such bureaucracies are necessary evils. In Europe, putting up with crusty, money-hungry UEFA is the price to be paid for sober administration of the Champions League and European Championships—on free TV (for now). By contrast, the allied organizations that look after soccer matters in Africa and South America, CAF and CONMEBOL, are almost fiendish in their levels of corruption. In those two regions, the price tag attached to semi-competent, graft-ridden chaos would appear rather high.

And then there is CONCACAF, whose reputations for scandal, skimming, and ridiculous footballing behaviors are more cartoonish than sinister. Be that as it may, we allow the Miami-based organization its foibles, its shady economic windfalls, in exchange for access to entertaining international soccer.

Formed in 1962 and originally based in Mexico City, the confederation today serves forty-one futbol-playing nations in North America, Central

America, and the Caribbean. Up until 1990, it clearly served Mexican fortunes first and foremost, especially during the 21-year reign of Mexican-born president Joaquín Soria Terrazas, and the arrangement did make a kind of bureaucratic, economic, and competitive sense. Mexico was the biggest, most successful footballing nation in the region. US broadcasters, for their part, had no interest in bidding on regional soccer events throughout the 1960s, 1970s, and 1980s. *Grupo Televisa* was more than happy to fill that void and maximize its own revenues by shaping tournament coverage around *El Tri* and Mexican media consumers.

Each and every confederation around the world exists to maximize revenues in a similar fashion. In following that north star here in the Western Hemisphere, CONCACAF has chased the money, better served those populations that have money, cozied up to its share of dictators, and elevated some real crooks. None more brazen than Jack Warner of Trinidad & Tobago, who succeeded Soria as president in 1990. Like *El Clásico Norteamericano* itself—and so much of our continental story—everything changed after 1990. As a first order of business, the new administration moved the confederation to South Florida, out from under pervasive Mexican pressures. Then Warner and his new vice president, the American Chuck Blazer, launched the Gold Cup, and the USMNT held up its end of the bargain. Its 1991 title, especially the semifinal win over Mexico, convinced US television networks to invest in future broadcast rights.

Without that Gold Cup, the United States and Mexico would not have jump-started and juiced their rivalry so quickly, or lucratively. Ditto for the four US Cup tournaments organized from whole cloth by the USSF starting in the mid-1990s. Everyone around the table at Sunday dinner—Grampa FIFA, the sibling federations north and south, all the extended relations in from Central America and the islands—saw the same thing: More *superclásicos* meant more eyeballs, more revenue.

So what if this regional soccer organization had been delinquent in not creating such a tournament for nearly thirty years? Let's turn a blind eye to the fact that, all across the nineties, Warner—a first-ballot Soccer Corruption Hall of Famer—ran the confederation like a mob boss. (He'd be indicted on charges of wire fraud, racketeering, and money laundering by the US Department of

Justice in 2015.[1]) Who cares if the broader futbol world thinks *CONCACAF* and imagines only substandard pitches, former presidents in handcuffs, the pelting of players with rocks and garbage, or the military escort of team buses to and from airports? [2]

The enduringly dodgy nature of CONCACAF has always overshadowed its simple incompetence and petty money-grubbing. But this much is also true: None of the region's post-1991 successes—from the cultivation of US vs. Mexico, to the cooperation between *Liga MX* and Major League Soccer, to regional Champions Cup and Nations League competitions, to ever more profitable television rights, to the hosting of World Cups in 1994 and 2026—would be possible without the confederation. In this story of Siblings, CONCACAF is the unpredictable, new-moneyed, oft-pickled uncle whose involvement in your family's dysfunctional reunions has, over the years, proved unavoidable.

In writing *Generation Zero*, I documented heaps of historical episodes that help convey and define just what a fabulously bizarre, garish, utterly newsworthy entity CONCACAF has shown itself to be these last sixty years—not just the organization but its member countries, their administrators, and fans. To best tell those stories, I coined a phrase that sums things up explicitly:

> CONCACAFkaesque, adj., 1) *bewilderingly dodgy, corrupt or otherwise substandard; slightly embarrassing but nevertheless compelling;* 2) *descriptive of match management, field conditions, stadium security and/or administrative ethics as rendered by game officials, futbol fans, federations and/or confederations in North America, Central America and the Caribbean; as in,* "The decision from Trinidad & Tobago's federation to effectively sell its World Cup qualification fixture in the spring of 1985 was predictably CONCACAFkaesque."

That last bit? Actual fact, allegedly. When T&T attempted to qualify for the 1986 Mexican *Mundial*, the Soca Warriors drew the United States and Costa Rica in a preliminary group stage. The T&T Football Federation, under the leadership of then-secretary Warner, resolved to sell its home fixture, and the associated home-field advantage, to the US Soccer Federation for a reported $40,000 in 1985. This episode has never been substantiated. Warner has bigger legal fish to fry, and the USSF has nothing to gain by fleshing out the arrangement. Nevertheless, both legs of home-and-home qualifiers *were* contested stateside[3] on May 15 (St. Louis) and May 19, 1985 (Torrance, California). Warner is alleged to have similarly laundered a World Cup home date to the Costa Rican federation the month before, for a sum that has never been determined. Both legs of that tie were held in San José.[4]

In revealing ways, the confederation has become a living, breathing, clownish, small-time illicit character in US-Mexico relations and the region's futbol culture at large. A great many things CONCACAFkaesque are still happening, or only now coming to light under current president, the Canadian Victor Montagliani. In May 2022, the Greenland F.A. applied for membership in CONCACAF, which does accept autonomous territories. (Denmark maintains sovereignty there.) Upon re-election in November 2024, Donald Trump began openly talking about "acquiring" Greenland. He was inaugurated on January 21, 2025. That same day, the GFA announced it would meet with Montagliani and the powers-that-be in Miami.[5] Credit the Greenlanders: They can read a room.

So could Chuck Blazer. He's the former US Soccer Federation functionary who saw leadership potential in Jack Warner, then convinced him to run for CONCACAF president back in 1989. Blazer managed his campaign. Upon Warner's election, the two quickly became the Butch & Sundance of confederation-style cash-skimming, bribe-taking, and influence-peddling.

Blazer served under Warner as general secretary until 2011, and he did so very capably. According to former Major League Soccer commissioner Doug Logan, Blazer "brought [US] soccer into the modern television age almost single-handedly."[6] He was also known as "Mr. 10 Percent," for the millions he misappropriated from TV and sponsorship deals. In 2012, his world came crashing down. The FBI and IRS had uncovered more than a decade of unpaid taxes on hidden, multimillion-dollar incomes. Blazer turned state's evidence. As a result, Warner today remains confined to the island nation of his birth, resisting extradition to the United States on those 2015 charges.[7] Blazer himself died of cancer in 2017, before his many indictments could be adjudicated.

The fall of Warner and Blazer made for scandalous headlines, but their rise also tells a relevant story. From CONCACAF's inception, Mexico had dominated the region competitively and commercially. Starting in 1990, Butch & Sundance transformed the regional body from an international guppy into a still-comical-but-hugely-profitable player—with the United States and its humungous media market at its core. These events turned the North American Derby into a cash cow. This evolution, of course, could not have taken place without the Yanks finally pulling their own weight competitively. But Blazer and Warner smartly leveraged that fact to create a far larger revenue pie than anyone had imagined possible. Their efforts produced an object lesson in successful *Soccernomics*, one that the US and Mexican federations, in addition to *Liga MX* and MLS, have sought to apply and exploit ever since. As partners. Because long-term rivalry, as we've learned, is just another form of co-dependence.

•••

Keen-eyed observers might notice the capitalization and italicization of a non-standard word late in the paragraph directly above. *Soccernomics* started out as a 2009 book from authors Stefan Szymanski and Simon Kuper that applied data and economic theory to, as its lengthy subhead explained, *Why England Loses, Why Germany and Brazil Win, and Why the U.S., Japan, Australia, Turkey—and Even Iraq—Are Destined to Become the Kings of the World's Most Popular Sport*.[8] It's a great read, almost uniformly insightful (*Iraq?*) and popular enough to spawn a series of follow-ups. One takeaway from all the various soccer-based installments: In futbol, economic rationales must stand in equilibrium with competitive incentives and the power of culture.

We've shared examples of these *Soccernomic* balancing acts several times already: the US Federation finally breaking the high-revenue habit of staging World Cup qualifiers in Los Angeles, in order to preserve home-field advantage; the FMF's calculated decision to hold so many *amistosos* north of its border, a cash addiction it has no intention of kicking.

For their own distinct reasons, each federation seeks to balance commerce with the will of its futbol community and the pursuit of victories. *El Federación* would never hold must-win World Cup qualifiers in enemy territory, despite the king's ransom such matches would bring in.

These incentives are pretty clear and obvious, and the Nations League, first contested in 2023, represents an instructive model because through this tournament, CONCACAF maintains these priorities on behalf of member federations. That's what a confederation *does*, or what it should do.

The Nations League format was pioneered in Europe by UEFA, but it ticks all the boxes here in North America as well. The event brings top regional sides together for meaningful friendlies in between World Cups, apart from WC qualifying. It increases the potential for US vs. Mexico engagement—two of the four editions have produced this specific ratings bonanza. Each Nations League tournament naturally creates content for CONCACAF to sell to broadcasters all over the region. Because the competition extends to all forty-one members, the multi-tiered tournament also helps the confederation fairly qualify teams for its premier extravaganza, the biennial Gold Cup.

Not one of these boxes gets ticked to the same economic effect without the involvement of the United States and its mega media market.

CONCACAF did conduct a formal championship prior to the Gold Cup. The *Campeonato de Naciones* was contested between 1963 and 1990. Not once did the Americans participate—because they never managed to qualify for the 6-team, round-robin field. This failure wasn't merely competitive, nor the fault of Team USA alone. Without access to US eyeballs and advertisers, the tournament never made money for anyone, outside of the Mexican federation and Televisa.

The Gold Cup reframed everything, starting in 1991. It recast the modern Derby as a competition between equals, but the tournament also set Chuck Blazer free. He could sell CONCACAF productions like Gold Cups and WC qualifiers to US broadcasters. The federation north of the border conjured the US Cup in the mid-1990s to sell the same thing to the same broadcasters. Likewise, FIFA awarded the 1999 Confederations Cup to Mexico in hopes that its newly invigorated rival would meet *El Tri* at the Azteca in a semifinal—which it did.

Today we can perhaps better understand why FIFA, starting in the futbol desert of the late 1980s, catered to and courted the US market with such vigor. In 2023, an extensive cross-section of US broadcasters shelled out $1.44 billion in annual rights fees to deliver soccer content to the same, formerly impoverished market. Let's detail the networks and properties to drive the point home: NBC (English Premier League), CBS/Turner (UEFA Champions League, Italian *Serie A*, USMNT and Women's National Team), ESPN (Spanish *La Liga*, German *Bundesliga*), Apple TV (MLS), Fox (FIFA World Cup in English), Telemundo (FIFA World Cup in Spanish) and CBS/Twitch (National Women's Soccer League).[9]

To contextualize: The National Hockey League, long considered the fourth major US sport, receives $625 million annually from its lone US television rights holder, Turner Sports.[10] Hockey defenders might argue that streaming deals featuring overseas leagues make the comparison akin to apples vs. oranges. And they would be right. Soccer's international profile and gender-inclusive scope deliver a larger, completely unique fan demographic to US broadcasters and their advertisers. Put another way, America's soccer-watching public today need not care about or fixate upon Major League Soccer alone, or even the national teams, in order to follow the game here. The collective appetite for MLS, for Mexican, English, Spanish, and German league soccer, for men's and women's World Cups, for the Euros and the *Copa América* clearly generates big money for networks—a figure exceeding $1.44 billion in annual advertising and subscription revenues, one assumes. That's how capitalism works.

FIFA foresaw, then helped create this return on investment when it awarded this country the 1994 World Cup. Ditto when it awarded Mexico the 1970 World Cup.

Many scratch their heads or voice displeasure at FIFA's relentless pursuit of similar long-term growth in the Middle East. It's the courtship of authoritarian governments that feels wrong, but such bureaucratic initiative should not surprise anyone familiar with FIFA or anyone living through late-stage capitalism. Besides, far more cultural soccer interest can be found across the Arab world today than existed in the United States back in 1988.

"It is not necessarily about the Qataris or Saudis or, by extension, Euro-dominated FIFA behaving badly," wrote Frank Foer in *The Atlantic*, prior to World Cup 2022. "It is us, as a global community of soccer consumers, actually confronting what it looks like when we rely utterly on a system that deprives people of rights beyond their economic function. That's not a 'soccer' system (or a futbol system) we're confronting. It's a capitalist system." [11]

•••

The *Soccernomic* motivations of CONCACAF, FIFA, and those federations representing Mexico and the United States shouldn't surprise us, either. They're all attempting the same gymnastics: to balance economic, competitive, and cultural incentives in ways we can understand—even in the event we should find the coddling of repressive regimes distasteful.

But what, then, to make of the Leagues Cup, this unprecedented cooperation of *Liga MX* and MLS? The incentives here aren't nearly so obvious. When the tournament launched in 2023, many observers didn't see the logic—and still don't. Unlike the Nations League, this wasn't an established format borrowed from UEFA. Nowhere else in futbol do first divisions in neighboring countries, in *any* two countries, cooperate on such a level.

CONCACAF already organizes a region-wide tournament for top finishers in regional first divisions. It's called the Champions Cup, a less glitzy but still economically fruitful version of the UEFA Champions League or CONMEBOL's *Copa Libertadores*. The main draw for the CONCACAF version is identical to that of the Leagues Cup: MLS clubs vs. *Liga MX* clubs. So, what gives? Is this outright duplication? What motivates this peculiar cooperation between what had been clear rival leagues, whose clubs feed opposite sides of the US-Mexico blood feud?

Major League Soccer, which has only been around since 1996, would potentially gain competitive legitimacy from this cooperation—provided its clubs win more than they lose. Accepting Jon Arnold's contention that Mexican fans prefer to look south while corporate directors look north, what precisely do *Liga MX* club owners expect to receive in this bargain?

"The conventional wisdom is, MLS gets culture and status, while *Liga MX* gets dollars. And that's true, but I think it's a little reductive," CONCACAF expert Arnold told me. "I would say that overall, yes: The leagues are stronger together. In theory. But I do think that an increased collaboration could come at the expense of the fans, mostly Mexican fans, who have been there the whole time. I might be trying to thread the needle there, but I think that's where I land."

Over its short lifespan, the Leagues Cup format has shown itself to be most flexible. It debuted in 2023, morphed prior to the 2024 edition and, at this writing, has been tweaked again ahead of Edition III. The general idea has not changed, though. The two leagues are intent on conducting a summer tournament in the United States, where league clubs face off in cross-border fashion first in group play, then in a knockout phase that crowns a champion. Both *Liga MX* and MLS were so committed to the original idea that they each went on month-long hiatus, for the entire month of August, to make the first two incarnations possible.

Every match those first two years was played in MLS stadia, obliging Mexican clubs to cede home-field advantage and spend weeks at a time on the road. That oddity—what strikes some as a bullying big-brother imposition on a younger sibling—hasn't changed and is unlikely to change, or so said *Liga MX* president Mikel Arriola when announcing the 2025 format: "We'll play midweek all summer so Mexican teams don't struggle," he told ESPN in December 2024, "and *Liga MX* games will be played on the weekends." [12]

Contesting all the matches in *El Norte* makes no competitive sense to me, as a consumer of regional club futbol. In the *Soccernomics* framework, this stipulation goes against the common-sense will to compete and win. Fans of first-division futbol in Mexico felt and continue to feel the same way.

But we skeptics, who'd been puzzling over these matters since the summer of 2023, had it all wrong. In the first place, *Liga MX* clubs play here all the time, a fact that researching this book has made crystal clear (to all of us). Revenue in US dollars is the Holy Grail. Holy Grail 1A would be the cultivation of new fans in the United States, Mexican American and otherwise. And hey, when Mexican clubs do manage to beat MLS rivals in the process, they bolster the *Liga MX* brand quite capably. The tournament, then, will always be a north-of-the-border affair. Playing all summer long, on weekdays, gives the schedule a whiff of UEFA Champions League stature. Indeed, starting in 2025, the two finalists and the winner of the third-place game automatically earn places in the CONCACAF Champions Cup.

●●●

These are the nuts and bolts, but they don't explore in much depth what this collaboration is *actually* about. Arnold and Marion Reimers both see more nuanced, longer-term planning from *Liga MX*, which has long billed itself—quite rightly, according to a decade of Neilsen ratings—as the most popular league on either side of the border. At the risk of being more reductive, the Leagues Cup is an attempt to reposition the league for future success, and Mexican Americans are again the focus of this effort. Arnold explains:

> Major League Soccer does get this cultural cachet from the partnership, but there's such a huge Mexican-American community in the States, a majority of which doesn't typically rate MLS as a top league. When Major League Soccer teams win a Leagues Cup [Inter Miami and Columbus Crew claimed the first two] they still sneer a little bit. If MLS teams *consistently* win, then you'll start to see this fan population say, *Oh, this is a league that I will probably start watching.*
>
> More to the point demographically, you're seeing more and more young Mexican Americans saying, *You know what? I love my dad's team, Chivas, but LAFC is pretty cool as well.* I think you're starting to see this fan base develop an allegiance for two clubs: one that's their local team and one that's their pop's or their mom's team.

Erick Calderon supports Arnold's view with numbers from the Pew Research Center. When second- and third-generation US-based Latinos become increasingly Americanized, their Spanish television viewership drops dramatically. By the second generation, 69 percent watch mostly in English; by the third generation, 83 percent prefer English-language programing.[13]

But soccer is different. According to Pew, 90 percent of Latino futbol fans, across generations, prefer to watch soccer broadcasts in Spanish. "The fact that Americanization has no significant effect on how Hispanics view and consume their sport," says Calderon, "speaks to the significance soccer has in their lives and how it is attached to their ethnicity."

"The other side of this," Arnold interjects, "which is also evolving and developing: Attendance in Mexico is dipping. The TV ratings are dipping. Some of the teams are signing the [Leagues Cup] deal to make some money, and I'm not even saying that in a cynical way. Some teams *need* to sign deals to survive, right? They're also signing deals that put their games behind paywalls. MLS made that same bet, but when you make that bet, you know you're not gonna get as many fans inside your stadium."

The revenue and attendance situations in *Liga MX* cities make finding new fans north of the border essential. And here we circle back to the digital revolution, which has eased fan access to every futbol league in the world that's worth a damn. In short, the two biggest North American leagues are joining forces to begin assembling a product that can compete in this more global marketplace.

"*Liga MX* is not only competing against MLS. It's competing against the Champions League," Reimers explains, and she would know. Her employer, TNT, broadcasts CL matches in Mexico.

> It's competing against the Premier League. It's competing against *La Liga*. You have people in Mexico, young men and women, young boys and girls, who are no longer rooting for América and Chivas. They are rooting for Barcelona and Real Madrid. This is the way entertainment is going. In Guatemala, there is no bigger sporting event than *El Clásico*. And I'm not talking about Comunicaciones [the biggest club in Guatemala]. I'm talking about Barcelona-Real Madrid. That is an issue because you need to bring more eyes to your product.
>
> You're not only competing against that. You're competing against Netflix. You're competing against Amazon Prime. You're competing against HBO Originals. You're competing against so many things, and *Liga MX* needs to be able to pay their players, which are incredibly overpriced. It needs to sustain a product that is very difficult to sustain on the model as it exists today. So, I think that having a commercial partner who has infrastructure and pays in dollars will always be a smart move. And Mexico has a lot of footballing culture that it can bring to the U.S. and start that inverse colonization, as we have talked about before.

This is a big swing from *Liga MX*. The risk, of course, is a dilution of what makes the Mexican soccer product *Mexican*. But the risks are bigger still for a league and federation whose own domestic partnerships—with each other; between clubs; among leagues, broadcasters, and clubs—have been compromised for decades.

"Mexico," Reimers says, "has a problem in terms of how its football is structured. You don't have an autonomous federation. They want to make us believe it is independent. It's not. You have owners making decisions over who's in the national team. Of course, owners that also have their own interests. But when all 18 of them sit down at the table, you have these little groups, these political feuds where this one has a problem with that one, and the financial interest of this one is aligned only with that one. This is one reason *Liga MX* has not grown. It is directly to do with why the men's national team will never grow—not until you have an independent federation."

• • •

Reimers believes (and it's hard to argue with her) that despite the titanic sums that media companies are paying for streaming rights these days, the future is more likely to bring a financial reckoning, as opposed to further expansion:

> I think these are difficult times for football and we'll remember them with an asterisk. When we were talking about Guatemalans loving the *Clásico*, I thought, well, the *Clásico* is to the Spanish language what Manchester City-Arsenal is to the Anglophone world. And this makes sense. It is cultural. I know people follow the EPL in Mexico, but not in the same way that they follow *La Liga*. Also, it's easier for any Mexican to say *Villarreal* than to say *Brighton and Hove Albion*!
>
> And just to anchor what I was mentioning before: The U.S. has a similar relationship to the English and the Premier League. But then they take the Premier League to Asia! The Premier League has such a grip on world soccer—it is such a powerhouse—that it will be very difficult to compete with in the future, if it goes as it is. I think that men's football has created a bubble and someday, sooner or later, it will explode, and it will not be a pretty thing to watch.

In the meantime, MLS and *Liga MX* have hatched the Leagues Cup as a hedge, as a regional strategy to establish a viable footing in this super-competitive, thoroughly global economic reality. Building two North American soccer products to compete with the Premier League juggernaut—or, to perhaps weather a cratering of rights fees, should the market tank—certainly better explains why these two league siblings have chosen to partner up. Or close ranks.

There are two more economic wrinkles to consider when we try to get our heads around the amplified collaboration of the continent's two major leagues. The first: Apollo Global Capital's proposed investment of $1.25 billion in *Liga MX*, a deal that fell apart in December 2024 when the assembled club directors failed to vote on the matter. League Commissioner Juan Carlos Rodriguez, formerly the president of sports enterprises at *Grupo Televisa*, immediately resigned.[14]

Apollo's cash-infusion deal ain't dead yet, or so indicated the cross-border media chatter when this book went to press. Any lingering optimism also makes sense because what the league had planned to do with that money—invest in on-field product (players) and physical infrastructure (stadiums), while centralizing *Liga MX* television and commercial operations—remains critical to its growth in the US and other Spanish-speaking markets.

"We know that we are the kings of a very unique hill which is Mexican soccer in the U.S.," then-Commissioner Rodriguez told *The Athletic* back in 2021.

> That means *Liga MX*, the Mexican national team, and any games that are played against MLS clubs. *Liga MX* is becoming more relevant [in the United States] due to the success of MLS. When we bought Euro [2020] and the UEFA Champions League [rights], we knew that we needed to increase the size of our footprint outside of Mexican Americans. That investment has always paid off.[15]

It is all about the next broadcast deal. Unfortunately, *Liga MX* has never spoken with one voice on such matters. Chivas has contracts of its own with Telemundo and Amazon. Club América has a separate and unique understanding with Televisa (its owner), which today also controls Univision (TUDN). "Bringing all teams together in one deal could have made the media rights . . . much more significant, especially in the U.S.," according to *The Athletic*'s Paul Tenorio and Adam Crafton, reporting on the failed Apollo proposal.

Why didn't club directors sign on the dotted line? Well, that question brings up the second wrinkle: The antitrust lawsuit Relevent Sports brought against the US Soccer Federation in 2019. Relevent had wished to stage an official Spanish *La Liga* match at Miami's Hard Rock Stadium, but the US Federation refused to sanction the match. FIFA sided with the USSF, citing the sovereignty of federations—to protect domestic league enterprises.[16] (Ever wonder why all those foreign club matches played here each summer are mere exhibitions, not official regular-season fixtures? That sovereignty is why.)

In the spring of 2024, when the US Supreme Court refused to hear the Federation's appeal of a District Court decision, Relevant prevailed. The effects of this ruling have not yet been felt. It's merely a matter of time.

"Club América needs to leave the *Estadio Azteca* during pre-World Cup renovations that begin this summer," Jon Arnold wrote when the decision came down. "Do you think they'd rather set up shop in Queretaro or Los Angeles? Would they make more money in Toluca or in Texas?" Relevant brought the suit in order to host official *La Liga* matches in Miami. That's sure to happen, perhaps as early as spring 2026. Ditto for Mexican clubs, who have, as we know, always coveted the US market. Can the EPL and *Bundesliga* be far behind?"[17]

●●●

Liga MX sees the same opportunity in the United States that *La Liga* and the EPL see. Its cooperation with Major League Soccer makes even more sense in this light. According to Arnold, though, Mexican clubs must first put their financial houses in order. Investment at the Apollo level would enable the culture change that Mexican first-division futbol desperately needs to compete—not with MLS, but with aggressive foreign competitors who want access to the North American futbol-watching market.

Mexican clubs today operate in strikingly disparate ways. Some of that imbalance is due to the wide array of bottom lines—what eighteen different clubs make from eighteen different broadcast deals and eighteen different stadium capacities. But many clubs simply aren't administered according to twenty-first-century standards.

"When executives speak about what *Liga MX* is getting from the Leagues Cup partnership, some of the language seems kind of fake—like *best practices*," Jon Arnold told me. "What does that even mean? Sounds like something you throw into a press release. But I think *Liga MX* teams *are* going to learn best practices from MLS, and I think that's very important going forward. Digital ticketing, for example. Lots of clubs don't have it. They didn't have it at *Estadio Azteca* till a couple years ago."

MLS clubs in small markets have done a pretty great job carving out market share. Liga MX clubs have never had to do that. They were the only games in town, but the market is changing. In May of 2025, the *Associated Press* reported that Mexican League Baseball teams in Tijuana, Mexico City, and Monterrey outdraw *Liga MX* clubs in Pachuca, Santos Laguna, Mazatlán, and Ciudad Juarez.[18] According to Arnold:

> The entertainment market in Mexico is flourishing, and many clubs don't know how to compete because they've never had to. I love the Azteca. I think they do a good job of making you feel the weight of the history there. But I've been to many games there—for América and Champions Cup matches, big games—and there were 20,000 people. It sucks to get to. The light rail is terrible. I can see how people might say, *Well, I'm gonna watch it at the bar with my buddy*. So, there are reasons people aren't going to games there. They're the same reasons people don't go to *Liga MX* games all over the country.
>
> If you solve those problems and make it fun to go and easy to get to, then you'll get a full Azteca again. People change; their desires change. The fan experience is a big thing now—especially for people who travel to the United States. When I lived in Tijuana, I can't tell you how many people were like, *Hey, you want to go over to the Padres game?* Petco Park in San Diego—beautiful facility. You can tap your phone to pay for everything, and now Xolos [the *Liga MX* club in Tijuana] bring that over. So many people from Monterrey spend their holidays in Texas, where maybe they go to a Texans game. More and more Mexicans recognize what the fan experience can be.
>
> So, how do these *Liga MX* teams reach these fans that they've neglected for so long? They really do need that knowledge and insight from some of these MLS teams.

Some of those best practices are already influencing the way Mexican club owners think, big picture. Exhibit A: Major League Soccer's central-ownership model, where all thirty-two teams are owned by the league itself. This structure allows MLS to speak with one voice on broadcast rights, player-salary structures, intellectual property, and sponsorships. The system has its detractors, but it does prevent any one club from accruing too much power and dominating MLS, on the field or off it.

The Apollo deal was meant to move the Mexican first division in a more cohesive direction. In the meantime, business as usual south of the border—freewheeling club owners who act only in their self-interest—has trickled down to adversely affect a remarkable spectrum of futbol matters, including national team performance. Most Mexicans will tell you that more of their countrymen should be playing in Europe, to better hone their skills at top clubs. One reason they don't? Eighteen *Liga MX* honchos following their own saints.

"You have owners who have price tags put on players' heads that are way above market value—because they want to make more money," Reimers explains.

> That's why lots of players don't go to Europe. The transfer fee is too high. There are other reasons. Players like being a big fish in a little pond . . . But otherwise, clubs are very much in a position where they do not want to let the players go unless they cash out big. And that has a direct impact on how talent is driven overseas, or not.

●●●

Here's one last "best" business practice to ponder: the *absence* of promotion and relegation. Major League Soccer has never featured this staple of futbol leagues the world over. North of the border, we don't call this *corruption* or *freewheeling self-centered ownership*. We call it protecting the value of clubs. Evidently, *Liga MX* clubs agree. Mexico's top division "paused" this promotion/relegation relationship with lower divisions during Covid-19, as a precautionary health measure. Six years later, despite some controversy, observers agree: It's unlikely to be revived.[19]

"It was a very different form of promotion and relegation going on in Mexico, not like in England or France," Arnold points out, adding yet another wrinkle: "I think the [Apollo] investments were meant to try and lay the groundwork for more foreign club ownership, but I also think the domestic owners are trying to protect their own investments. If I own Chivas and they're trash, which sometimes they are, there are real consequences with relegation—potentially, even more money to be lost if this deal eventually comes through.

"To some extent, it's cold capitalism. But I think there are a lot of things about the fan experience, about the way clubs do social media, about marketing the teams in specific markets, where clubs look at MLS and say, *Man, these guys do have it figured out.*"

MLS commissioner Don Garber clearly supports the Leagues Cup enterprise. He backs private equity investments in *Liga MX* as well. And why not? The two leagues are partners now, facing an onslaught of foreign challengers on "American" shores. What's more, MLS—acting through its media and marketing arm, Soccer United Marketing—did a similar deal in 2012 with the Rhode Island-based private equity firm Providence, before repurchasing that stake in 2017.[20]

In early December 2024, before the Apollo deal was tabled, Garber told a press gathering:

> *Liga MX* has been on air in our country since way before Major League Soccer. They just went about it differently. So, I don't know that much is really going to change. We helped them with the organization of their new structure because it mirrors very much what MLS is all about. I think it's going to lead to more cooperation between MLS and *Liga MX*, as opposed to less.
>
> This is a story about getting our region to come together and in essence be able to have the same significance, the same importance that UEFA has in Europe. And you can't just hope for that. You have to drive it, you've got to engage it. The World Cup being across all three countries is example number one.

The biggest takeaway from all these maneuvers may be rhetorical. Garber simply does not talk about *Liga MX*, or Mexico (or Canada) like he's discussing competitors. Not anymore.

• • •

Rafa Marquez is a thoroughly modern figure. In the twenty-first century, no one has wielded more influence on the fortunes and reputations of Mexican soccer. The modern game is a global game, so it follows that Rafa made much of his mark, for himself and his countrymen, abroad. In 1999, he left the security of domestic futbol for the French club AS Monaco. Following the World Cup trauma of 2002, he moved to F.C. Barcelona, where the polished center back appeared 243 times for one of history's finest club sides. To the extent that Mexican players have taken their talents abroad, Hugo Sanchez and Marquez are the models. Manchester United star Javier "Chicharito" Hernández, in particular has cited Marquez as his inspiration in this regard.[21] Not every foreign adventure went to plan. After an unhappy two-year stint in MLS, with New York Red Bulls—the worst decision of his career, he later told ESPN Deportes [22]—Rafa returned home to finish his playing days where they started, with Atlas of Guadalajara.

While his resume is among the most cosmopolitan ever built by a Mexican footballer, the Michoacán native has very mixed feelings about the idea of leaving or forsaking Mexico in search of something better. Marquez told Grant Wahl for the *Good Rivals* doc:

> My father was the eldest child growing up and he suffered the abandonment of my grandfather migrating to the United States. He had to become the man of his house, to provide for his brother and bring home the daily bread. I'll always remember, every night, my father telling us about what he endured when our grandfather abandoned us. He always told us that we had to value what we have, and that stuck with me. That's the issue the United States carries for me. Without blaming it or fearing it, the United States caused pain in my family because of that abandonment.[23]

> The first time I ever heard of or knew about the United States, it was because I had family members living there. We only saw them on important dates like Christmas. And I wondered why they lived there. Then I began to understand it better. I saw the United States as a place where people went in search of something better, and maybe they did indeed progress. I saw that when they returned. You could tell the difference in the clothes and shoes they wore. The gifts they would bring back. But their attitudes had changed, too. They were superior, simply because they were living in the United States, and I didn't like that this had happened with members of my own family.

> Ultimately, we've always seen the U.S. as the place where dreams of a better life come true. But personally I know that these dreams can also be achieved here in Mexico, and I have achieved them.

Marquez cuts a complex and candid figure. Looking back on his 2002 performance in South Korea—90 minutes of footballing tragedy on a Shakespearian scale—he refuses to pull punches: "We did not want to play the U.S. because they are an uncomfortable rival. We would rather lose to anyone than the United States. Playing against the U.S. is more than a match. It's rivalry. It's passion."[24]

Handsome to the point of elegance, Rafa also speaks with a calm and clarity that exudes a sort of nobility. The human element with this guy is always right there on the surface. It's hard not to admire him.

At the same time, do take a moment to appreciate how many of the story elements related above—the man's family background, his professional decision-making—were predicated on *Soccernomic* and straight-up money factors.

In the modern futbol world, this should not surprise us. Economic components combine to influence most everything in today's beautiful game, including *El Clásico*. The emotion and fire of this storied competition remain. They will always remain. But if the dollars and everyone's pursuit of them don't sit at the center of US-Mexico conversations, they are never far away.

One wonders what Rafa Marquez thinks about all this cross-border, market-driven cooperation—in light of his fraught history with the United States and his future role as Javier Aguirre's heir apparent. World Cup 2026 is another cooperative and highly commercial enterprise. Once the tournament is finished, it's reasonable to expect that professional club soccer will go forward as an ever-more continental undertaking because the dollars demand it.

Post World Cup, on behalf of the national team he is poised to inherit, Rafa will be spending a lot of time and energy in the United States. He will manage the men in green during friendly internationals, of course. The manager and his *Federación* colleagues will also scour the southern United States, meeting and convincing young Mexican Americans to compete for *El Tricolor*.

"Our scouting division was set up three years ago [2018]. We developed a strategy in which there are scouts in many different parts of the U.S.," explains Jorge Tello Hernandez, speaking to the Spanish sports daily *La Marca*.[25] From 2019 to 2023, Tello led the FMF scouting department. Today, he's with Club Necaxa.

Nowadays the Mexican talent that's developing in the U.S. has been doing so for 15–20 years. So much so that U.S. youth leagues are as strong as any others worldwide. Players are often not Mexican and neither are their parents. Maybe they have roots and they have the legal right to become Mexican citizens. But they have no real links to Mexico and they don't visit, so it's not that simple. Still, we want to showcase our soccer project, and if it suits them on a sporting level, they can choose to play for Mexico.

I wish Rafa Marquez all the best in his prospective role with the national team because accommodating the American economic and cultural monolith is not something for which he's shown much patience or enthusiasm through the years. And managing *La Selección,* even in the best and simplest of times, is plenty hard enough.

10

The Unlikely, Once-Marginalized Custodians of a Rivalry Most Fierce

The North American Derby does fascinating things to the footballing attachments of young Latinas. Meet Alexandra, whom Professor Erick Calderon interviewed in May of 2024. The date is relevant. Two months before, *El Tri femenil* had shocked the four-time world champion Americans in a group-stage match at the CONCACAF W Gold Cup.

Calderon asked Alexandra whether, as a Mexican American, she experienced any feelings of conflict when these two national teams squared off.

"Yes. I have it every time," she replied.[1]

> Where it's like, oh, I'm supporting the U.S., but internally I feel like I should be supporting Mexico and knowing more about the Mexico team . . . And for some reason, I just haven't done it. But now that María Sánchez has come into the Wave [San Diego's National Women's Soccer League club], I'm like, oh, she's in the Mexico team. Okay, now I really *really* have to learn and start getting into the Mexican national team—but also, I want to get into the *Liga [MX] femenil* . . . especially now because the Wave is gonna play them.

A startling collection of what I shall term "demographic truths," plus a similar number of marketing strategies based on those understandings, crystallizes for us in the world of North American women's soccer.

The Wave, like all National Women's Soccer League clubs, does face Mexican squads each summer during the NWSL x Liga MX Femenil Summer Cup, first contested in 2024. This north-south cooperation was modeled by the Leagues Cup in 2023. As we learned in Chapter 9, *Liga MX* is involved largely for fan development.

Alexandra has demonstrated and articulated precisely how those matches foster her preference for Mexican sides.

Note the key role played by San Diego's NWSL entry, The Wave. After two failed attempts at professional club soccer early in the millennium, the NWSL is having a moment. It's growing. It's on TV. The established cachet attached to US Women's National Teams has finally filtered down to the club level.[2]

At the same time, the unique structure of Alexandra's fandom also substantiates how these "American" success stories have benefited the Mexican national team program and club teams south of the border.

We've asserted that a legitimate women's *clásico* does not yet exist between the United States and Mexico, and that remains true. As Marion Reimers explained, "in futbol, the big rivals are those who can beat you." As NBA Logo and Laker legend Jerry West has made very clear through the years, "Everyone kept talking about the rivalry we had with the Celtics [during the 1960s]. They beat us seven times in a row in the NBA finals. That doesn't sound like a rivalry to me."[3]

In time, though, the *dos a cero* from March 2024—just the second victory for *El Tricolor* in forty-three meetings—may prove as influential as the USMNT's Gold Cup win over Mexico in 1991. We're not there yet. But an extraordinary fan foundation has been laid for the *El Clásico femenil,* north of the border, on account of yet another fascinating tangle of identity politics.

● ● ●

According to Calderon, young Latinas have "relied on the USWNT for years now as an identity figure . . . a peculiar one because it does not stop at ethnicity. The USWNT plays a bigger role socially in the United States as they have contributed to the advancement of women's sports nationally, have fought for equitable fair pay, and are routinely activist for LGBTQ+ rights.

Supporting them is not just a way of manifesting national pride, but a way of supporting feminism. It is because of this that Mexican-American women find themselves caught in a struggle with identity when they face the Mexican women's national team."[4]

The derby *femenil* may remain in the formative stages, but it already lives up to one important principle: Rivalry in and of itself is an intimate, unspoken form of interdependence.

Most of the young women who've latched onto US national team players, alongside fair pay and social-justice causes, are futbol fans fundamentally. But remember that Calderon's master's thesis—*Navigating identity through soccer in Southern California*—concentrated on the habits and attitudes of Mexican Americans. We are familiar with folks rooting for *El Tri* as a means of cultural expression and devotion. We get the idea that while some Mexican Americans may root for both men's national teams, most favor *La Selección* when the North American *Clásico* is renewed.

Calderon, now an ethnic studies professor at Shasta College, has uncovered a new twist. He found that young Latinas often root for the Mexican men's national team while at the same time being inclined toward the US Women's National Team. For now.

Meet Jasmine, who juggles loyalties in this fashion but doesn't know quite what to think about them. "I ask myself that quite a bit," she told Calderon.[5]

Mary is less conflicted. "If men are playing, I cheer for Mexico. If the women are playing, I cheer for the USA. But the last game they played, [the Mexican women] won," she told Calderon in April 2024. "I cannot tell you the amount of pride I felt. That was nothing like I ever felt for a USA game. I'm getting goosebumps talking about it . . . So much pride in being *Mexicana*—to know that's, like, an option for people. It makes me so happy."

As the professor neatly sums up, "Every other aspect and way of living may be contested, but soccer remains intact as a way of displaying ethnic attachment." [6]

Such attachment represents one of the few reliable through lines when it comes to women's soccer in North America, where today, templates and expectations are recast daily and often fly in the face of conventional wisdom.

In terms of the *clásico,* the role of Big Sister is clearly played by the United States—a mirror-image of the men's derby. Alexandra and her mates bring to light how differently they follow club and national team soccer compared to established (read: male) norms.

Women have traditionally not closely followed team sports with their eyeballs, that is, their viewing habits.[7] Until Caitlin Clark showed up in 2024, men accounted for 70 percent of WNBA viewership.[8] If that, too, is changing—if women start watching soccer and basketball on TV—the economic and societal implications are rather staggering.

"I'd have to check the numbers, but there are more men watching women's sports in Mexico today," Reimers reported to me in 2024.

> I expect that to change, but I think that's a vicious circle—because women are still taught that this is an arena we should not enter. And it has to do with, how should I say this: Very marked and very monolithic ways of understanding the fun of watching sports. Yes. It's like, for example, you have a girl who goes out to the street and she's wearing her Guns N' Roses T-shirt, which she bought in H&M. And you have this guy coming over saying, *Oh, you're not a Guns N' Roses fan. I want you to tell me the name of six albums and their producers.* I know that guy, those guys. It's like, you need a membership to be accepted into this very masculine idea of what it should be like to be a sports fan.

Yes, boys and girls, ladies and gentlemen, mansplaining in futbol remains an issue that knows no borders!

> The idea that you can never change your team. Why not? If a team of mine is being bought by a state that does not respect human rights, that kills journalists, that doesn't allow homosexuality, that brings women back how many hundred years, and I don't agree with that—why can't I change?! And why am I supposed to know every lineup from 1982 up until now? Why am I not allowed just to enjoy?
>
> It's this membership kind of thing, but women are not like that. No. We're not taught to be like that.
>
> Maybe it will change, but it's a sticking point right now that I think exists—no one really wants to talk about it because it's very sensitive. But then again,

you have this project in Portland [Oregon], The Sports Bra, no? The first bar dedicated only to women's sports. I think that's really cool. I'd like to see a bar that is also dedicated to women being able to go and watch sports in their own way and write their own history and understand their own rituals.

What would this mean? I'm not sure. But today the standard is this stereotypical guy thing where everyone is yelling and drinking beer and eating wings. And it's just a very narrow way of appreciating sport. There have to be other ways to—monetize is a very sterile word—but there has to be another way to do it.

•••

A decade ago, most observers would have argued the Mexican national team had a very, very long way to go before it reached some degree of competitive parity with the Americans. But the scale and speed of change in the women's game—along paths many students of the male game do not recognize—have narrowed the gap between siblings, as *El Tri*'s upset victory in February 2024 reinforced so meaningfully. As further illustrated by the USWNT's substandard showing in Australia at the 2023 Women's World Cup.

My advice: *Buckle up*, because the paradigm shifts aren't done with women's soccer.

From the moment women's international futbol formalized itself during the 1980s, the American Way has prevailed. Through 2023, this not-so-controversial historical judgment held water on the two fronts that matter most. In the competitive crucible, the United States established itself as the finest side in the world. It won four of the eight World Cups contested since the tournament launched in 1991. The Stars & Stripes also claimed four Olympic gold medals over the same span.

Second, in terms of top-tier talent development, the US collegiate system played the central role in enabling this competitive success. American universities turned out a remarkably steady stream of superstars and otherwise useful internationals over the course of four decades. These programs also trained up hundreds more national team stalwarts who just happen to hail from, and ultimately represent, other footballing nations around the world.

Our friend Dr. Andrei Markovits spells out these facts of footy life in his seminal study, *Women in American Soccer and European Football: Different Paths to Shared Glory*. His book, updated and resissued in 2024, also accurately predicted that this US-dominated status quo stood on the verge of great change.

And so it has come to pass. Today, European clubs and national team programs are turning out better players, in higher volumes, fetching unprecedented transfer fees compared to their North American counterparts.[9] Naomi Girma's million-dollar Chelsea deal is the exception, but take note of who shelled out in January 2025 to sign the Yank defender! NWSL clubs cannot afford that kind of money. Not yet.

The biggest, richest clubs Over There have finally bought into the women's game, something the male-dominated, hidebound Euro futbol establishment had steadfastly refused to do throughout the twentieth century.[10] Hell, Real Madrid did not field its *Feminino* incarnation until 2020.

This sea change, which started to take hold circa 2010, has resulted in far more sustainable financial models for European women's clubs, by virtue of their association with deep-pocketed, brand-name organizations like Manchester City, Bayer Leverkusen, Olympic Lyon, and F.C. Barcelona. It has also meant access to the powerhouse youth academies funded and administered by those clubs.[11]

There was a time, not so long ago, when the United States was home to the best professional club soccer on the planet, and it wasn't close. Current USWNT manager Emma Hayes, a British subject, crossed the Atlantic to coach here during that heyday. She led the Chicago Red Stars from 2008 to 2010 in Women's Professional Soccer (WPS), the league that NWSL replaced in 2013. Next, she served as technical director at another WPS franchise, the Western New York Flash.

In 2026, the technical quality on display in the NWSL, to say nothing of *Liga MX feminil* (LMXF), does not compare well with the soccer product in English, French, and Spanish leagues. In fact, where did Hayes coach before she accepted the USWNT posting? Chelsea, which, in addition to splashing cash, operates a 70-year-old academy system that most NWSL clubs can only dream about. At this writing, there are fourteen NWSL franchises. Three have affiliations with MLS clubs, and only seven have in-house academies in place.[12]

Starting in 1985, American soccer pioneered and modeled the international standard for women and how to sustain it. There were legal and cultural factors that fostered this success: Title IX (the 1972 civil rights legislation that protects people from discrimination based on sex in education programs or any activities that receive federal financial assistance), the unisexual Youth Soccer Revolution, and the domestic college system (arguably a product of Title IX). They all provided young US women bountiful opportunities to play the game relatively free of stigma or structural barriers.

And let us remember another Markovits maxim: Wherever men's soccer has been historically weak—the United States is Exhibit A, but Norway, Australia, and Japan also fit this bill—women enjoyed the societal elbow room to excel.

Even Yankee obstinacy regarding the calendar served to benefit women's futbol stateside. "It has helped build the sport. It allows women, for example, to go to Europe, play for a while and then come back," Reimers says. "When they return, they have played in the UEFA Champions League. They can bring that expertise back—and they are always willing to bring that expertise back.

"Today they will not be bringing knowledge from the U.S. over there, but the other way around."

Next year's Women's World Cup in Brazil will tell us how well the USWNT has managed and responded to this transition. Hayes is clearly an excellent coach. She has worked hard to integrate a new generation of players into the national team—players who have already adapted to the new normal. This younger generation of US talent is professionalizing earlier and partaking of the college experience less and less. Lily Yohannes turned pro at age fifteen, while Claire Hutton and Jaedyn Shaw took that plunge—straight from their club teams—at seventeen. Lindsey Heaps and the Thompson twins, Gisele and Alyssa, both went professional at eighteen. Several current USWNT rosterees did play college ball: Korbin Albert, Michelle Cooper, Ally Sentnor, Catarina Macário, Teirna Davidson, and Emily Sams. They're all a bit older, but not one played the full four years.

While matters are evolving quickly, it says here that European national teams will enjoy a meaningful developmental and technical advantage until such time as the NWSL puts the necessary academy infrastructure fully in place.

•••

Several of these tectonic movements work to the substantial benefit of the Mexican women's national team and the country's nine-year-old first division. Because LMXF was created as a wholly owned subsidiary of *Liga MX*, each club already maintains a functioning academy system. As was the case in Europe, Mexican clubs were not required to create new training facilities and staff them.

Mexico's turn-of-the-century repositioning on dual nationality continues to pay dividends on the futbol front. The Mexican American population grows the pie when it comes to identifying and courting potential *El Tri* talent north of the border.

During its first two seasons of operation, *Liga MX feminil* restricted to four the number of foreign women any team might carry on its roster. More critically, the league counted Mexican American dual nationals as foreigners. That bylaw was declared null and void in 2019.[13]

European pros are not exactly clamoring to play in LMXF, but Mexican Americans definitely are. In 2024–25, they accounted for 25 percent of roster spots on the league's best three teams. More than a third of the top side, Club América Feminil, is US born, according to Calderon, who adds, "These results have spilled over into the Mexican women's national team who today [2025], with 12 Mexican-American players, compose more than half of the team. From those 12, seven are products of Southern California." [14]

Such progress bodes very well for the *superclásico feminil*, of course. Even more intriguing? The USWNT appears beatable for the first time ever.

LMXF was founded only in 2017. The ability of the league and national team to attract and develop domestic players alongside Mexican Americans has some partisans thinking beyond US vs. Mexico. "There is the possibility," Reimers told me, lowering her voice to create a mock conspiratorial tone, "that Mexican women will be a big protagonist at the World Cup before the men will."

That degree of fast-track evolution would send shockwaves through the Mexican futbol community, which Reimers calls the country's "last trench of *machismo*."

While Mexico's sporting patriarchy is one reason no Title IX equivalent was ever enacted there, Second-Wave Feminism did animate *Copa 1971*.

This unofficial women's world cup tournament—the subject of a wondrous, eponymous 2023 documentary film—attracted four national teams from Europe, Argentina, and host Mexico.[15] The United States did not participate. Denmark won it, beating Mexico in the final before a crowd of 110,000.

The motion picture didn't merely tell this previously untold story. The producers uncovered match and period footage that had gone unreleased for fifty years. It's a bit mind-boggling that such an event actually took place, twenty years ahead of the inaugural Women's World Cup, drawing crowds to *Estadio Azteca* every bit as large as had cheered *El Tri* and Brazil the year before.

It's even weirder, and a bit sinister, that history, FIFA, and football associations in all six countries nearly erased the whole kit and caboodle.

Set aside their sour, self-serving motivations. As was the case in Europe, neither the futbol establishment in Mexico nor the broader culture there was anywhere near ready to welcome, much less foster women's soccer.[16] Not just during the 1970s, but all through the 1980s, 1990s, and well into the twenty-first century.

•••

In these pages, we have made productive use of *Perspectives on the US-Mexico Soccer Rivalry: Passion and Politics in Red, White, Blue and Green*, edited by Jeffrey Kassing and Lindsey Meân. When the subject is women's soccer, the anthology's 2016 publication date is particularly pertinent. The years prior gave almost no hint of the growth to come in Mexican women's soccer. On the contrary, they painted a comparatively grim, downtrodden picture, as if the period between *Copa 1971* and the founding of LMXF featured nothing but patriarchal backlash.

That's not far from reality. *Liga MX feminil* did not exist, of course. In *Red, White Blue and Green*, the only references to Mexican club soccer were those *Federación* efforts to place national team prospects in the NWSL.

Like the US Men's National Team prior to 1990, Mexico turned out some very talented players prior to 2016. Foremost among them was Maribel Domínguez Castelán, who scored a record eighty-two times for her country, mainly in the service of overmatched incarnations of *La Selección*. She did find the mark in *El Tri*'s first-ever victory over the United States, a 2–1 decision in a

2010 World Cup qualifier in Cancún. Otherwise, much of Mexico didn't know what to make of Domínguez or athletic women like her.

Domínguez's national team colleague, Mónica González, explained that widely held ambivalence this way: "They are worried about the lesbian label. People tell girl players that they are boys, and it can become a self-fulfilling prophesy," she explained to ESPN in 2016. "It's just not accepted; the girls are doing something prohibited." [17]

The man in charge of *El Tri feminil* throughout this period (1998–2016), former national team player Leonardo Cuéllar, spent much of his career at the nexus of Mexican American soccer relations. He made his name at Pumas, in the old *Priméra*, and he subbed on for *La Selección* late in the infamous November 1980 match in Fort Lauderdale. By that time, he played his club soccer in the North American Soccer League with the San Diego Sockers. The Mexico City native finished his career in the obscure Western Alliance, one of the regional leagues that popped up following NASL's demise.

Unfortunately, Cuéllar proved himself ineffective and strangely passive in his role with the women's national team. In 2015, he was content to farm out player development to indifferent NWSL clubs. As Dan Lauletta reported in *The Equalizer*: "Not a single player who played for the Mexico women's national team in 2015 played a single minute in the NWSL in 2015. Cuéllar explained that he had no communication with the team coaches . . . but didn't blame them; rather he felt that his players needed to step up their play to make the club rosters." [18]

"The clubs are not at fault," Cuéllar told Lauletta. "I think we need to challenge our players to be on the [NWSL] level."

Harsh. But Lauletta did not disagree with *El Mister's* broad assessment of the Mexican talent pool. After singling out Verónica Pérez, Teresa Noyola, and Mónica Ocampo as the most impressive *mexicanas* at the 2015 World Cup in Canada, he went on to conclude that, so far as NWSL clubs are concerned, "Mexico is not exactly stocked with coveted players."

According to Mónica González, a native of Corpus Christi, Texas, who appeared eighty-three times for *El Tri feminil* between 1998 and 2011, outsourcing player development made sense in the pre-LMXF era. "I think it's easier to walk over to your neighbor's ranch and pick his corn than have to grow your own," she told ESPN.[19]

What a difference a decade makes. Contrast these dire assessments with the can-do vibe following the February 2024 *dos a cero*. The FMF has stepped up recruitment of transnational prospects, to great effect for club and country. Thanks to its academy systems, *Liga MX feminil* is turning out young players of quality, upgrading the national team and changing domestic attitudes toward gender and sport. The league's open, enthusiastic interdependence with the NWSL forecasts a growth potential and competitive ceiling for Mexico that feels comparable to that of Canada, a country with the third largest player pool in women's soccer worldwide. Spurred on by Mexico's obvious strides, Canada launched its own domestic concern, The Northern Super League, in April of 2025.

Machismo-fueled indifference toward women's soccer is not a phenomenon peculiar to Mexico. The British, French, German, and Spanish futbol establishments were equally detached—until they weren't.

By the same token, women's futbol isn't going anywhere if it's relying on male fans to grow the sport. As it is, men cannot keep up with the viewing and rooting options delivered by today's digital broadcast smorgasbord. Female fans clearly represent the optimal and logical growth demographic here.

Have women typically supported women's professional sports in terms of viewership? No. Not anywhere really, as Dr. Markovits confirmed for me in January 2025. Not in numbers that have ever enabled clubs and leagues to effectively gather eyeballs, attract advertisers, turn profits, and thrive.

At this writing, for the first time anywhere, those demographic numbers appear to be shifting. The rise of Mexican women's soccer and the NWSL have each shown how quickly and unpredictably this strand of the game can establish new norms, new institutions, and move forward. But it's women themselves, on the field and in the continental audience, who will make these leagues succeed.

●●●

Here's what you won't read in any account of American-born women who went south to play for the Mexican women's national team: *Wow, the USWNT whiffed on that one. They should never have let HER get away.*

The great preponderance of top-flight *mexicanas* still choose and will continue to choose Team USA if they have the chance and the bloodlines. Ashley Sanchez and Sofia Huerta are two current examples.[20] Each looked past the *El Tri* option, just as Catarina Macário looked past representing Brazil. The US Women's National Team continues to offer all three far better chances to further their professional careers, to consistently compete for, and to win international trophies.

On the men's side of the ledger, we encounter another, equally stark mirror image. For all the choices over which young Mexican Americans and their families reportedly agonize, *El Tricolor* and the *Federación* have yet to lose a highly sought-after Mexican American male to the *gringos*. Striker Ricardo Pepi would be the first, and his status as an actual "star who got away" remains pending, as he fights for minutes and continues to mature at Dutch club PSV Eindhoven.

Pepi was born in January 2003, so his best days may still rise to meet him. In the meantime, for young male dual nationals of quality, the perceived strength of *La Selección* and, to a complementary extent, *Liga MX*, continue to carry the day. Some of that decision-making is cultural—the same process Mexican American futbol fans must navigate, for identical reasons of heritage.

But young soccer prospects are also *working a system*, playing one national team program against the other, trying to best position themselves for career success.

The competition to sign young Mexican American talent is fierce and potentially alienating. The young men over whom federations and clubs make such a fuss often indicate they feel *Ni de aquí, ni de allá*—"Not from here, or from there." [21] Reimers once again puts it best: "Who are we to judge those personal decisions? We start using this lame, patriotic, nationalistic discourse and we feel entitled to decide on other people's nationality."

Be that as it may, most highly touted, dual-national prospects don't seek to settle questions of identity and nationality. Far from it. The rules governing national team affiliation only encourage these young men and women to have it both ways, to play it both ways—right up until the twelfth-hour moment when they formally commit to one senior national team or another.

•••

The FIFA rules are unisex. They do not bind a youth player—meaning those twenty-one years old or fewer—to any country according to U-17 or U-19 national team participation. Competitors are "cap-tied" only once they turn twenty-one and appear for a senior national team in a FIFA-sanctioned match.[22] Even then, cap-tied players can petition FIFA for a one-time switch of nationality, if they so choose.

In light of this forgiving framework, young national-team prospects would be foolish to commit to the United States or Mexico before they had to. Accordingly, before these questions of nationality are settled, federation coaches and scouts woo young up-and-comers and make promises about World Cup participation, about national team places, and about what positions they can expect to play. Promises they *know* cannot be kept. Players, for their own part, accept the flattery and make similar non-binding declarations in return.

"It's no surprise that Mexico would now be looking here for players," Tony Lepore, director of talent identification for the US Federation, told Grant Wahl in 2021. "In the U.S., we have some of the largest scouting events globally, so you have scouts from so many other national teams on hand, given the number of multi-nationals we have here. I think right now, in our youth national team, in that player pool, we have 60–70 players who are dual U.S-Mexico.[23]

"For U.S. Soccer it's never any pressure, you know. Instead, it's empathy and understanding about what it means to have a connection in your heart with two different national teams. Based on your family, based on your heritage. In the end, it's this connection that they feel in their heart that will drive their decisions."

Claiming to know what's in someone else's heart is an elaborate and highly speculative exercise, especially for young stars who routinely ping back and forth between youth national teams.

Consider the path taken by Alex Zendejas, born in Ciudad Juárez, raised across the river in El Paso, and today scoring goals as an attacking midfielder for the biggest club in Mexico, América. He played on the U-15 and U-17 US national teams alongside contemporaries Christian Pulisic and Tyler Adams. When the Mexican U-21 team came calling in 2020, he exercised his dual-national right to appear in two friendly internationals vs. Qatar and China.

A year later, when he appeared for the senior Mexican national team in friendlies against Ecuador and Guatemala, many assumed Zendejas had made his choice. But those fixtures were not FIFA-sanctioned. At least, that's what Zendejas and his lawyers argued—and the folks in Zurich agreed. When the midfielder appeared in two legit *amistosos* for the senior USMNT in January of 2023, only then was he officially cap-tied (though today he still maintains his 1-time switch [24]—like a savvy NBA coach who saves his last challenge, or a disillusioned college basketball sophomore who ponders a change of scenery in the Name, Image & Likeness Era).

Did the *El Tri* brain trust ever see this guy starting or contributing to the Mexican national team? Probably not. And *that* is likely what drove the decision-making—not the young man's heart, nor the legal nuances of what makes a friendly international official or not. Either way, the Zendejas Saga demonstrates how the system as it exists today obligates scouts, federation youth coaches, and senior national team managers to play a painstaking, not very honest game of strategic gestures, two-faced whispers, and brown-nosing. Because such behavior tends to keep players where they *want* to be: *Ni aquí, ni allá*.

Would Zendejas and his legal team have pressed the point about those friendlies if the diminutive midfielder had been earning big minutes for *El Tri*? Doubtful. If the minutes aren't there, if too many established studs are playing ahead of you in your preferred position on the field, maybe it's time to explore options.

Lepore's comments show public respect for the cultural questions, but both federations clearly encourage dual nationals to walk both sides of the street. Not against the rules, or the spirit of those rules, but this surplus of leeway—juiced by wave after wave of empty adulation—makes it easy for young players to overvalue their bargaining positions.

●●●

Young phenoms possess a shelf life—every footballer has one. Thus, it's wise that they negotiate their professional paths as prudently as possible, from positions of power and choice. One never knows how or how long the ball will bounce.

Stars & Stripes *Mister* Mauricio Pochettino chose to leave Zendejas off the 2025 Nations League roster. The América man was subsequently named to the preliminary 50-man Gold Cup player pool, but his World Cup 2026 prospects were very much in doubt at this writing, with half a dozen attacking midfielders standing in his way.

After their one-time transfers are exhausted, there is no going back for footballing pros, men or women.

Ever heard of Edwin Lara? What about Jesse González or Abraham Romero? Each was born in this country and played youth internationals for both federations. Lara exercised his one-time switch option, while Romero and Gonzalez were only rumored to have considered such a measure. In the end, none of the three men ever played a senior international for the US or *El Tricolor*.

As Lepore attests, as many as 100 dual nationals participate in the various US Federation youth teams at any one time. Only a handful will ever compete for the United States or Mexican senior national teams. And yet, the posturing doesn't stop—not from U-17 team managers, who strongly and publicly suggest these players are difference-makers. Not from the competitors themselves, who assert bedrock love of [insert-country-here] depending on which Federation or media outlet is asking. Everyone seems to read from the same scripts. Until such time that, having made a decision and come to regret it, they file their respective one-time switch applications with FIFA.

In the early 2020s, this circus swirled around Lompoc, California-born Julián Araujo, who left high school to join the FC Barcelona Residency Academy in Casa Grande, Arizona. The lad played on five different US youth national teams, made his cap-tying senior appearance in 2020, and played regularly at right back for the L.A. Galaxy in MLS. When Berhalter didn't name him to the 2021 Gold Cup roster, he bolted—filing his one-time switch and joining Tata Martino's *Selección*.[25] Thirteen appearances later, having spent a season with

La Liga club Las Palmas, and another with EPL club Bournemouth, Araujo has not nailed down the starting right-back position with *El Tri*.

How do we know this?

Because, at this writing, reports are bubbling up that Phoenix-born Richie Ledezma is considering a switch from Red, White & Blue to Red, White & Green. According to Herc Gomez in April 2025, speaking behind a big desk on ESPN FC, Pochettino considers the PSV man a central midfielder, not a right back—where Sergiño Dest is still to return from long-term injury, and Joe Scally, despite his *Bundesliga* pedigree (Borussia Mönchengladbach), has not impressed.

This speculative punditry from Gomez might have been undertaken in earnest. Or, Ledezma rumors may have been the flavor of the month, requisite content for an insatiable medium. Either way, let's agree that "love of country" has little to do with where Ledezma ends up. The young man wants to play in a World Cup.

Now sift into these capsule case studies the conventional wisdom that the US Soccer Federation isn't doing enough to seek out and foster Mexican American talent in this country.[26] This charge has been levied for years. Forget for a moment about how expensive club soccer might be here. Clearly there are a great deal of national-team opportunities that Mexican Americans today entertain and *may see fit to spurn*, opting instead for the rival national team.

Does it make sense to spend more Federation dollars and man-hours uncovering additional players of value, only to have a healthy portion of them ultimately declare for *El Tri*?

Here's another uncomfortable truth. The entire Mexican futbol establishment relies on the Mexican American population to show up en masse, over and over again, and pay for their international friendly and Leagues Cup tickets in US currency. The Federation and *Liga MX* cater to and court this population over the airwaves, 24/7, with the help of mega-channel TUDN and its advertisers. They've also been conducting youth tryouts across SoCal, Arizona, and Texas for decades, fostering the impression among dual nationals (and their parents) that legitimate pathways to *La Selección* are there for the taking.

Youth clubs in these regions are no less eager to leverage the heritage angle. San Diego Surf S.C. routinely holds "Mexican American ID Camps" where boys and girls ages 12–15 are encouraged to come try out—at $100 per session, according to the 2025 ad I saw in the *Soccer America* daily newsletter. The boy featured in the advertisement was wearing the latest *El Tri* away kit.

More specifically, back in September of 2015, the *Fresno Bee* reported on Leonardo Cuéllar's arrival in Riverdale, California. Still the manager of *El Tri feminil*, *El Mister* had shown up to sign autographs and promote The Pink Cup, a tournament-cum-scouting combine sponsored by the FMF ($150 per team). The story read, "Athletes who are eligible for the Mexican National team, Cuéllar said, may be called for a tryout to one of the country's four squads: U-15, U-17, U-20 and the senior team . . . Cuéllar and his staff also will host a coaches clinic on Saturday, Nov. 7. The cost is $100 per person." [27]

I wonder how much of this "scouting" doesn't boil down to formulaic community outreach and fan development. Nothing ties Mexican Americans to their ancestral culture like futbol, and parents anywhere will spend beyond their means to give their kids a chance at success, much less soccer stardom. "Premier" clubs routinely sell a very similar brand of hope and striving to parents across the United States.

•••

Competition for professional-grade, US-based futbol talent proceeds along two basic pathways: The federation track—where Mexico and the United States each recruit, then groom prospects for youth national teams—and the professional club track comprising academies operated by Major League Soccer and *Liga MX* franchises. There does exist a separate universe of so-called "elite" youth academies that operate privately and regionally, for a fee, ultimately feeding both tracks.

On account of so many dual nationals born and raised north of the border, Mexican clubs draw heavily but strategically from this US-based talent pool. *Liga MX* maintains a 9:7 rule, which limits the number of foreigners on senior rosters (to 9) and mandates that no more than 7 non-Mexicans take the field at any one time. Mexican Americans are considered foreigners—*unless* they are registered with the FMF before the age of 19.[28] This canny carve-out, and the pull of family heritage, makes the professional futbol life in *Liga MX* more attractive and accessible.

"It's easier for me to make a phone call to Mexico and get opportunities for one of my kids to be seen by professional clubs than it is here in the United States," says Jesse Cadena, president of Phoenix-based Tuzos Mesa Academy, speaking to former MLS broadcaster John Shrader, now with the College of Journalism and Mass Communications at the University of Nebraska-Lincoln.[29]

On the flip side, according to Jesse Magallon of Ozzy's Laguna F.C. in Santa Ana, California, plenty of new arrivals want their children to stay in the United States. "There are the parents," he told Shrader, "that think, 'Well, we immigrated here to find a better life, and you want to go back to Mexico. How does that make any sense?' Well, the profession that makes the most money in Mexico is soccer. So, when you send your kid back to Mexico, it's with that expectation."

In February 2025, DC United signed Sacramento-born Fidel Barajas on loan from Chivas of Guadalajara, with an option to extend through the entirety of the MLS season.[30] A dual national, Barajas had spent time in the San Jose Earthquakes academy system before turning pro with the USL Charleston Battery at sixteen. The USL Championship named him its 2023 Young Player of the Year—and off he went to Real Salt Lake for six months, then to Chivas for a $4 million transfer fee. A Mexican youth international who had also made appearances for the US U-17 national team, Barajas played five *Liga MX* matches for Chivas off the bench. He was one of eleven Yanks on Liga MX rosters to start the 2024 *Torneo Apertura*—but the young Californian reportedly struggled to adapt to life in Guadalajara. Now he's back in MLS.

The Barajas Saga is not uncommon. As Mexican scout Jorge Tello pointed out, these dual nationals aren't Mexican *per se*; many have never set foot in the country. Upon arrival, these teenagers are thrown into that cultural deep end—while simultaneously competing tooth and nail for minutes with an entirely new corps of competitors.

Observe here a list of those MLS players who went the opposite way, to *Liga MX*, during the January 2025 transfer window: Omar Campos, LAFC to Cruz Azul (transfer); Héctor Herrera, Houston Dynamo to Toluca (free transfer); Alan Pulido, Sporting KC to Guadalajara (transfer); Miguel Tapias, Minnesota United to Guadalajara (transfer). These Mexican nationals were joined by Argentinian Emiliano Rigoni, Austin FC to León (free transfer); two

Colombians, Cristian Dájome, D.C. United to Santos Laguna (free transfer) and Jesús Murillo, LAFC to FC Juárez (free transfer); and Uruguayan Matías Cóccaro, CF Montreal to Atlas FC (loan).

The organism is well served when North America's two major leagues enjoy this sort of talent exchange—allowed, as a practical matter, by Major League Soccer's atypical schedule.

When a veteran like Cóccaro requires a period of international adjustment, we are not so surprised. Born in 1997, the Uruguayan showed up in Montreal by way of Argentine club Huracán in 2024. Less than a year later, he was shipped off to the GDL.

Barajas was born in 2006. Just a kid. Upon joining Chivas, the young dual national discovered he was more comfortable playing "here" than "there".

In January 2018, Landon Donovan made the late-career decision to spend his final professional minutes in *Liga MX*, with León. Comfortable as a pro on either side of the border, he required no adjustment period. Competitively, his move proved to be a nothingburger, something of a stunt. Near the season's end, a month before World Cup 2018, Donovan did an English-language commercial for Wells Fargo where, green scarf extended over his head, he encouraged viewers to root for *El Tri* in Russia: "Anyone in need of a team to root for, join us in cheering for the Mexican national team. *Vamos Mexico*!"

The Stars & Stripes had failed to qualify for this *Mundial* by virtue of a crushing loss to Trinidad & Tobago the previous October. In the States, Donovan's bank spot went over like a lead balloon. On the platform formerly known as Twitter, he heard it from former national team colleagues Carlos Bocanegra ("Really?") and Taylor Twellman ("I'd rather cut off my own toe"), plus thousands more naysaying USMNT zealots. ESPN's Sebastian Salazar had this to say: "Please don't do it U.S. fans. The rivalry, with all its rancor & spite, is THE defining element of futbol in our region. Watering it down for beer/banks won't enrich the rivalry."

Turns out there's a shelf life for goodwill, too. When the 2018 season concluded, Donovan promptly retired.

"To say this was controversial would be an understatement," Reimers adds. "The correct adjective would be *opportunistic*. It's a discourse matter. Supporting the Mexican team does not mean supporting Mexicans. He said,

'I grew up with Mexicans. I get along with them.' That's alright. Perhaps I'm being shortsighted here, but I don't consider Landon Donovan to be a leading voice in public discourse on supporting Mexican migrants."

Herc Gomez was more direct: "That would not happen on the Mexican side," he told Grant Wahl in 2021. "You will not find Rafa Marquez or Osvaldo Sanchez doing that, no matter how much money they offered them." [31]

●●●

It may seem a bit "in the weeds" to spend so much space at the end of this book talking about obscure teenage fans of the *El Clásico Norteamericano*, alongside equally adolescent, unproven youth prospects who may never play a minute for any of the four senior national teams. Yet these are the Siblings who have not retired, the ones most likely to shape the rivalry going forward. Born in this century, tempered by years of Youth National Team Hopscotch, they are the derby's would-be custodians, and, in that respect, the 2026 World Cup is a sort of testing ground, perhaps even a tryout.

Here's what I mean: In June, the two men's programs will attempt to go as deep into the tournament as possible—to achieve competitive glory for themselves, for their respective nations, but also to earn the future commitments of youth internationals and soccer lovers still making up their minds. The women will follow suit at World Cup 2027.

Vegas-born Herculez Gomez, a product of both MLS and Liga MX, is spot on regarding these matters, in the broader sense. South of the border, there does not exist a critical mass of young players who cannot decide where to play their international futbol. To a one they aspire to *El Tri*.

North of the border is where these hyper-ticklish, existentially gnarly choices regarding loyalties, service, devotion, colors, and national-team participation are being made. So let me be clear: It's critical to the North American Derby that the US Men's National Team impresses this June and July. Not because Major League Soccer might go away if it doesn't, or NBC might not renew its EPL contract if the Yanks crash out at the group stage. But because an entire generation of young Mexican American players will be further encouraged to look south.

And that would put *Der Klassiker's* healthy, quite delectable equilibrium at risk.

By the same token, a shocking semifinal appearance from *El Tri feminil* in Brazil would supply the women's *clásico* a humungous boost. World Cup performance matters. As we learned in 2002.

I'll admit, dear readers, that I don't much like the idea that private ambitions might result in such flexible, fickle stances on nationality, identity, or rooting interests. It makes me a bit queasy to process these individual player profiles, especially when I'm obliged to contrast quite reasonable professional calculations with so much public badge-kissing and one FIFA switch after another.

But this is the futbol world we live in today.

The flavor of the month for spring 2025: Jonathan Germán "JoGo" Gómez Mendoza, who's still only 23 years old as you read this. Nonetheless, the left back from North Richland, Texas wasn't cap-tied at this writing, despite having competed for both senior national teams—in unofficial friendlies—and having logged more than eighty appearances in *La Liga* (Real Sociedad, Mirandés) and the Greek Super League (PAOK).

So, what is JoGo thinking right now? Here is the parlor game we play in 2026. What are his family members and coaches and ex-national team confidants whispering in his ear? How will World Cup 2026 performances—from the USMNT and *La Selección;* from the various positional competitors ahead of him in national team depth charts—affect his decision-making thereafter? Suppose he has already declared for one national team or the other. Time to use that one-off switch?

Herculez Gomez, no relation, told hosts of the *Futbol Asada* podcast in March 2025:

> I do speak to these guys before decisions get made. And sometimes they straight up ask, *What do you think?* These players—Efraín Álvarez, Brandon Vasquéz, Julián Araujo—they come out and say it: *Where should I play?* That's how difficult a decision this is.[32]
>
> I have love for two countries. I have love for two cultures, and I feel like I'm on an island. There's nothing like being a Chicano where you feel like sometimes you're not Mexican enough. And then, even where you live, you're not American enough. You're like, *What the fuck am I then?* So,

when it comes to making the choice, you've gotta go into it calculated and sometimes cold. And that's a shitty thing for fans to hear. It really is. I mean, I see this all the time. *We don't want you if you don't want to be here.* Right?

It's that rhetoric, you know, that blurs the lines of xenophobia. It sounds very much like a "get out of the country if you don't want to be here" type thing. When a Mexican fan hears that you're having doubts about where you want to go, well, *I don't fucking watch you then.* Right? I understand that sentiment from the fans.

I would add: How else *could* fans react if, as we've learned, rooting interests are so inextricably tied to identity?

Perhaps I'm old fashioned, but I'm a Red Sox junkie because I grew up in Greater Boston. I'm a Tottenham Hotspur man—not because I'm a masochist (!)—but owing to the fact that my U-14 club team toured England in 1978, and Peter Shreeves, then Spurs reserve manager, put us through the training paces one lucky day. Later in life, I did a semester of university abroad and was placed, quite randomly, in North London.

Readers of *Sibling Rivalry* should agree that I admire Mexican futbol a great deal. But I back the Stars & Stripes come hell or high water. And I inherited these rooting interests—that is, my own sporting identity—on account of the cold, hard facts of geography.

But you know what? Identity doesn't give a damn about geography. Not today.

●●●

Midway through World Cup 2002, I showed up at Loggia Glen Cove—the Italian-American social club serving this Long Island, N.Y. community—to catch an early morning broadcast of Mexico vs. Italy, the final group-stage match live from Oita, Japan. *El Tri's* last game before everything went sideways in the Round of 16.

My family was staying with friends. I could have watched the game at their home, in my pajamas: by the early twenty-first century, World Cup games *were* on network TV. But I wanted a more communal experience. Sure enough, at the crack of dawn, I found two dozen elderly Italian Americans in place at the club, sipping espresso, smoking unfiltered cigarettes, and generally luxuriating in their shared heritage. The perfect place to enculturate on the soccer front.

With ten minutes gone, three Mexican dudes in their twenties slipped in and quietly took their seats behind me, near the back. Our rooting interests were quickly made plain, but we also made friends. We managed our divergent matters of identity on the fly, with simple handshakes, smiles, and nods, the act of sipping coffee together, and quietly taking the piss out of our elderly, ornery hosts.

A draw would have seen both teams advance, and all was sweetness and light until *El Tri* went ahead in the 34th minute. The goal prompted smiles but otherwise respectful, muted celebrations from my new Mexican comrades. Everywhere else inside the club, audible grumbling commenced. Come the second half, agitated arm-waving ensued. Accusations were advanced. Ten minutes from full time, the Italians earned a free kick in a dangerous, central position. Vincenzo Montella and Alessandro Del Piero argued over who would take it. The old Italian men of Glen Cove argued along with them. Montella prevailed, only to hammer the ball directly into the wall—at which point the room erupted in shouts of recrimination. Several ashtrays and tiny coffee cups were hurled at the television set. When I looked around, our silent Mexican cheering section had vanished. Two minutes later, Del Piero equalized, peace was restored, and both countries went through to the knockout phase.

You know the rest.

I share this story to spotlight my belief that, if the *superclásico* is left to futbol fans—as en-masse custodians of this sporting trust, which borders on the sacred—we'll be fine. True aficionados will maintain the spirit of rivalry in more pure and sensible ways than federations, scouts, media, club owners, or players. Even though, oddly, these professional competitors are the elemental focus of our obsessions.

"These days," the late, great Grant Wahl said for himself, on camera, during his own documentary, "we're seeing so many examples of the cooperation between the neighbors, the United States and Mexico, especially through soccer. The only concern I have is that it dulls the rivalry. I hope that isn't the case, because I think this rivalry is one of the best things in sports."[33]

If we futbol freaks are in charge of vibe maintenance, Grant, I worry less. Even if the mansplaining and wing-eating are getting old.

Followers of the Beautiful Game, as we've detailed, can undergo long-term evolutions on reams of delicate subjects. Perhaps their loyalties ebb and flow in terms of intensity. Maybe, on occasion, large fan populations fall victim to mass delusion or, as Grant referenced, boredom. But because identity is so powerful, the faithful actually *can* be counted upon, more reliably and reasonably, to determine what's in their hearts, what family heritage truly means in the greater scheme, and how much geography should affect these matters of allegiance.

Early in this narrative, I reported that national team players saw the US-Mexico rivalry and competitive parity coming well before their partisans did—because pros are conditioned to not get carried away by delusion and emotion. Nevertheless, these are the same men and women who, today, routinely and intentionally sublimate their identities to better position themselves vocationally—to participate in World Cups, to make more money, or secure more prestigious club careers—with less and less fidelity to those badges on their chests. Yeah, the ones they're always smooching.

That sounds plainly calculating to me, and damned cold.

Until you hear someone like *El Chicharito* weigh in on the matter: "I love this thing between Mexico and the US, because unconsciously, indirectly, we've helped them tremendously to grow," Hernández told Wahl in 2021. "And they've done the same for us. And that's why rivalries are cool. That's what makes them what they are." [34]

I was similarly thunderstruck by something Ricardo Pepi's dad, Daniel, revealed during the *Good Rivals* doc. He appeared next to his brother, each of them kitted out in USMNT gear. Daniel, in particular showed himself to be very practical and eloquent on these matters of national team fandom, despite his place in the eye of a hurricane:

> He's my son, a center-forward for the United States, but we have to remember that it's soccer. It's a sport. The fact that he is representing the U.S. doesn't make him any less Mexican. He lives and breathes like all Mexicans. We feel that emotion. And now it's a different emotion because, like I said, we've always supported Mexico. But now it's our turn to support the U.S.[35]

Here's our answer! Put the moms and dads in charge. Or perhaps Papa Pepi himself.

Of course, I make fun. No one is in charge of the North American Derby, this messy unmanageable inheritance that is headed in directions we couldn't possibly predict. Not the fans, not the players, not their parents or their federations. These footballing relations between the United States and Mexico, such a fluid and prickly state of affairs, should not be viewed as a geopolitical hornet's nest, or even a complexity to be solved. Rather, as we've come to expect, our Sibling Rivalry requires a shared stewardship and responsibility.

Notes

Chapter 1

1. MediaTempo.com, "Raúl Cárdenas, Former Coach of El Tri, has Passed Away," March 26, 2016, https://www.mediotiempo.com/futbol/liga-mx/fallecio-raul-cardenas-ex-dt-del-tri (May 20, 2025).

2. J. Ventura, "Una triste realidad para nuestro futbol," *La Afición*, November 24, 1980, 1(N).

3. Doug Bandow, "750 Bases in 80 Countries Is Too Many for Any Nation: Time for the US to Bring Its Troops Home," October 4, 2021, https://www.cato.org/commentary/750-bases-80-countries-too-many-any-nation-time-us-bring-its-troops-home (May 20, 2025); David Vine, "Where in the World Is the U.S. Military," Politico.com, https://www.politico.com/magazine/story/2015/06/us-military-bases-around-the-world-119321 (May 20, 2025); Mohammed Hussein and Mohammed Haddad, "Infographic: US Military Presence around the World," https://www.aljazeera.com/news/2021/9/10/infographic-us-military-presence-around-the-world-interactive (May 20, 2025).

4. Grant Wahl, producer, "Good Rivals," documentary, Amazon Prime Video, 2022, https://www.amazon.com/Good-Rivals-Season-1/dp/B0B8PJSRK1.

5. Wahl, "Good Rivals."

6. E. Avelar, "Estados Unidos no asusta ni debe presionarnos," *La Afición*, April 19, 1997, 2–3(N).

7. Michael Whalen, documentary producer, "Gringos at the Gate," 2012, https://vimeo.com/230095655.

8. Greg Grandin, *The End of the Myth: From the Frontier to the Border Wall in the Mind of America* (New York City: Metropolitan Books), 88.

9. Wahl, "Good Rivals."

10. Wahl, "Good Rivals."

11. Susan Fiske, *Envy Up, Scorn Down: How Comparison Divides Us* (New York City: Russell Sage Foundation, 2011), 2.

12 Kevin Baxter, "Visa Approval Crisis Threatens to Cost 2026 World Cup and L.A. Olympics Millions," *Los Angeles Times*, https://www.latimes.com/sports/story/2025-01-29/sports-visas-delay-olympics-world-cup (May 20, 2025).

Chapter 2

1 Hunter Shobe and Geoff Gibson, "Place, Nation, and the Mexico–US Soccer Rivalry: Dual Citizens, Home Stadiums, and Hosting the Gold Cup," in *Perspectives on the U.S.-Mexico Soccer Rivalry; Passion and Politics in Red, White, Blue and Green*, ed. Jeffrey W. Kassing and Lindsey J. Meân (New York City: Palgrave Macmillan, 2016), 54.

2 "Border Crossing Data Annual Release: 2023–2024," Bureau of Transportation Statistics, U.S. Department of Transportation, February 18, 2025, https://www.bts.gov/newsroom/border-crossing-data-annual-release-2023–2024 (May 21, 2025).

3 Grant Wahl, producer, "Good Rivals," documentary, Amazon Prime Video, 2022, https://www.amazon.com/Good-Rivals-Season-1/dp/B0B8PJSRK1.

4 Andy Hall, "Which Players Have Been Naturalized to Play for Mexico?" Diario AS, September 6, 2023, https://en.as.com/soccer/which-players-have-been-naturalized-to-play-for-mexico-n/ (May 21, 2025).

5 Alexi Lalas, State of the Union Podcast, Fox Sports, March 26, 2024.

6 Futbol Asada podcast, Cabra Sports, March 9, 2025.

7 Andrei Markovits and Steven Hellerman, *Offside: Soccer and American Exceptionalism* (Princeton: Princeton University Press, 2001), 128–61.

8 Alex Silverman, "MLS Sets Attendance Record in 2024 with 5% Uptick over Last Season," *Sports Business Journal*, https://www.sportsbusinessjournal.com/Articles/2024/10/22/mls-attendance?origin=serp_auto (May 21, 2025).

9 Roxane Coche and Oscar Guerra, "Food-Ball: Tailgates that Enculturate Before US–Mexico Fútbol Matches," in *Perspectives*, 223–4.

10 Coche and Guerra, "Food-Ball," 224.

11 Erick Calderon, "*Existimos porque resistimos*: Navigating Identity through Soccer as a Chicanx in Southern California" (Masters Thesis, University of California San Diego, 2024), 3.

12 Wahl, "Good Rivals."

13 Wahl, "Good Rivals."

14 Wahl, "Good Rivals."

15 Wahl, "Good Rivals."

16 Wahl, "Good Rivals."

17 Wahl, "Good Rivals."

18 Wahl, "Good Rivals."

19 Wahl, "Good Rivals."

20 Martín del Palacio, "El mundo no se acabó, la vida tiene que seguir," *La Afición*, June 18, 2002, 8.

21 Xavier Velasco, "Remember the Alamo," *La Afición*, June 16, 2002, 8.

Chapter 3

1 Erik Francisco Lugo, "Mexico—International Results," 1927–2025, https://www.rsssf.org/tablesm/mex-intres.html.

2 Francisco, "Mexico—International Results."

3 Tariq Panja and Rory Smith, "For Turkish Germans, Heart Overrules Home at Euro 2024," *New York Times*, https://www.nytimes.com/2024/06/22/world/europe/european-championship-euros-germany-turkey.html (May 21, 2025).

4 Lindsey J. Meân and Raquel Herrera, "Gendered Nations: Media Representations of the Men's and Women's US–Mexico Soccer Rivalry," in *Perspectives on the US-Mexico Soccer Rivalry: Passion and Politics in Red, White, Blue, and Green*, ed. Jeffrey W. Kassing and Lindsey J. Meân (New York City: Palgrave Macmillan, 2016), 99.

5 John Grahmlich, "What the Data Says about Gun Deaths in the U.S.," https://www.pewresearch.org/short-reads/2025/03/05/what-the-data-says-about-gun-deaths-in-the-us (May 21, 2025).

6 Sylvia Clark, "Mariachi Music as a Symbol of Mexican Culture in the United States," *Sage Journals*, 2015, https://web.archive.org/web/20150626072816/http://ijm.sagepub.com/content/23/3/227.short (May 21, 2025).

7 Jon Arnold, "Mexico Is Missing the Flavor," *Get CONCACAFed*, March 2023.

8 Grant Wahl, "The 2013 Night Graham became San Zusi and Panama's Pitch Invader Plan Went Awry," 2017, https://www.foxsports.com/stories/soccer/the-2013-night-graham-became-san-zusi-and-panamas-pitch-invader-plan-went-awry (May 18, 2025).

9 Patrick Thomas Ridge, "Mexico 'on Top': Queering Masculinity in Contemporary Mexican Soccer Chronicles," in *Perspectives*, 123–34.

10. Andrew Cawthorne and Andrew Mills, "Argentina and Mexico Fans' Rivalry Rocks Qatar," https://www.reuters.com/lifestyle/sports/mexico-argentina-fans-bring-feisty-rivalry-qatar-2022-11-26 (May 18, 2025).

11. Ridge, "Mexico 'on Top,'" 123–34.

12. Pablo Maurer, "San Diego FC Coach, Sporting Director Denounce Homophobic Chants at Inaugural Home Match," https://www.nytimes.com/athletic/6169617/2025/03/02/san-diego-fc-denounces-homophobic-chants/ (May 21, 2025).

13. Herculez Gomez, Threads post, March 2, 2025, https://www.threads.com/@herculezg/post/DGydB83tktc.

14. Ridge, "Mexico 'on Top,'" 123–34.

15. Ridge, "Mexico 'on Top,'" 123–34.

16. "Messi: There Is No Comparison between Argentina and Mexico," Associated Press, April 18, 2025, https://apnews.com/article/messi-argentina-mexico-rivalidad-b7207430529409da4438ab6a6dc98 (May 21, 2025).

17. Juliana Menasce Horowitz, "How Mexicans See America," May 1, 2013, https://www.pewresearch.org/global/2013/05/01/how-mexicans-see-america/ (May 21, 2025).

18. Jacob Poushter, Jordan Lippert, and Sarah Austin, "How Mexicans and Americans View Each Other and their Governments' Handling of the Border," August 12, 2024, https://www.pewresearch.org/short-reads/2024/08/12/how-mexicans-and-americans-view-each-other-and-their-governments-handling-of-the-border/ (May 21, 2025).

Chapter 4

1. Leigh Thelmadatter, "The Miners Who Brought British Culture to Mexico," 2021, https://mexiconewsdaily.com/mexicolife/the-miners-who-brought-british-culture-to-mexico/ (May 21, 2025).

2. Nia Griffiths, "How Many Football Teams Are Called Arsenal?" February 14, 2021, https://dailycannon.com/2016/11/how-many-football-teams-called-arsenal (May 21, 2025).

3. Andy Markovits and Steven Hellerman, *Offside: Soccer and American Exceptionalism* (Princeton: Princeton University Press, 2001), 128–61.

4. Hillary Mantel, "Why I Became a Historical Novelist," https://www.theguardian.com/books/2017/jun/03/hilary-mantel-why-i-became-a-historical-novelist (May 21, 2025).

5. Matthew Brown, "The Pioneering British," *Sports in South America: A History* (Yale University Press, 2023), 48–68. https://doi.org/10.2307/j.ctv36xw849.6.

6. Brown, *Sports in South America*, 48–68.

7   Brown, *Sports in South America*, 48–68.

8   "The Giants Who Opened Doors," Fifa.com, https://web.archive.org/web/20160409081002/http://www.fifa.com/news/y=2008//news=the-giants-who-opened-doors-772969.html (May 21, 2025).

9   Brown, *Sports in South America*, 48–68.

10 Kieran McGovern, "1928 FIFA Congress," November 5, 2022, https://medium.com/the-story-of-football/the-1928-fifa-congress-566198e5114a (May 21, 2025).

11 Daniel Creel, "Overview: The American Soccer League, 1921–1934," April 27, 2022, https://www.ussoccerhistory.org/overview-the-american-soccer-league-1921-1934 (May 21, 2025).

12 "The American Footballer Who Got USA to Italy '34," Fifa.com, May 24, 2024, https://www.fifa.com/en/tournaments/mens/worldcup/articles/usa-mexico-qualifying-play-off.

13 Luigi Ruggieri, "Un experto italiano y Correa creen que nuestra oncena ganará a la americana," *La Afición*, May 23, 1934, 4.

14 Tony Cirino, *U.S. Soccer Vs. The World* (Leonia: Damon Press, 1983), 69–89.

15 Per Ed Farnsworth, "1934: USA vs. Mexico and the "Little Truck," *Society of American Soccer History*, October 8, 2015, https://www.ussoccerhistory.org/1934-usa-mexico-and-the-little-truck (May 21, 2025).

16 Ruggieri, "Por jugar brusco perdió México con Estados Unidos," *La Afición*, May 25, 1934, 2.

17 Roger Magazine, Sergio Varela Hernández, and Aldo Bravo, "A Resistance to Rivalry: The US–Mexico Soccer Matchup Through the Eyes of Mexican Sports Journalists, 1934–2013," in *Perspectives on the U.S.-Mexico Soccer Rivalry: Passion and Politics in Red, White, Blue, and Green,* edited by Jeffrey W. Kassing and Lindsey J. Meân (New York City: Palgrave Macmillan, 2016), 93–4.

18 Magazine et al., "A Resistance to Rivalry," 94–5.

19 Magazine et al., "A Resistance to Rivalry," 98.

20 "Una gran sorpresa se van a llevar los futbolistas de Estados Unidos," *La Afición*, September 11, 1937, 1, 4.

21 Magazine et al., "A Resistance to Rivalry," 78.

22 "Tbe History and Liga MX," https://golazomexicano.wordpress.com/the-history-and-liga-mx/ (May 22, 2025).

23 Barnaby Lane, "Who Founded Liga MX? The Origins of Mexico's Top Soccer League," March 7, 2025, https://www.si.com/soccer/who-founded-liga-mx-origins-mexico-top-soccer-league (May 22, 2025).

24 Hal Phillips, *Generation Zero: Founding Fathers, Hidden Histories & The Making of Soccer in America* (Nantucket: Dickinson-Moses Press, 2022), 46–78.

25 Cardozo Calderón, *La selección nacional: Con el orgullo a media can- cha. (1923–1970), Crónicas del futbol mexicano* (Mexico: Clío, 2000), 178.

26 James Hilsum, "World Cup 2026 Schedule: Mexico City's Azteca to Host Opening Match, Final Set for New Jersey's MetLife Stadium," April 2, 2024, https://www.tntsports.co.uk/football/world-cup/2026/world-cup-2026-schedule-mexico-city-s-azteca-to-host-opening-match-final-set-for-new-jersey-s-metlif_sto10009705/story.shtml (May 22, 2025).

27 Andrea Flores, "Remembering the Tlatelolco Massacre, and the Questions that Remain," https://www.latimes.com/delos/story/2023-10-02/tlatelolco-massacre-matanza-55th-anniversary (May 22, 2025).

28 Michael Lewis, "40 Years On: How New York Cosmos Lured Pelé to a Football Wasteland," https://www.theguardian.com/football/blog/2015/jun/02/40-years-on-how-new-york-cosmos-lured-pele-to-a-football-wasteland (May 22, 2025).

29 "Tbe History and Liga MX."

30 Calderón, *La selección nacional*, 162.

31 Calderón, *La selección nacional*, 162.

32 "MLS Continues Exploring Shift to International Soccer Calendar," April 10, 2025, https://www.mlssoccer.com/news/mls-continues-exploring-shift-to-international-soccer-calendar (May 22, 2025).

Chapter 5

1 Susan Fiske, *Envy Up, Scorn Down: How Comparison Divides Us* (New York City: Russell Sage Foundation, 2011), 2.

2 Fiske, *Envy Up, Scorn Down*, 2.

3 Greg Grandin, *The End of the Myth: From the Frontier to the Border Wall in the Mind of America* (New York City: Metropolitan Books), 152–3.

4 Carrie Gibson, *El Norte: The Epic and Forgotten Story of Hispanic North America* (New York City: Atlantic Monthly Press, 2019), 204–6.

5 Gibson, *El Norte*, 208.

6 Gibson, *El Norte*, 210.

7 Grant Wahl, "In Ever-Changing USA Landscape, USMNT vs. Mexico a Complex Rivalry," https://www.si.com/soccer/2015/10/05/usa-mexico-rivalry-mexican-americans-concacaf-cup (May 22, 2025).

8. "Biography of Florencio Xatruch," https://redhonduras.com/en/biography/biography-florencio-xatruch/ (May 22, 2025).

9. Grandin, *End of the Myth*, 156.

10. John Mason Hart, *Revolutionary Mexico: The Coming and Process of the Mexican Revolution* (Oakland: University of California Press, 1987), 235.

11. Gibson, *El Norte*, 307–9.

12. Gibson, *El Norte*, 309.

13. Gibson, *El Norte*, 358–9.

14. Gibson, *El Norte*, 352–56.

15. Andy Markovits, Rebecca Shippen, and Jillian Victor, "Envy and Scorn as Primary Markers of the Pervasive Antipathy in College Football's Rivalry Games: The University of Michigan as a Representative Microcosm," *Sport in Society* 20 (2017), https://www.tandfonline.com/doi/full/10.1080/17430437.2017.1326758.

16. Grant Wahl, producer, "Good Rivals," documentary, Amazon Prime Video, 2022, https://www.amazon.com/Good-Rivals-Season-1/dp/B0B8PJSRK1.

17. Grahame Jones, "This is Much Worse than Trash Talking," *LA Times*, https://www.latimes.com/archives/la-xpm-1998-feb-16-sp-19859-story.html (May 22, 2025).

18. Erick Calderon, "*Existimos porque resistimos*: Navigating Identity through Soccer as a Chicanx in Southern California" (Masters Thesis, University of California San Diego, 2024), 7–8, 22.

Chapter 6

1. Andy Markovits and Steven Hellerman, *Offside: Soccer and American Exceptionalism* (Princeton: Princeton University Press, 2001), 7–51.

2. Miguel Delaney, "Fifa Is Losing Its Dignity as Infantino Bows to Trump's 'Maga World Cup' Dream," *The Independent*, March 20, 2025, https://www.independent.co.uk/sport/football/donald-trump-fifa-world-cup-2026-gianni-infantino-b2718552.html (May 22, 2025).

3. Leander Schaerlaeckens, "Gianni Infantino and Donald Trump Have Taken the 2026 World Cup for Themselves," *The Guardian*, https://www.theguardian.com/football/2025/mar/12/gianni-infantino-donald-trump-2026-world-cup (May 22, 2025).

4. Hal Phillips, *Generation Zero: Founding Fathers, Hidden Histories & The Making of Soccer in America* (Nantucket: Dickinson-Moses Press, 2022), 66.

5. John Cassidy, "FIFA's Sepp Blatter Has Finally Met His Match," *New Yorker*, May 28, 2015, https://www.newyorker.com/news/john-cassidy/fifas-sepp-blatter-has-finally-met-his-match (May 22, 2025).

6 Hal Phillips, "England May Have Wrexham AFC (Est. 1864) . . . We Have the Baltimore Blast," https://genzero.halphillips.net/england-has-wrexham-afc-est-1864-we-have-the-baltimore-blast (May 22, 2025).

7 "Get to Know Your Cup," January 31, 2023, https://www.ussoccer.com/stories/2023/01/get-to-know-your-cup (May 22, 2025).

8 "American Soccer League I (1921–1933)," https://soccerhistoryusa.org/asha/asl.html (May 22, 2025).

9 "History, Foundation," https://www.clubnecaxa.mx/contenidos/historia (May 22, 2025).

10 Jon Arnold, "Welcome to Wrexcaxa?" May 1, 2024, https://getconcacafed.substack.com/p/welcome-to-wrexcaxa (May 22, 2025).

11 Colin Jose, *The American Soccer League: The Golden Years of American Soccer 1921–1931* (Lanham, MD: Scarecrow Press, 1998), 124.

12 Jose, *The ASL*, 126.

13 Phillips, *Generation Zero*, 194–210.

14 Kutis History, https://www.kutissoccer.com/about (May 22, 2025).

15 Jonah Fontela, "St Louis Kutis & a Father-to-Son Cup Triumph," https://www.ussoccer.com/stories/2023/04/st-louis-kutis-a-father-to-son-cup-triumph (May 22, 2025).

16 David Keyes, "Fútbol Americano: Immigration, Social Capital, and Youth Soccer in Southern California" (University of California San Diego dissertation, 2015).

17 Phillips, *Generation Zero*, 39–69.

18 Phillips, *Generation Zero*, 25.

19 U.S. Census, "Population Growth and Distribution," https://www2.census.gov/prod2/decennial/documents/42189394n1-26ch1.pdf (May 22, 2025).

20 Society of American Soccer History, "USMNT Results: 1970–1979," https://www.ussoccerhistory.org/usnt-results/usmnt-results/usmnt-results-1970–1979 (May 22, 2025).

21 SASH, "USMNT Results."

22 United Press International, "U.S. and Mexico Tie, 0-0, In World Cup Soccer," https://www.nytimes.com/1976/10/04/archives/us-and-mexico-tie-00-in-world-cup-soccer.html (May 22, 2025).

23 Michael Lewis, "40 Years Later: 1980 U.S. Olympic Team Recalls Moscow Boycott, Meeting President Jimmy Carter," https://www.ussoccer.com/stories/2020/07/40-years-later-1980-us-olympic-team-recalls-moscow-boycott-meeting-president-jimmy-carter (May 22, 2025).

24 Men in Blazers podcast, Wondery, 2016.

Chapter 7

1. Jerry Seinfield, "Seinfeld," 1995, https://www.youtube.com/watch?v=we-L7w1K5Zo.

2. Kevin Baxter, "For Soccer He Traded His OC Life for Mexico. Now He Shows Young Players They Can Stay," *LA Times*, https://www.latimes.com/sports/soccer/story/2019-08-31/michael-orozco-pathway-to-professional-soccer-orange-county-sc (May 22, 2025).

3. Tariq Panja and Rory Smith, "For Turkish Germans, Heart Overrules Home at Euro 2024," *NY Times*, https://www.nytimes.com/2024/06/22/world/europe/european-championship-euros-germany-turkey.html (May 22, 2025).

4. Isaac Stanley-Becker, "World Cup Players Says He Is 'a German When We Win' but 'an Immigrant When We Lose,' Quits National Team," *Washington Post*, https://www.washingtonpost.com/news/morning-mix/wp/2018/07/23/quitting-national-team-world-cup-player-says-he-is-a-german-when-we-win-but-an-immigrant-when-we-lose (May 22, 2025).

5. Andy Markovits and Steven Hellerman, *Offside: Soccer and American Exceptionalism* (Princeton: Princeton University Press, 2001), 7–51.

6. Desmond Morris, *The Soccer Tribe* (New York City: Rizzoli International Publications, 1981), 21–2.

7. Robert Cialdini and J. T. Lanzetta, "Basking in Reflected Glory: Three (Football) Field Studies," *Journal of Personality and Social Psychology* 34, no. 3 (1976): 366–75.

8. Juan Javier Pescador, "Global Fútbol, the Masked Fan, and Flat Screen Arenas: Mexican Soccer Communities in the USA and the Genesis of the Tricolor Brand in Global Landscapes, 1970–2012," in *Perspectives on the U.S.-Mexico Soccer Rivalry; Passion and Politics in Red, White, Blue and Green*, ed. Jeffrey W. Kassing and Lindsey J. Meân (New York City: Palgrave Macmillan, 2016), 262.

9. Pescador, "Global Fútbol, the Masked Fan, and Flat Screen Arenas," in *Perspectives*, 257–8.

10. Dave Wilt, "The Films of El Santo," https://terpconnect.umd.edu/~dwilt/santo.html (May 22, 2025).

11. Massimo Dutto and Giorgio Vegetti, *80 anni di Monza* [*80 years of Monza*], 1992.

12. "Recognizing and Naming America: Waldseemüller's 1507 Map," *Library of Congress*, https://www.loc.gov/collections/discovery-and-exploration/articles-and-essays/recognizing-and-naming-america (May 22, 2025).

13. Erick Calderon, "*Existimos porque resistimos*: Navigating Identity through Soccer as a Chicanx in Southern California" (Masters Thesis, University of California San Diego, 2024), 12–13.

14. Nick Miller, "World Cup Willie, Striker and Ciao: Best World Cup Mascots," June 7, 2014, https://www.espn.com/soccer/story/_/id/37395176/world-cup-willie-striker-ciao-best-world-cup-mascots (May 22, 2025).

15 Hal Phillips, *Generation Zero: Founding Fathers, Hidden Histories & The Making of Soccer in America* (Nantucket: Dickinson-Moses Press, 2022), 258.

16 Grant Wahl, producer, "Good Rivals," documentary, Amazon Prime Video, 2022, https://www.amazon.com/Good-Rivals-Season-1/dp/B0B8PJSRK1.

17 E. Porta, "Una derrota que nos llama a reflexionar: E.U. 2, México 0," *La Afición*, July 6, 1991, 7.

18 Jeff Carlisle and Tom Marshall, "U.S.-Mexico Oral History as Told by the Players Who Created It," *ESPN.com*, October 1, 2015, https://www.espn.com/soccer/story/_/id/37431298/us-mexico-oral-history-told-players-involved (May 22, 2025).

19 Randy Harvey, "Mexico Gets 3–0 Win, but Cup's Empty," *LA Times*, https://www.latimes.com/archives/la-xpm-1991-03-15-sp-116-story.html (May 22, 2025).

20 "USMNT Results 1990–1999, 2000–2009," *Society of American Soccer History*, https://www.ussoccerhistory.org/usnt-results.

21 M. Flores, "Campeón de oro," *La Afición*, July 26, 1993, 5.

22 Roger Magazine, Sergio Varela Hernández, and Aldo Bravo, "A Resistance to Rivalry: The US–Mexico Soccer Matchup Through the Eyes of Mexican Sports Journalists, 1934–2013," in *Perspectives on the U.S.-Mexico Soccer Rivalry; Passion and Politics in Red, White, Blue and Green*, ed. Jeffrey W. Kassing and Lindsey J. Meân (New York City: Palgrave Macmillan, 2016), 83.

23 E. Avelar, "Puede ser una revancha muy preciosa," *La Afición*, July 1, 1995, 5.

24 Wahl, "Good Rivals."

25 Flores, "Adiós MMB," *La Afición*, July 18, 1995, 6.

26 Joel Brinkley, "4-Year Fight in Florida 'Just Can't Stop Drugs,'" *NY Times*, https://www.nytimes.com/1986/09/04/us/4-year-fight-in-florida-just-can-t-stop-drugs.html (May 22, 2025).

27 Douglas Jehl, "Buchanan Takes Aim at Wilson," *LA Times*, https://www.latimes.com/archives/la-xpm-1992-03-09-mn-2550-story.html (May 22, 2025).

28 Greg Grandin, *The End of the Myth: From the Frontier to the Border Wall in the Mind of America* (New York City: Metropolitan Books, 2019), 232.

29 Paul Theroux, *On the Plain of the Snakes: A Mexican Road Trip* (New York City: Penguin, 2019).

30 Roxane Coche and Oscar Guerra, "Food-Ball: Tailgates That Enculturate Before US–Mexico Fútbol Matches," in *Perspectives*, 237.

31 Wahl, "Good Rivals."

Chapter 8

1. Jeffrey Kassing, "An (Im)penetrable Fortress: The Mythology of Estadio Azteca in the US–Mexico Men's National Team Soccer Rivalry," in *Perspectives on the US-Mexico Soccer Rivalry; Passion and Politics in Red, White, Blue and Green*, ed. Jeffrey W. Kassing and Lindsey J. Meân (New York City: Palgrave Macmillan, 2016), 175–76.

2. Jeff Carlisle and Tom Marshall, "U.S.-Mexico HHistory as Told by the Players Who Created It," *ESPN.com*, October 1, 2015, https://www.espn.com/soccer/story/_/id/37431298/us-mexico-oral-history-told-players-involved (May 22, 2025).

3. Hunter Shobe and Geoff Gibson, "Place, Nation, and the Mexico–US Soccer Rivalry: Dual Citizens, Home Stadiums, and Hosting the Gold Cup," in *Perspectives*, 58.

4. SASH, "USMNT Results," https://www.ussoccerhistory.org/usnt-results/usmnt-results (May 22, 2025).

5. "England National Football Team All-time Record," EUFootball.info, https://eu-football.info/_matches.php?id=60 (May 22, 2025).

6. Grant Wahl, "U.S. Victory at Estadio Azteca No Longer an Impossible Feat," SI.com, https://www.si.com/soccer/2013/03/26/us-mexico-estadio-azteca-world-cup-qualifier (May 22, 2025).

7. Grant Wahl, producer, "Good Rivals," documentary, Amazon Prime Video, 2022, https://www.amazon.com/Good-Rivals-Season-1/dp/B0B8PJSRK1.

8. Jeff Carlisle and Tom Marshall, "U.S.-Mexico Oral History as Told by the Players Who Created It," *ESPN.com*, October 1, 2015, https://www.espn.com/soccer/story/_/id/37431298/us-mexico-oral-history-told-players-involved (May 22, 2025).

9. Wahl, "Good Rivals."

10. Stephen P. Andon, "Dos-A-Cero: US Soccer Mythology and Columbus, Ohio," in *Perspectives*, 148–54.

11. Mark Ziegler, "USA Savors Sweet Clincher—USA 2 Mexico 0," *San Diego Union-Tribune*, September 4, 2005, C-1.

12. S. Reiset, "Columbus Crew, la 'casa del terror' para el Tri," *Mediotiempo*, S.A. (February 9, 2009), http://www.mediotiempo.com/futbol/seleccion-mexicana/noticias/2009/02/07/columbus-crew-la-casa-del-terror-del-tri (May 22, 2025).

13. Aaron Gordon, "Mexico Wins Mexican-American Stadium War," April 9, 2013, https://www.buzzfeed.com/aarongordon/what-the-georgia-dome-could-learn-from-the-best-stadium-in-n (May 22, 2025)

14. Carlisle and Marshall, "Oral History."

15. Carlisle and Marshall, "Oral History."

16. Grant Wahl, "How Far They've Come, State of USA vs. Mexico," https://www.si.com/soccer/2015/10/06/usa-mexico-rivalry-2005-si-vault-usmnt (May 22, 2025).

17 Carlisle and Marshall, "Oral History."

18 Arnoldo Rivera, "Aztecazo! Mexico 1—Costa Rica 2," *La Nación*, June 17, 2001, https://web.archive.org/web/20170322202903/http://www.nacion.com/ln_ee/2001/junio/17/deportes1.html (May 22, 2025).

19 Roberto Velázquez Bolio, "Gringos sin chiste," *La Afición*, August 10, 2011, 2.

20 Wahl, "Good Rivals."

21 Barak Fever, "La Contra columna: Wake Up America!" *La Afición*, August 11, 2011, 3.

22 Carlisle and Marshall, "Oral History."

23 Grant Wahl, "How Far They've Come: State of USA vs. Mexico Rivalry, 10 Years Ago," SI.com, March 28, 2005, https://www.si.com/soccer/2015/10/06/usa-mexico-rivalry-2005-si-vault-usmnt (May 22, 2025).

Chapter 9

1 "Nine FIFA Officials and Five Corporate Executives Indicted for Racketeering Conspiracy and Corruption," Justice.gov, May 27, 2015, https://www.justice.gov/usao-edny/pr/nine-fifa-officials-and-five-corporate-executives-indicted-racketeering-conspiracy-and (May 23, 2025).

2 Hal Phillips, *Generation Zero: Founding Fathers, Hidden Histories & The Making of Soccer in America* (Nantucket: Dickinson-Moses Press, 2022), 279–96.

3 "USMNT Results: 1980–1989," https://www.ussoccerhistory.org/usnt-results/usmnt-results/usmnt-results-1980-1989/ (May 23, 2025).

4 "CONCACAF Nations Cup 1985," https://www.rsssf.org/tablesc/conca85.html (May 23, 2025).

5 Seth Vertelney, "Greenland Set for Talks to Join Concacaf, Still Probably Not Joining United States," https://prosoccerwire.usatoday.com/story/sports/2025/01/23/greenland-set-for-talks-over-joining-concacaf/77911305007/ (May 23, 2025).

6 Michael Carlson, "Chuck Blazer Obituary," https://www.theguardian.com/football/2017/jul/13/chuck-blazer-obituary (May 23, 2025).

7 "Former FIFA Vice President, Austin Jack Warner, Continues His Fight Against Extradition to US," June 29, 2023, https://www.caribbeantoday.com/sections/news-2/former-fifa-vice-president-austin-jack-warner-continues-his-fight-against-extradition-to-us (May 23, 2025).

8 Stefan Szymanski and Simon Kuper, *Soccernomics* (Bold Type Books, 2009).

9. Grant Wahl, "Fútbol with Grant Wahl," August 19, 2022, https://grantwahl.substack.com/p/friday-newsletter-the-us-has-gone (May 23, 2025).

10. "NHL Thriving as It Hits Midway Point of Current Media Rights Deal," November 23, 2024, https://www.spglobal.com/market-intelligence/en/news-insights/research/nhl-thriving-as-it-hits-midway-point-of-current-media-rights-deal (May 23, 2025).

11. Frank Foer, "A Spectacle of Scoundrels," November 17, 2022, https://www.theatlantic.com/international/archive/2022/11/qatar-hosting-fifa-world-cup-soccer/672171/ (May 23, 2025).

12. Lizzy Becherano, "Leagues Cup Scraps Mid-summer Pause to MLS, Liga MX Seasons," December 15, 2024, https://www.espn.com/soccer/story/_/id/42994380/leagues-cup-scraps-pause-mls-liga-mx-seasons (May 23, 2025).

13. Erick Calderon, "*Existimos porque resistimos*: Navigating Identity through Soccer as a Chicanx in Southern California" (Masters Thesis, University of California San Diego, 2024), 23.

14. Paul Tenorio and Adam Crafton, "Liga MX Controversy Explained: How a $1.25bn Deal Collapsed—and What Happens Now," https://www.nytimes.com/athletic/6000252/2024/12/17/ligamx-rodriguez-mls/ (May 23, 2025).

15. Felipe Cardenas, "'Univision Is Becoming the Home of Soccer': How the Spanish-Language Network Is Growing Its Viewer Base in the U.S.," https://www.nytimes.com/athletic/2840626/2021/09/21/univision-is-becoming-the-home-of-soccer-how-the-spanish-language-network-is-growing-its-viewer-base-in-the-u-s/ (May 23, 2025).

16. Jeff Carlisle, "USSF, Relevent Settlement Clears Path for Foreign League Games," April 10, 2025, https://www.espn.com/soccer/story/_/id/44610691/ussf-relevent-settlement-clears-path-foreign-league-games (May 23, 2025).

17. Jon Arnold, "América in Atlanta? Chivas in Cali? Liga MX Regular Season Games Could Come to the U.S.," April 24, 2024, https://getconcacafed.substack.com/p/america-in-atlanta-chivas-in-cali (May 23, 2025).

18. Carlos Rodríguez, "Mexican Baseball League's Recent Growth in Attendance Now Rivals Soccer Clubs," April 16, 2025, https://apnews.com/article/robinson-cano-diablos-rojos-mexican-baseball-league-52db4cef1eaf7360ecdf642ee51938fb (May 23, 2025).

19. Alex Donaldson, "Liga MX, FMF Brought before CAS over Promotion-Relegation Decision," May 21, 2025, https://www.sportcal.com/news/liga-mx-fmf-brought-before-cas-over-promotion-relegation-decision (May 23, 2025).

20. "MLS Reacquires Soccer United Marketing Stake," June 21, 2017, https://media.sportbusiness.com/news/mls-reacquires-soccer-united-marketing-stake/ (May 23, 2025).

21. Tom Marshall, "What Chicharito's Galaxy Move Means to the Future of MLS and Mexican Soccer," January 24, 2024, https://www.espn.com/soccer/story/_/id/37580907/what-chicharito-galaxy-move-means-future-mls-mexican-soccer (May 23, 2025).

22. Tom Marshall, "Rafa Marquez Regrets Red Bulls Move, Hoping for World Cup Finale," April 17, 2018, https://www.espn.com/soccer/story/_/id/37551405/rafa-marquez-regrets-red-bulls-move-hoping-world-cup-finale (May 23, 2025).

23. Grant Wahl, producer, "Good Rivals," documentary, Amazon Prime Video, 2022, https://www.amazon.com/Good-Rivals-Season-1/dp/B0B8PJSRK1.

24. Wahl, "Good Rivals."

25. "Jorge Tello: 'There's a Real Battle with the United States to Win Players,'" https://www.marca.com/mx/futbol/seleccion-mx/2023/04/23/644542ea268e3ee1558b45e9.html (May 23, 2025).

Chapter 10

1. Erick Calderon, "*Existimos porque resistimos*: Navigating Identity through Soccer as a Chicanx in Southern California" (Masters Thesis, University of California San Diego, 2024), 44–8.

2. Asli Pelit and Meg Linehan, "NWSL Requested Permission to Start a New Second Division. What Does it Mean for Women's Soccer?" https://www.nytimes.com/athletic/6311310/2025/04/26/nwsl-second-division-womens-soccer-explained (May 23, 2025).

3. "Celtics City," HBO documentary series, 2025, Episode 1.

4. Calderon, "Navigating Identity," 46.

5. Calderon, "Navigating Identity," 46.

6. Calderon, "Navigating Identity," 50.

7. Andy Markovits, *Women in American Soccer and European Football: Different Paths to Shared Glory* (Nantucket: Dickinson Moses, 2023), 138–9.

8. Keith Nissen, "Viewership of Women's Sports in the US is on the Rise," December 19, 2024, https://www.spglobal.com/market-intelligence/en/news-insights/research/viewership-of-womens-sports-in-the-us-is-on-the-rise (May 23, 2025).

9. Markovits, "Different Paths," 75.

10. Markovits, "Different Paths," 83–4.

11. Markovits, "Different Paths," 80.

12. Cesar Hernandez, "How NWSL, Its Players Plan to Thrive Without College Drafts," March 7, 2025, https://www.espn.com/soccer/story/_/id/44045194/how-nwsl-players-plan-thrive-college-drafts (May 23, 2025).

13 Hernandez, "Can Liga MX Femenil Grow to Rival the Power of NWSL?" September 13, 2024, https://www.espn.com/soccer/story/_/id/41105869/can-liga-mx-femenil-grow-rival-power-nwsl (May 23, 2025).

14 Calderon, "Navigating Identity," 47.

15 "Copa '71," documentary film, New Black Films, 2024, https://www.youtube.com/watch?v=c4jJvY4uM3M.

16 Markovits, "Different Paths," 85–6.

17 Jeff Carlisle, "Once-Reluctant Volunteer Monica Gonzalez Helps Kids on Global Scale," October 14, 2015, https://www.espn.com/espnw/w-in-action/2015-summit/story/_/id/13880118/monica-gonzalez-turns-gonzo-soccer-worldwide-success (May 23, 2025).

18 Dan Lauletta, "The Lowdown: Has NWSL Helped Canada, Mexico?" http://equalizersoccer.com/2015/06/30/the-lowdown-has-nwsl-helped-canada-mexico/ (May 23, 2025).

19 Tom Marshall, "Monica Gonzalez Urges Mexican Federation to Seize Opportunity to Promote Women's Game," April 15, 2016, http://www.espn.com/espnw/sports/article/15204801/monica-gonzalez-urges-mexican-federation-seize-opportunity-promote-women-game (May 23, 2025).

20 Nina Friend, "USWNT's Ashley Sanchez and Sofia Huerta on their Dual Identities as Mexican Americans," July 2, 2023, https://www.nbcsports.com/on-her-turf/news/uswnt-womens-world-cup-ashley-sanchez-sofia-huerta-mexican-americans (May 23, 2025).

21 Hernandez, "Vazquez Chose U.S. over Mexico but Soon May Call Europe Home," June 23, 2023, https://www.espn.com/soccer/story/_/id/37899796/brandon-vazquez-usmnt-mexico-gold-cup-starter (May 23, 2025).

22 "FIFA Publishes Explainer on Eligibility to Play for Representative Teams," January 28, 2021, https://inside.fifa.com/legal/media-releases/fifa-publishes-explainer-on-eligibility-to-play-for-representative-teams (May 23, 2025).

23 Grant Wahl, producer, "Good Rivals," documentary, Amazon Prime Video, 2022, https://www.amazon.com/Good-Rivals-Season-1/dp/B0B8PJSRK1.

24 Jaime Uribarri, "USMNT Beat Mexico for Club América Winger Alejandro Zendejas," March 14, 2023, https://www.mlssoccer.com/news/usmnt-beat-mexico-for-club-america-winger-alejandro-zendejas (May 23, 2025).

25 Tom Bogert, "Official: Julian Araujo Declares for Mexico, Files Switch from USMNT," October 5, 2021, https://www.mlssoccer.com/news/official-julian-araujo-declares-for-mexico-files-switch-from-usmnt (May 23, 2025).

26 Ramon Antonio Vargas, "US Latinos Are Soccer-Mad. Why Isn't That Reflected in the World Cup Squad?" November 15, 2022, https://www.theguardian.com/football/2022/nov/15/usmnt-qatar-world-cup-2022-soccer-latino-players (May 23, 2025).

27 Angel Moreno, "Mexico Women's Soccer Coach Leonardo Cuellar Looks to Recruit Valley," September 28, 2015, https://www.fresnobee.com/sports/soccer/article36887691.html (May 23, 2025).

28 "How Many Foreign Players Is Each Liga MX Team Allowed to Have?" https://www.marca.com/en/football/liga-mx/2023/06/29/649d6591e2704edb8c8b45a2.html (May 23, 2025).

29 John Shrader, "The Border War for Young Mexican American Soccer Players: How Family and National Identity Play Out on the Field," in *Perspectives on the U.S.-Mexico Soccer Rivalry; Passion and Politics in Red, White, Blue and Green*, ed. Jeffrey W. Kassing and Lindsey J. Meân (New York City: Palgrave Macmillan, 2016), 17–20.

30 "D.C. United Makes Bold Bet on Fidel Barajas," February 27, 2025, https://onefootball.com/en/news/dc-united-makes-bold-bet-on-fidel-barajas-40766251 (May 23, 2025).

31 Wahl, "Good Rivals," 2022.

32 Futbol Asada podcast, Cabra Sports, March 9, 2025.

33 Wahl, "Good Rivals," 2022.

34 Wahl, "Good Rivals," 2022.

35 Wahl, "Good Rivals," 2022.

Bibliography

Arace, Michael. "How the Columbus Crew Climbed from Near Extinction to the Top of American Soccer." *Columbus Dispatch*, July 14, 2024.

Arnold, Jon. "América in Atlanta? Chivas in Cali? Liga MX Regular Season Games could Come to the U.S.," April 24, 2024. https://getconcacafed.substack.com/p/america-in-atlanta-chivas-in-cali.

Arnold, Jon. "Mexico Is Missing the Flavor." *Get CONCACAFed*, March 2023.

Arnold, Jon. "Welcome to Wrexcaxa?" May 1, 2024. https://getconcacafed.substack.com/p/welcome-to-wrexcaxa.

Associated Press. "Messi: There Is No Comparison between Argentina and Mexico," April 18, 2025. https://apnews.com/article/messi-argentina-mexico-rivalidad-b7207430529409da4438ab6a6dc98.

Baxter, Kevin. "For Soccer He Traded His OC Life for Mexico. Now He Shows Young Players They Can Stay." *LA Times*, August 31, 2019. https://www.latimes.com/sports/soccer/story/2019-08-31/michael-orozco-pathway-to-professional-soccer-orange-county-sc.

Baxter, Kevin. "Visa Approval Crisis Threatens to Cost 2026 World Cup and L.A. Olympics Millions." *LA Times*, January 29, 2025. https://www.latimes.com/sports/story/2025-01-29/sports-visas-delay-olympics-world-cup.

BBC.com. "A Piece of Britain Lost in Mexico," May 20, 2018. https://www.bbc.com/travel/article/20180520-a-piece-of-britain-lost-in-mexico.

Becherano, Lizzy. "How do Dual Nationals Decide between the USMNT and Mexico," July 7, 2024. https://www.espn.com/soccer/story/_/id/40401190/how-dual-nationals-decide-usmnt-usa-mexico-pepi-ochoa-barajas.

Becherano, Lizzy. "Leagues Cup Scraps Mid-summer Pause to MLS, Liga MX Seasons." *ESPN*, December 1, 2024. https://www.espn.com/soccer/story/_/id/42994380/leagues-cup-scraps-pause-mls-liga-mx-seasons.

Blakemore, Erin. "The Largest Mass Deportation in American History," March 23, 2018. https://www.history.com/news/operation-wetback-eisonhower-1954-deportation.

Bogert, Tom. "Official: Julian Araujo Declares for Mexico, Files Switch from USMNT." MLSsoccer.com, October 5 2021. https://www.mlssoccer.com/news/official-julian-araujo-declares-for-mexico-files-switch-from-usmnt.

Brinkley, Joel. "4-Year Fight in Florida 'Just Can't Stop Drugs'." *NY Times*, September 4, 1986. https://www.nytimes.com/1986/09/04/us/4-year-fight-in-florida-just-can-t-stop-drugs.html.

Brown, Matthew. "The Pioneering British." In *Sports in South America: A History*, 48–68. Yale University Press, 2023.

Calderón, Cardozo. *La selección nacional: Con el orgullo a media cancha. (1923–1970), Crónicas del fútbol mexicano*, 178. Mexico: Clío, 2000.

Calderon, Erick. "*Existimos porque resistimos:* Navigating Identity through Soccer as a Chicanx in Southern California." Master's Thesis, University of California San Diego, 2024.

Cardenas, Felipe. "Univision is Becoming the Home of Soccer: How the Spanish-Language Network Is Growing its Viewer Base in the U.S." *The Athletic*, September 21, 2021. https://www.nytimes.com/athletic/2840626/2021/09/21/univision-is-becoming-the-home-of-soccer-how-the-spanish-language-network-is-growing-its-viewer-base-in-the-u-s/.

Caribbean Today. "Former FIFA Vice President, Austin Jack Warner, Continues His Fight Against Extradition to US," June 29, 2023. https://www.caribbeantoday.com/sections/news-2/former-fifa-vice-president-austin-jack-warner-continues-his-fight-against-extradition-to-us.

Carlisle, Jeff. "Once-reluctant Volunteer Monica Gonzalez Helps Kids on Global Scale." *ESPN.com*, October 14, 2015. https://www.espn.com/espnw/w-in-action/2015-summit/story/_/id/13880118/monica-gonzalez-turns-gonzo-soccer-worldwide-success.

Carlisle, Jeff. "U.S.-Mexico Oral History as Told by the Players Who Created It." with Tom Marshall for *ESPN.com*, October 15, 2015. https://www.espn.com/soccer/story/_/id/37431298/us-mexico-oral-history-told-players-involved.

Carlisle, Jeff. "USSF, Relevent Settlement Clears Path for Foreign League Games." *ESPN.com*, April 2025. https://www.espn.com/soccer/story/_/id/44610691/ussf-relevent-settlement-clears-path-foreign-league-games.

Carlisle, Jeff. "U.S. Soccer, MLS-owned Soccer United Marketing Parting Ways after Nearly 20 Years," May 23, 2021. https://www.espn.com/soccer/story/_/id/37617549/us-soccer-mls-owned-soccer-united-marketing-parting-ways-nearly-20-years.

Carlson, Michael. "Chuck Blazer Obituary." *Guardian*, July 13, 2017. https://www.theguardian.com/football/2017/jul/13/chuck-blazer-obituary.

Cassidy, John. "FIFA's Sepp Blatter Has Finally Met His Match." *New Yorker*, May 28, 2015. https://www.newyorker.com/news/john-cassidy/fifas-sepp-blatter-has-finally-met-his-match.

Cawthorne, Andrew, and Andrew Mills. "Argentina and Mexico Fans' Rivalry Rocks Qatar." *Reuters*, November 11, 2026. https://www.reuters.com/lifestyle/sports/mexico-argentina-fans-bring-feisty-rivalry-qatar-2022-11-26.

"Celtics City." HBO Sports Documentaries, Ringer Films/Words+Pictures 2025, Episode 1.

Cialdini, Robert, and J. T. Lanzetta. "Basking in Reflected Glory: Three (football) Field Studies." *Journal of Personality and Social Psychology* 34, no. 3 (1976): 366–75.

Cirino, Tony. *U.S. Soccer Vs. The World*, 69–89. Leonia: Damon Press, 1983.

Clark, Sylvia. "Mariachi Music as a Symbol of Mexican Culture in the United States." *Sage Journals*, 2015. https://web.archive.org/web/20150626072816/http://ijm.sagepub.com/content/23/3/227.short.

ClubNecaxa.com. "History, Foundation." https://www.clubnecaxa.mx/contenidos/historia.

"Copa '71." Documentary film. New Black Films, 2024. https://www.youtube.com/watch?v=c4jJvY4uM3M.

Crafton, Adam. "Donald Trump, Jared Kushner and the Race to Host the 2026 World Cup," November 4, 2024. https://www.nytimes.com/athletic/5891523/2024/11/04/donald-trump-united-states-world-cup-2026/.

Creel, Daniel. "Overview: The American Soccer League, 1921–1934," April 27, 2022. https://www.ussoccerhistory.org/overview-the-american-soccer-league-1921-1934.

David, Rick. Men in Blazers podcast interview, Wondery, 2016.

Dávila, Marco. "World Cup 2010: Mexico's Great Love-Hate Relationship with Argentina." *Guardian*, June 26, 2010. https://www.theguardian.com/football/blog/2010/jun/26/world-cup-2010-mexico-argentina.

Davis, Noah. "Not Just Another Game." *SB Nation*, March 26, 2013. https://www.sbnation.com/longform/2013/3/26/4136238/usmnt-vs-mexico-soccer-rivalry-history-world-cup-qualifying.

Delaney, Miguel. "Fifa Is Losing Its Dignity as Infantino Bows to Trump's 'Maga World Cup' Dream." *The Independent*, March 20, 2025. https://www.independent.co.uk/sport/football/donald-trump-fifa-world-cup-2026-gianni-infantino-b2718552.html.

Donaldson, Alex. "Liga MX, FMF Brought before CAS over Promotion-Relegation Decision." *SportCal*, May 21, 2025. https://www.sportcal.com/news/liga-mx-fmf-brought-before-cas-over-promotion-relegation-decision.

Dutto, Massimo, and Giorgio Vegetti. *80 anni di Monza* [*80 years of Monza*], 1992.

EUFootball.info. "England National Football Team All-Time Record." https://eu-football.info/_matches.php?id=60.

Farnsworth, Ed. "1934: USA vs. Mexico and the 'Little Truck.'" *Society of American Soccer History*, October 8, 2015. https://www.ussoccerhistory.org/1934-usa-mexico-and-the-little-truck/.

Fifa.com. "The American Footballer Who Got USA to Italy '34," May 24, 2024. https://www.fifa.com/en/tournaments/mens/worldcup/articles/usa-mexico-qualifying-play-off.

Fifa.com. "FIFA Publishes Explainer on Eligibility to Play for Representative Teams," January 28, 2021. https://inside.fifa.com/legal/media-releases/fifa-publishes-explainer-on-eligibility-to-play-for-representative-teams.

Fifa.com. "The Giants Who Opened Doors," May 21, 2008. https://shorturl.at/wGvZM.

Fifa.com. *Orozco*: "Everybody Talks About My Goal at Azteca," October 21, 2016. https://inside.fifa.com/tournaments/mens/worldcup/2018russia/news/orozco-everybody-talks-about-my-goal-in-the-azteca-2845246.

Fiske, Susan. *Envy Up, Scorn Down: How Comparison Divides Us*, 2, 4. New York City: Russell Sage Foundation, 2011.

Flores, Andrea. "Remembering the Tlatelolco Massacre, and the Questions That Remain," October 2, 2023. https://www.latimes.com/delos/story/2023-10-02/tlatelolco-massacre-matanza-55th-anniversary.

Foer, Frank. "A Spectacle of Scoundrels." *The Atlantic*, November 17, 2022. https://www.theatlantic.com/international/archive/2022/11/qatar-hosting-fifa-world-cup-soccer/672171/.

Fontela, Jonah. "St. Louis Kutis & a Father-to-Son Cup Triumph." U.S. Soccer Federation. https://www.ussoccer.com/stories/2023/04/st-louis-kutis-a-father-to-son-cup-triumph.
Friend, Nina. "USWNT's Ashley Sanchez and Sofia Huerta on Their Dual Identities as Mexican Americans." NBCSports.com, July 2, 2023. https://www.nbcsports.com/on-her-turf/news/uswnt-womens-world-cup-ashley-sanchez-sofia-huerta-mexican-americans.
Gibson, Carrie. *El Norte: The Epic and Forgotten Story of Hispanic North America*, 204–6, 208, 210, 307–9, 358–9, 362–6. New York City: Atlantic Monthly Press, 2019.
Gomez, Herculez. Interview by *Futbol Asada* podcast, Cabra Sports, March 9, 2025.
Gordon, Aaron. "Mexico Wins Mexican-American Stadium War." *Buzzfeed*, 2013. https://www.buzzfeed.com/aarongordon/what-the-georgia-dome-could-learn-from-the-best-stadium-in-n.
Grahmlich, John. "What the Data Says about Gun Deaths in the U.S." *Pew Research Center*. https://www.pewresearch.org/short-reads/2025/03/05/what-the-data-says-about-gun-deaths-in-the-us.
Grandin, Greg. *The End of the Myth: From the Frontier to the Border Wall in the Mind of America*, 88, 152–3, 156. New York City: Metropolitan Books, 2019.
Griffiths, Nia. "How Many Football Teams are Called Arsenal?" *Daily Cannon*, February 14, 2021. https://dailycannon.com/2016/11/how-many-football-teams-called-arsenal.
Hall, Andy. "Which Players Have Been Naturalized to Play for Mexico?" *Diario AS*, September 6, 2023. https://en.as.com/soccer/which-players-have-been-naturalized-to-play-for-mexico-n/.
Hart, John Mason. *Revolutionary Mexico: The Coming and Process of the Mexican Revolution*, 235. Oakland: University of California Press, 1987.
Harvey, Randy. "Mexico Gets 3-0 Win, but Cup's Empty." *LA Times*, March 15, 1991. https://www.latimes.com/archives/la-xpm-1991-03-15-sp-116-story.html.
Hernandez, Cesar. "Can Liga MX Femenil Grow to Rival the Power of NWSL?" *ESPN.com*, September 13, 2024. https://www.espn.com/soccer/story/_/id/41105869/can-liga-mx-femenil-grow-rival-power-nwsl.
Hernandez, Cesar. "How NWSL, Its Players Plan to Thrive without College Drafts." *ESPN.com*, March 7, 2025. https://www.espn.com/soccer/story/_/id/44045194/how-nwsl-players-plan-thrive-college-drafts.
Hernandez, Cesar. "Vazquez Chose U.S. over Mexico but Soon May Call Europe Home." *ESPN.com*, June 23, 2023. https://www.espn.com/soccer/story/_/id/37899796/brandon-vazquez-usmnt-mexico-gold-cup-starter (May 23, 2025).
Hilsum, James. "World Cup 2026 Schedule: Mexico City's Azteca to Host Opening Match, Final Set for New Jersey's MetLife Stadium," April 2, 2024. https://www.tntsports.co.uk/football/world-cup/2026/world-cup-2026-schedule-mexico-city-s-azteca-to-host-opening-match-final-set-for-new-jersey-s-metlif_sto10009705/story.shtml.
Horowitz, Juliana Menasce. "How Mexicans See America." *Pew Research Center*, May 1, 2013. https://www.pewresearch.org/global/2013/05/01/how-mexicans-see-america/.
Jehl, Douglas. "Buchanan Takes Aim at Wilson." *LA Times*, March 9, 1992. https://www.latimes.com/archives/la-xpm-1992-03-09-mn-2550-story.html.
Justice.gov. "Nine FIFA Officials and Five Corporate Executives Indicted for Racketeering Conspiracy and Corruption," May 27, 2015. https://www.justice.gov/usao-edny/pr/

nine-fifa-officials-and-five-corporate-executives-indicted-racketeering-conspiracy-and.

Kassing, Jeffrey W., and Lindsey J. Mêan, eds. *Perspectives on the U.S.-Mexico Soccer Rivalry Passion and Politics in Red, White, Blue, and Green*. New York City: Palgrave Macmillan, 2016.

— Andon, S. "Dos-A-Cero: US Soccer Mythology and Columbus, Ohio," 147–70.
— Coche, R., and O. Guerra. "Food-Ball: Tailgates that Enculturate Before US–Mexico Fútbol Matches," 223–4, 265–80.
— Grainey, T. "Women's Soccer in Mexico: A Unique Spin on the Rivalry with the USA," 25–40.
— Kassing, J. "An (Im)penetrable Fortress: The Mythology of Estadio Azteca in the US–Mexico Men's National Team Soccer," 170–89.
— Magazine, R., S. Varela, and A. Bravo. "A Resistance to Rivalry: The US–Mexico Soccer Matchup Through the Eyes of Mexican Sports Journalists, 1934–2013," 73–89, 93–4, 98.
— Mêan, L., and R. Herrera. "Gendered Nations: Media Representations of the Men's and Women's US–Mexico Soccer Rivalry," 99.
— Pescador, J. J. "Global Fútbol, the Masked Fan, and Flat Screen Arenas: Mexican Soccer Communities in the USA and the Genesis of the Tricolor Brand in Global Landscapes, 1970–2012," 243–61.
— Ridge, P. T. "Mexico 'on Top': Queering Masculinity in Contemporary Mexican Soccer Chronicles," 123–41.
— Schrader, J. "The Border War for Young Mexican American Soccer Players: How Family and National Identity Play Out on the Field," 3–1.
— Shobe, H., and G. Gibson. "Place, Nation, and the Mexico-US Soccer Rivalry: Dual Citizens, Home Stadiums and Hosting the Gold Cup," 54.

Keyes, David. "Fútbol Americano: Immigration, Social Capital, and Youth Soccer in Southern California." University of California San Diego dissertation, 2015.

La Afición, via Periodicals Archive at the National Autonomous University of Mexico, Mexico City:

— Avelar, E. "Estados Unidos no asusta ni debe presionarnos," April 19, 1997.
— Avelar, E. "Puede ser una revancha muy preciosa," July 1, 1995.
— Bolio, R. V. "Gringos sin chiste." *La Afición*, August 10, 2011.
— del Palacio, M. "El mundo no se acabó, la vida tiene que seguir," June 18, 2002.
— Fever, B. "*La Contra columna*: Wake Up America!" August 11, 2011.
— Flores, M. "Adiós MMB," July 18, 1995.
— Flores, M. "Campeón de oro," July 26, 1993.
— Porta, E. "Una derrota que nos llama a reflexionar: E.U. 2, México 0," July 6, 1991.
— Ruggieri, L. "Por jugar brusco perdió México con Estados Unidos," May 2, 1934.
— Ruggieri, L. "Un experto italiano y Correa creen que nuestra oncena ganará a la americana," May 23, 1934.
— Velasco, X. "Remember the Alamo," June 16, 2002.
— Ventura, J. "Una triste realidad para nuestro futbol," November 24, 1980.
— "Una gran sorpresa se van a llevar los futbolistas de Estados Unidos," September 11, 1937.

Lalas, Alexi. *Alexi Lalas' State of the Union Podcast*. Fox Sports, March 26, 2024.

Lane, Barnaby. "Who Founded Liga MX? The Origins of Mexico's Top Soccer League." *Sports Illustrated*, March 7, 2025. https://www.si.com/soccer/who-founded-liga-mx-origins-mexico-top-soccer-league.

Lauletta, Dan. "The Lowdown: Has NWSL Helped Canada, Mexico?" *The Equalizer*, June 30, 2015. http://equalizersoccer.com/2015/06/30/the-lowdown-has-nwsl-helped-canada-mexico/.

Lewis, Michael. "40 Years Later: 1980 U.S. Olympic Team Recalls Moscow Boycott, Meeting President Jimmy Carter." https://www.ussoccer.com/stories/2020/07/40-years-later-1980-us-olympic-team-recalls-moscow-boycott-meeting-president-jimmy-carter.

Lewis, Michael. "40 Years On: How New York Cosmos Lured Pelé to a Football Wasteland." *Guardian*, June 2, 2015. https://www.theguardian.com/football/blog/2015/jun/02/40-years-on-how-new-york-cosmos-lured-pele-to-a-football-wasteland.

Littleton, Cynthia. "Ryan Reynolds and Rob McElhenney Buy Stake in Mexico's Club Necaxa." *Variety*, April 29, 2024. https://variety.com/2024/biz/news/ryan-reynolds-rob-mcelhenney-club-necaxa-eva-longoria-wrexham-1235985035/.

Lugo, Erik Francisco. "Mexico—International Results, 1927–2025." https://www.rsssf.org/tablesm/mex-intres.html.

Jones, Grahame. "This Is Much Worse than Trash Talking." *LA Times*, February 16, 1998. https://www.latimes.com/archives/la-xpm-1998-feb-16-sp-19859-story.html.

Jose, Colin. *The American Soccer League: The Golden Years of American Soccer 1921–1931*, 124, 126. Lanham, MD: Scarecrow Press, 1998.

Mantel, Hilary. "Why I Became a Historical Novelist." *Guardian*, June 3, 2017. https://www.theguardian.com/books/2017/jun/03/hilary-mantel-why-i-became-a-historical-novelist.

Marca.com. "How Many Foreign Players Is Each Liga MX Team Allowed to Have?" *Marca*, June 29, 2023. https://www.marca.com/en/football/liga-mx/2023/06/29/649d6591e2704edb8c8b45a2.html.

Marca.com. "Jorge Tello: 'There's a Real Battle with the United States to Win Players,'" March 23, 2023. https://www.marca.com/mx/futbol/seleccion-mx/2023/04/23/644542ea268e3ee1558b45e9.html.

Markovits, Andrei. *Women in American Soccer and European Football: Different Paths to Shared Glory*, 7, 80, n83–4, 138–9. Nantucket: Dickinson-Moses Press, 2023.

Markovits, Andrei, and Steven Hellerman. *Offside: Soccer and American Exceptionalism*, 7–51, 128–61. Princeton: Princeton University Press, 2001.

Markovits, Andrei, Rebeeca Shippen, and Jillian Victor. "Envy and Scorn as Primary Markers of the Pervasive Antipathy in College Football's Rivalry Games: The University of Michigan as a Representative Microcosm." *Sport in Society* 20 (2017). https://www.tandfonline.com/doi/full/10.1080/17430437.2017.1326758.

Marshall, Tom. "Monica Gonzalez Urges Mexican Federation to Seize Opportunity to Promote Women's Game." *ESPN.com*, April 15, 2016. http://www.espn.com/espnw/sports/article/15204801/monica-gonzalez-urges-mexican-federation-seize-opportunity-promote-women-game.

Marshall, Tom. "Rafa Marquez Regrets Red Bulls Move, Hoping for World Cup Finale." *ESPN.com*, April 17, 2018. https://www.espn.com/soccer/story/_/id/37551405/rafa-marquez-regrets-red-bulls-move-hoping-world-cup-finale.

Marshall, Tom. "What Chicharito's Galaxy Move Means to the Future of MLS and Mexican Soccer." *ESPN.com*, January 24, 2024. https://www.espn.com/soccer/story/_/id/37580907/what-chicharito-galaxy-move-means-future-mls-mexican-soccer.

Martinez, Fidel. "Latinx Files: Why I'm Taking a Break from the Mexican Men's National Soccer Team." *LA Times*, September 12, 2024. https://www.latimes.com/delos/newsletter/2024-09-12/mexico-soccer-el-tri-dissapointment-decepcion-nacional-latinx-files.

Maurer, Pablo. "San Diego FC Coach, Sporting Director Denounce Homophobic Chants at Inaugural Home Match." *The Athletic*, March 2, 2025. https://www.nytimes.com/athletic/6169617/2025/03/02/san-diego-fc-denounces-homophobic-chants/.

McGovern, Kieran. "1928 FIFA Congress." *Medium*, November 5, 2022. https://medium.com/the-story-of-football/the-1928-fifa-congress-566198e5114a.

MediaTempo.com. "Raúl Cárdenas, Former Coach of El Tri, has Passed Away," March 26, 2016. https://www.mediotiempo.com/futbol/liga-mx/fallecio-raul-cardenas-ex-dt-del-tri.

Miller, Nick. "World Cup Willie, Striker and Ciao: Best World Cup Mascots," June 7, 2014. https://www.espn.com/soccer/story/_/id/37395176/world-cup-willie-striker-ciao-best-world-cup-mascots.

MLSsoccer.com. "MLS Continues Exploring Shift to International Soccer Calendar," April 10, 2025. https://www.mlssoccer.com/news/mls-continues-exploring-shift-to-international-soccer-calendar.

Moreno, Angel. "Mexico Women's Soccer Coach Leonardo Cuellar Looks to Recruit Valley," September 28, 2015. https://www.fresnobee.com/sports/soccer/article36887691.html.

Morris, Desmond. *The Soccer Tribe*, 21–2. New York City: Rizzoli International Publications, 1981.

Navarro, Andrea. "Televisa Chairman Azcarraga Resigns Amid FIFA Bribery Probe." *Bloomberg*, October 24, 2024. https://www.bloomberg.com/news/articles/2024-10-24/televisa-chairman-azcarraga-steps-down-amid-fifa-bribery-probe.

Nissen, Keith. "Viewership of Women's Sports in the US Is on the Rise." SP Global.com, December 19, 2024. Shttps://www.spglobal.com/market-intelligence/en/news-insights/research/viewership-of-womens-sports-in-the-us-is-on-the-rise.

Onefootball.com. "D.C. United Makes Bold Bet on Fidel Barajas," February 27, 2025. https://onefootball.com/en/news/dc-united-makes-bold-bet-on-fidel-barajas-40766251.

Panja, Tariq, and Rory Smith. "For Turkish Germans, Heart Overrules Home at Euro 2024." *New York Times*, June 22, 2024. https://www.nytimes.com/2024/06/22/world/europe/european-championship-euros-germany-turkey.html.

Pelit, Asli, and Meg Linehan. "NWSL Requested Permission to Start a New Second Division. What Does It Mean for Women's Soccer?" *The Athletic*, April 26, 2025. https://www.nytimes.com/athletic/6311310/2025/04/26/nwsl-second-division-womens-soccer-explained.

Phillips, Hal. *Generation Zero: Founding Fathers, Hidden Histories & The Making of Soccer in America*, 25, 39, 46–78, 66, 194–210. Nantucket: Dickinson-Moses Press.

Poushter, Jacob, Jordan Lippert, and Sarah Austin. "How Mexicans and Americans View Each Other and their Governments' Handling of the Border." *Pew Research Center*, August 12, 2024. https://www.pewresearch.org/short-reads/2024/08/12/how-mexicans-and-americans-view-each-other-and-their-governments-handling-of-the-border/.

Powell, Robert Andrew. *This Love Is Not For Cowards: Salvation and Soccer in Cuidad Juárez*. New York City: Bloomsbury USA, 2012.

RedHonduras.com. "Biography of Florencio Xatruch." https://redhonduras.com/en/biography/biography-florencio-xatruch/.

Reiset, S. "Columbus crew, la 'casa del terror' para el Tri." *Mediotiempo*, S.A., February 9, 2009. http://www.mediotiempo.com/futbol/seleccion-mexicana/noticias/2009/02/07/columbus-crew-la-casa-del-terror-del-tri.

Rivera, Arnoldo. "Aztecazo! Mexico 1—Costa Rica 2." *La Nación*, June 17, 2001. https://web.archive.org/web/20170322202903/http://wvw.nacion.com/ln_ee/2001/junio/17/deportes1.html.

Rodríguez, Carlos. "Mexican Baseball League's Recent Growth in Attendance Now Rivals Soccer Clubs." *Associated Press*, April 16, 2025. https://apnews.com/article/robinson-cano-diablos-rojos-mexican-baseball-league-52db4cef1eaf7360ecdf642ee51938fb.

Sandalow, Brian. "Soldier Field Ready to Combat Homophobic Slurs at Mexico National Team Soccer Match." *Sun-Times*, May 30, 2024. https://chicago.suntimes.com/soccer/2024/05/30/u-s-soccer-soldier-field-ready-to-combat-homophobic-slurs-at-mexico-national-team-soccer-match?

Schaerlaeckens, Leander. "Gianni Infantino and Donald Trump Have Taken the 2026 World Cup for Themselves." *Guardian*, March 12, 2025. https://www.theguardian.com/football/2025/mar/12/gianni-infantino-donald-trump-2026-world-cup.

Silverman, Alex. "MLS Sets Attendance Record in 2024 with 5% Uptick over Last Season." *Sports Business Journal*, October 22, 2024. https://www.sportsbusinessjournal.com/Articles/2024/10/22/mls-attendance?origin=serp_auto.

Soccer History USA. "American Soccer League I (1921–1933)." https://soccerhistoryusa.org/asha/asl.html.

Society of American Soccer History. "USMNT Results: 1970–1979." https://www.ussoccerhistory.org/usnt-results/usmnt-results/usmnt-results-1970-1979.

SP Global. "NHL Thriving as It Hits Midway Point of Current Media Rights Deal," November 23, 2024. https://www.spglobal.com/market-intelligence/en/news-insights/research/nhl-thriving-as-it-hits-midway-point-of-current-media-rights-deal.

SportBusiness.com. "MLS Reacquires Soccer United Marketing Stake," June 21, 2017. https://media.sportbusiness.com/news/mls-reacquires-soccer-united-marketing-stake/.

Stanley-Becker, Isaac. "World Cup Players Says He Is 'a German When We Win' but 'an Immigrant When We Lose,' Quits National Team." *Washington Post*, July 23, 2018. https://www.washingtonpost.com/news/morning-mix/wp/2018/07/23/quitting-national-team-world-cup-player-says-he-is-a-german-when-we-win-but-an-immigrant-when-we-lose.

Straus, Brian. "For USMNT, a Vital Point Gained but Opportunity Squandered as Azteca's Mystique Wanes." *Sports Illustrated*, March 2, 2022. https://www.si.com/soccer/2022/03/25/usmnt-mexico-draw-world-cup-qualifying-azteca.

Surendran, Shwetha. "Report: U.S. Travel System Not Ready for World Cup, Olympics." *ESPN*, February 19, 2025. https://www.espn.com/olympics/story/_/id/43923123/us-travel-system-not-ready-world-cup-olympics.

Szymanski, Stefan, and Simon Kuper. *Soccernomics: Why England Loses, Why Germany and Brazil Win, and Why the U.S., Japan, Australia, Turkey—and Even Iraq—Are Destined to Become the Kings of the World's Most Popular Sport*. Bold Type Books, 2009.

Tenorio, Paul, and Adam Crafton. "Liga MX Controversy Explained: How a $1.25bn Deal Collapsed—and What Happens Now." *The Athletic*, December 17, 2024. https://www.nytimes.com/athletic/6000252/2024/12/17/ligamx-rodriguez-mls/.

Thelmadatter, Leigh. "The Miners Who Brought British Culture to Mexico." *Mexico News Daily*, 2021. https://mexiconewsdaily.com/mexicolife/the-miners-who-brought-british-culture-to-mexico/.

Theroux, Paul. *On the Plain of the Snakes: A Mexican Road Trip*. New York City: Penguin, 2019.

Tonoli, Amanda. "It's What Gives Columbus a Color and a Voice and a Sense of Pride." *Columbus Business Journal*, July 11, 2024. https://www.bizjournals.com/columbus/news/2024/07/11/crew-mls-all-star-game-lowercom-field.html.

United Press International. "U.S. and Mexico Tie, 0-0, In World Cup Soccer," October 4, 1976. https://www.nytimes.com/1976/10/04/archives/us-and-mexico-tie-00-in-world-cup-soccer.html.

Uribarri, Jaime. "USMNT Beat Mexico for Club América Winger Alejandro Zendejas." MLSsoccer.com, March 14, 2023. https://www.mlssoccer.com/news/usmnt-beat-mexico-for-club-america-winger-alejandro-zendejas.

U.S. Census. "Population Growth and Distribution." https://www2.census.gov/prod2/decennial/documents/42189394n1-26ch1.pdf.

U.S. Department of Transportation. "Border Crossing Data Annual Release: 2023–2024." Bureau of Transportation Statistics, February 18, 2025. https://www.bts.gov/newsroom/border-crossing-data-annual-release-2023-2024.

U.S. Library of Congress. "Recognizing and Naming America: Waldseemüller's 1507 Map." https://www.loc.gov/collections/discovery-and-exploration/articles-and-essays/recognizing-and-naming-america.

U.S. Soccer Federation. "Get to Know Your Cup," January 31, 2023. https://www.ussoccer.com/stories/2023/01/get-to-know-your-cup.

Vargas, Ramon Antonio. "US Latinos Are Soccer-Mad. Why Isn't That Reflected in the World Cup Squad?" November 15, 2022. https://www.theguardian.com/football/2022/nov/15/usmnt-qatar-world-cup-2022-soccer-latino-players.

Vertelny, Seth. "Club America President Open to Playing Liga MX Games in United States." *Pro Soccer Wire*, May 23, 2024. https://prosoccerwire.usatoday.com/2024/05/23/club-america-president-liga-mx-games-usa/.

Vertelny, Seth. "Greenland Set for Talks to Join Concacaf, Still Probably Not Joining United States." *Pro Soccer Wire*, January 23, 2025. https://prosoccerwire.usatoday.com/story/sports/2025/01/23/greenland-set-for-talks-over-joining-concacaf/77911305007/.

Wahl, Grant. "The 2013 Night Graham became San Zusi and Panama's Pitch Invader Plan Went Awry." *SI*, June 30, 2017. https://www.foxsports.com/stories/soccer/the-2013-night-graham-became-san-zusi-and-panamas-pitch-invader-plan-went-awry.

Wahl, Grant. "Fútbol with Grant Wahl," August 19, 2022. https://grantwahl.substack.com/p/friday-newsletter-the-us-has-gone.

Wahl, Grant, producer. *Good Rivals*. Documentary film. Amazon Prime Video, 2022.

Wahl, Grant. "How Far They've Come, State of USA vs. Mexico." *SI*, October 6, 2015. https://www.si.com/soccer/2015/10/06/usa-mexico-rivalry-2005-si-vault-usmnt.

Wahl, Grant. "In Ever-Changing USA Landscape, USMNT vs. Mexico a Complex Rivalry." *SI*, October 5, 2015. https://www.si.com/soccer/2015/10/05/usa-mexico-rivalry-mexican-americans-concacaf-cup.

Wahl, Grant. "U.S. Victory at Estadio Azteca No Longer an Impossible Feat." *Sports Illustrated*, March 26, 2013. https://www.si.com/soccer/2013/03/26/us-mexico-estadio-azteca-world-cup-qualifier.

Whalen, Michael, producer. *Gringos at the Gate*. Documentary film, 2012.

Wilt, Dave. "The Films of El Santo." https://terpconnect.umd.edu/~dwilt/santo.html.

Ziegler, Mark. "USA Savors Sweet Clincher—USA 2 Mexico 0." *San Diego Union-Tribune*, September 4, 2005, C-1.

Index

1928 Olympic Football Tournament   70
1972 Munich Olympics   3
1972 US Olympic Team   126
1979 *Coppa Italia* match   142
1988 Seoul Olympiad   40
1991 US Men's National Team   14
1992 Barcelona Olympiad   40
1999 Confederation Cup   7, 32, 87, 154, 170, 188
1999 FIFA Women's World Cup   124
1999 U-17 World Cup   35
2008 Summer Olympiad   134
2024 CONCACAF Champions Cup   62
2024 *Torneo Apertura*   220

ABA Sport   146
acculturation   30
Adams, Tyler   53, 216
Adidas   146, 216
African World Cup   145
Aguirre, Javier   7, 10, 34, 36, 44, 46, 201
Airbnb   44
Albinegros de Orizaba of Veracruz   67–8
Algeria   102
Algerian Football Federation   49
Álvarez, Efraín   223
American GI Forum   99
American Immigration Council   98
Americanization   109, 192
American League of Professional Football   117
American Soccer Cred   161
American Soccer League (ASL)   71, 79, 113, 117–20, 165

American Youth Soccer Organization (AYSO)   122
amistoso   31, 125, 177, 179, 187, 216
Andon, Stephen P.   168, 169
Anglo-Texans   94
Apollo Global Capital   195, 196, 198, 199
Araujo, Julián   217, 218, 223
Arena, Bruce   36, 162, 165, 166, 174
Argentina   26, 46, 52, 56–8, 60–2, 69–72, 80, 103, 128
Arnold, Jon   53, 57, 103–5, 118, 190, 192, 196, 198
Arriola, Mikel   191
Asian World Cup   10
AS Monaco   200
Aspe, Alberto García   13, 32–3, 151
assimilation   109
Atlantic Coast League   119
autonomy/autonomous   76, 79, 93–5, 97
Azteca, *see* Estadio Azteca

Baja California   95
Balboa, Marcelo   160
Barajas, Fidel   220, 221
Barón, Miguel Mejía   151
Basking in Reflected Glory (BIRG)   138
Battle of Churubusco   13, 94, 170
Bavarian United   116
Beasley, DeMarcus   177
Beckham, David   57
beisbol   8

Belgium   15, 25, 72, 89
Belo Horizonte   40
Berhalter, Gregg   41, 52, 163, 217
Bethlehem Steel FC   118
Big Bend National Park   ix
Black Stars of Ghana   145
Blanco, Cuauhtémoc   33
Blatter, Sepp   115
Blazer, Chuck   184, 186, 187
Bocanegra, Carlos   221
Bolio, Velasquéz Roberto   178, 179
Borgetti, Jared   176
Bornstein, Jonathan   134
Bradley, Bob   178
Bravo, Aldo   75, 150
Brazil   26, 33, 47, 55, 56, 69, 77, 87, 103, 120, 131, 143, 170, 179, 209, 223
Brazilian World Cup   40, 83, 145
Brent Spence Bridge   163
The British Club   67
British Empire   66
Brooklyn Bridegrooms   117
Buchanan, Pat   152
Buenos Aires club   46, 60, 69, 81, 149
Burr, Aaron   93
Bush, George H.W.   42, 152
Butch & Sundance   186, 187

Cadena, Jesse   210, 220
Calderon, Erick   30, 31, 109, 146, 192, 203–5
California   28, 34, 99, 109, 152
Caligiuri, Paul   104, 168
Campeonato de Naciones   188
Campos, Jorge   167
Canada   34, 41, 42, 63, 141, 153, 212, 213
Cañedo, Guillermo   84
Cantor, Andrés   38
Cardenas, Raúl   3, 7, 15
Cardoso, Johnny   53
Cardozo, Calderón   80
Carter, Jimmy   1, 128
Castelán, Maribel Domínguez   211
Castillo, Edgar   177
C.F. Pachuca   67, 68

Chicago National Soccer League   117
Chicago Red Stars   19, 208
Chilean World Cup   84
Chivas   19, 45, 55, 195, 198, 220, 221
Chyzowych, Walt   3
Cialdini, Robert   138
Cirino, Tony   74
Ciudad Juarez   23, 215
Civil War, American   13, 68
Clark, Caitlin   206
Clark Thread Co   117
Clásico Norteamericano   18, 26, 72, 93, 147, 184, 222
Cleveland Rams   74
Clinton, Bill   152, 153, 155
Clinton Administration   150
Club América   3, 24, 29, 45, 60, 68–9, 107, 195, 196
Club Atlético San Lorenzo de Almagro   15–16
Club León   78
Club Monza   142
Club Necaxa   117, 118, 201
Club Puebla   78
Club Unión De Curtidores   129
Club World Cup   114
Cobbs, Joe   10, 12, 17, 25, 26, 42, 49, 62, 90–2, 136, 162, 163, 167, 170, 173
Cóccaro, Matías   221
Coche, Oscar   30, 155
Coche, Roxane   29
codependence/co-dependent   26, 87, 113, 173
Cold War   4, 62, 169, 175
Colombia   15, 34
Columbus, Ohio   28, 47, 68, 161, 162, 164, 167, 169, 174, 181
Columbus, Christopher   159, 160
Columbus Crew   53, 67, 166
Company of the Gentlemen Adventurers   65
CONCACAF   11, 32, 34, 39, 54, 67, 80, 83, 85, 86, 126, 149, 164, 166, 175, 183–6, 188, 190
CONCACAFkaesque   185, 186

Index

Congress, U.S.   94, 98
CONMEBOL   82, 183, 190
containment strategy   152
Copa 1971   210, 211
Copa América   26, 31, 44, 70, 71, 189
   1995   12, 30, 151, 154
   2001   34
   2024   57
Copa InterAmericana   14
Copa Libertadores   15, 85, 190
Copa México   118
The Cornish   65, 66
Corona, Joe   177
Cortés, Hernán   159
Cortina, Germán Nuñez   69
Costa Rica   15, 84, 89, 129, 149, 154, 166, 175, 176, 185
Cotton Bowl stadium   103, 127
Cramer, Dettmar   126
Cruz, José G.   140
Cruz Azul   3, 220
Cuba   73, 83
Cuéllar, Leonardo   212, 219
Curry Silver Tops   74

Dájome, Cristian   221
Dallas   47, 51, 125, 127
Dalymount Park   vi
Davies, Charlie   172
Davis, Ricky   129
del Palacio, Martín   38
Del Piero, Alessandro   225
Dempsey, Clint   169, 179
Deportivo Toluca F.C.   107
Der Klassiker   26, 144, 164, 222
Der Nordamerikanische Klassiker   87
desmadre   57–60, 174
Dest, Sergiño   218
Díaz Ordaz, Gustavo   81
Dinétah   23
Di Stéfano, Alfredo   39
Domínguez Castelán, Maribel   211, 212
Donelli, Aldo   73–4

Donovan, Landon   34–6, 104, 167, 169, 178, 221, 222
Dos a Cero!   ix, 28, 34–6, 54, 129, 149, 162–4, 167–9, 175, 176, 181, 182, 204
Doyle, John   149
Draper, Don   92
dual national   24, 25, 94, 108, 136, 210, 214, 216–21

Eagle Man   52
The Eagles (*Las Aguilas*)   60, 69
Eastern Professional Soccer League (EPSL)   119
Eison, Matthew   52, 54, 55, 172
El Chicharito   226
El Clásico   159, 193, 194, 201
El Clásico femenil   204
El Economista   94
El fútbol siempre da revanche   28
El Mister   14, 148, 212, 219
El Paso   23, 215
El Principito   45
el pueblo mexicano   15, 79
El Salvador   86, 96, 154
El Santo   139, 140
El Tri femenil   203, 212, 219, 223
enculturation   30
England   vi, vii, ix, 71, 102, 137, 166, 224
English Football Association (FA)   40, 71, 116
entraîneur   14
envy   17, 18, 25, 40, 61, 62, 90, 92, 93, 100, 101, 104, 106
ESPN   29, 148, 174, 191, 212, 221
Estadio Akron   43–5, 50, 54, 56, 164
Estadio Azteca   viii, 1, 2, 9, 11, 33, 45, 55, 61, 81, 124, 125, 129, 133, 149, 160–2, 164, 170–3, 175–7, 180, 182, 188, 196, 197, 211
Estadio Cuauhtémoc   81
Estadio Nez   131
Estadio Nou Camp   81

Estadio Parque Asturias 77
Estadio Parque España 77
Estadio Parque Necaxa 77
Estadio Rommel Fernández 55
Estados Unidos Mexicanos 32, 41
Europe 8, 41, 47, 82, 86, 108, 142, 178, 183, 188, 198, 210, 211
European soccer confederation (UEFA) 48
Eusebio 14, 83
Existimos porque resistimos 31

F.A. Cup 70
Fall River Marksmen 72
Fan ID system 59
F.C. Barcelona 34, 102, 173, 193, 200, 208, 217
FC Barcelona Residency Academy 217
F.C. Cincinnati 19, 164
F.C. San Diego 59
Federación 3, 9, 15, 24, 38, 45, 46, 77, 78, 86, 125, 174, 211, 214
Federación de Futbol Mexicano (FMF), see Mexican Football Federation (FMF)
federal Bracero Program 99
Fédération Internationale de Football Association 15
Feilhaber, Benny 134
Fever, Barak 179
Fielder, Bill 73
FIFA 11, 15, 19, 22, 24, 69–73, 77, 80, 82, 83, 86, 88, 113–15, 119, 122, 147, 157, 188, 189, 196
First World War 68, 97
Fiske, Susan 17, 18, 90, 93
Flores, Salvador 98, 121
Foer, Frank 189
Fort Lauderdale 1–5, 86, 129, 147, 212
fortress 81, 134, 165, 171, 174
France/French 14, 15, 25, 26, 33, 49, 58, 72, 77, 102, 145
Friedel, Brad 167
Ft. Lauderdale Strikers 83

Fuerza 68, 118
fußballtrainer 14

Galacticos tradition 39
Gallagher, Jimmy 73
Gallina, Francesco 82
Garber, Don 171, 172, 199
García, Hector 99
García Aspe, Alberto 12, 32–3, 151
de la Garza, Rodolfo 95
Garza Gutiérrez, Raphael 68–70, 72, 76-78
GDL, The (Guadalajara) 44, 45, 53, 171, 221
Generation Zero: Founding Fathers, Hidden Histories & The Making of Soccer in America (Phillips) 112, 171, 185
Germans/Germany 14, 36, 48, 69, 102, 135, 162, 179
Giants Stadium 49, 104, 129, 178
Gibson, Carrie
  El Norte: The Epic and Forgotten History of Hispanic North America 13, 22–3, 95, 98, 164, 173, 191
Gibson, Geoff 161
Gilded Age 97
Girma, Naomi 208
Glen Cove, N.Y. 224, 225
Glover, Amy 15, 22, 23, 58, 94, 143, 175
Gold Cup 14, 31, 35, 47, 56, 147–9, 181, 184, 188, 204
  1991 16, 149
  1993 11
  1999 32
  2009 178
  2011 178, 179
  2021 217
Gomez, Herculez 27, 59, 177, 179, 180, 218, 222, 223
Gómez, Jonathan 223
Gonsalves, Billy 73

González, Jesse 217
Gonzalez, Jonathan 23, 24
González, Mónica 212
Grandin, Greg 97
   The End of the Myth 13, 94, 153
Grant, Ulysses S. 13
Great Depression 98, 118
Greater Boston 43, 224
Greenland F.A. 186
gringos 9, 35, 39, 44, 51, 69, 90, 95, 101, 127, 140, 150, 170, 172, 177, 178, 214
Grupo Televisa 118, 184, 195
Guadalajara 9, 22, 35, 43–8, 50–2, 55, 57, 58, 78, 93, 98, 131, 139, 140, 164, 220
Guardado, Andrés 45
Guarneros, Salvador 84
Guatemala/Guatemalans vi, 70, 96, 132, 175, 193, 194, 216
Guerra, Oscar 29, 30
Guerra, Roxane 155
Gulati, Sunil 16, 166, 174
Gunners, The 66

Hahn, Craig 52, 54
Hamilton, Alexander 93
Hard Rock Stadium 196
Hatfields & McCoys 151
Hayes, Emma 208, 209
Heaps, Lindsey 209
Helm, John 37
Hernández, Javier "Chicharito" 200, 226
Hernandez, Luis 36
Hernández, Sergio Varela 75, 150
Herrera, Raquel 49
Historic Crew Stadium 181
Home Nations 71
Honduras/Hondurans 86, 96, 149, 154, 176–7
Hoppe, Matthew 134
Huerta, César 54
Huerta, Sofia 214
Hutton, Claire 209

identity 11, 30, 49, 63, 134–6, 139, 145, 160, 161, 167, 205, 224
Indomitable Lions of Cameroon 145
Infantino, Gianni 114
Institutional Revolutionary Party (PRI) 21
interdependence 17, 103, 205, 213
Inter Miami 62
International Olympic Committee (IOC) 70, 71, 80
Ireland/Irish vi, ix, 102
Irvine Strikers 13
Italian-American social club 224
Italian World Cup of 1934 73
Italy/Italian vii, 15, 16, 26, 73, 74, 82, 114, 142, 144, 179, 224

Jalisco State 22, 45, 51
Japan/Japanese 6–8, 32–4, 100, 209, 224
John Reid Act of 1924 98
Jones, Cobi 37, 170
J&P Coats F.C. 118
Juárez, Ciudad 9, 23, 24, 46, 197, 215, 221

Kassing, Jeffrey 30, 160, 161, 211
Kehoe, Bob 124
Keough, Harry 98, 120
Keough, Ty 3, 98, 99, 121, 128–31
Keyes, David
   Fútbol Americano: Immigration, Social Capital, and Youth Soccer in Southern California 122
Klinsmann, Jurgen 177
Krumpe, Paul 28
Ku Klux Klan 98
Kuper, Simon 187

La Afición 4, 12, 38, 39, 73–5, 77, 86, 131, 148, 149, 151, 155, 179
La Albiceleste 56, 61
La Brigada De Oro 29
La Canarinha 115
La Celeste 71
L.A. Coliseum 11, 35, 125, 129, 148, 156

L.A. Galaxy 217
La Guerra Fria 169, 175
La Iglesia Metodista del Divino Salvador 65
Lalas, Alexi 26, 27, 109, 156, 160, 173–5
La Liga 44, 189, 193, 194, 196, 218, 223
La Liga Amateur de Veracruz 78
La Liga Mayor 78
La Liga Occidental de Jalisco 78
La Madre Patria 38
La Marca 105, 201
Lambeau Field 169
La Nación 175
La Opinión 180
La Priméra División de México 79
Lara, Edwin 217
Lara, Juan Carreño 72
Las Aguilas 9, 68, 76
La Selección 11, 14, 15, 24, 33, 41, 44, 45, 78, 83, 85, 104, 106, 108, 128, 129, 140, 144, 151, 174, 176, 178, 179, 202, 205, 211, 212, 214, 217, 218, 223
LA Times 19, 109
Latin America 57, 61
Latino heritage 99
LaVolpe, Ricardo 169
Leagues Cup 29, 41, 93, 103, 190–2, 194, 196, 199, 204, 218
Ledezma, Richie 218
León 46, 47, 67, 81, 129, 220–1
Lepore, Tony 216, 217
Les Bleus 25, 145
Levy, Juliette 13
Liga Mayor 78
Liga MX 9, 23, 24, 29, 41, 58, 60, 79, 93, 101, 103, 171, 185, 187, 190–9, 204, 210, 214, 218–21
Liga MX feminil (LMXF) 208, 210, 211, 213
Ligue 1 14
Lincoln, Abraham 98
Little League baseball 79, 122
Lockhart Stadium 1, 4
Longoria, Eva 118

Los Angeles 28, 29, 82, 84, 127, 148, 156, 187, 196
Los Canaleros 54
Los Contrachos 96
Los Electricistas 118
Los Yanquis 12, 128, 176
lucha libre 47, 51, 52, 139

Macário, Catarina 209, 214
McBride, Brian 36, 162
McCullers, Mark 166
Mac Donald, Duncan Mac Comish 68
Macías, Alberto 167
McIlhenny, Rob 116
McKennie, Weston 53, 163
Madison Square Garden 82
Mad Men 92
Magallon, Jesse 220
Magazine, Roger 75, 76, 150
Major Indoor Soccer League 129, 131
Major League Soccer (MLS) 19, 23, 24, 29, 31, 59, 66, 88, 105, 124, 134, 163, 165, 185, 186, 189, 190, 192, 193, 196–9, 219, 221–2
Malin, Seamus vi, 155
Mantel, Hilary 67, 128
Mao 14
Mapfre Stadium 160–3, 165, 168, 169, 181
Maracana Stadium 170
Maradona 57, 61, 161, 170
mariachi 50, 51
Markovits, Andrei 17, 18, 90–2, 101–4, 112, 208–9, 213
  Offside: Soccer and American Exceptionalism 100, 137
  Women in American Soccer and European Football: Different Paths to Shared Glory 208
Marquez, Rafa 24, 32–4, 36, 37, 45, 162, 169, 181, 199–202, 222
Marsch, Jesse 42
Marta 14
Martino, Tata 57, 217
Meân, Lindsey J. 30, 49, 211

Medford, Hernán   175
Mendoza, Gómez   223
Mendoza, Ruben   98, 99, 120, 121, 123, 124
Men in Blazers   129
Men's National Team, *see* US Men's National Team (USMNT)
Messi, Leo   58, 62, 88
Mexican American   23, 29, 31, 47, 99
Mexican Football Federation (FMF)   3, 15, 19, 41, 44, 45, 47, 49, 70, 76–80, 84, 127–9, 149, 151, 187, 201, 213, 219
Mexican League of Association Football   66
Mexican National Team   ix, 1, 6, 15, 16, 21, 23, 27, 31, 37, 43, 47, 49, 51, 70, 76, 79, 83, 103, 144, 163, 170, 174–6, 179, 180, 195, 203, 207, 216, 219, 221
Mexican *Priméra*   7, 14, 29, 71, 78, 82, 113, 118, 120
Mexican Revolution of 1910   97
Mexican War   13
Mexican World Cup   82, 141
Mexico/Mexican   vii, viii, ix, x, 1–19, 22–39, 41–63, 66–70, 72, 76–81, 84, 86, 87, 91, 94–7, 107–9, 112, 117, 118, 120, 125–7, 129–31, 133, 142, 143, 149, 154, 164, 166, 167, 175, 176, 179, 181, 183, 184, 186, 190, 193, 194, 200, 215, 220, 226, 227
  broadcast sector   8
  clubs   29, 196
  El Tri Feminil   11, 210, 212, 219, 223,
  fans   15, 27, 34, 58, 60, 90, 103, 116, 139
  futbol community   3, 37, 83
  media   8, 10, 150
  Spanish-speaking economy   8
Mexico Cricket Club   67
Miami Toros   83
Michigan *vs.* Ohio State   18
migration   17, 98, 99, 152, 154

Milla, Roger   145
Milutinovic, Bora   14–17, 82, 148, 149
Montella, Vincenzo   225
Monterrey   19, 45, 48, 62, 78, 83, 125–7, 174, 197
Montevideo   69, 70
Moorhouse, George   73
Morales, María Guadalupe Sánchez   18
Morales, Ramon   36
Morris, Aidan   53, 54
Morris, Desmond   138
  The Soccer Tribe   137
Moscow   129
Mou   14
Moyers, Steve   130
Mundial   15, 57, 71, 82, 84, 86, 114, 128, 136, 142, 185, 221
Munich, Bayern   101
Murillo, Jesús   221
Murray, Bruce   148
Mussolini, Benito   114

Nacho Libre   140
NAFTA   26, 42, 153, 154
NASL   4, 12, 82, 83, 115, 121, 124, 128, 129, 131, 142, 165, 194, 212
National Amateur Cup   119
National Autonomous University of Mexico   75
National Challenge Cup   117, 119
National Football League   2, 9, 118
National Hockey League   189
National tribe   138
NBA   40, 88, 204, 216
NBA Dream Team   144
NBC   4, 189, 222
New Jersey   94, 124, 129
New York Red Bulls   200
New York Yankees   vii, 46, 101, 173
New Zealand   35, 44, 55
NFL   74, 171, 172, 181
NFL Chicago Bears   115
Nicaraguan Democratic Party   95, 96

Ni de aquí, ni de allá 214
Nike 146
North American Derby ix, 11, 19, 26, 34, 43, 65–102, 131, 154, 162, 181, 187, 203, 222, 227
North American Football Confederation 79
North American Football Union 73, 80, 83
North American futbol culture 6
Northern Kentucky University 10
Northern Super League 213
Noyola, Teresa 212
Nueva Espana 23
NWSL 19, 88, 106, 204, 208, 209, 211–13
NX Football USA 118

Oakland Raiders 1
López Obrador, Andrés Manuel 153, 176
Ocampo, Mónica 212
Ohio State Fairgrounds 161
Old Enemy 38
Olympic Games 40, 81, 82, 131
Olympic movement 24, 137
Olympic tournament, 1980 129
Orozco, Michael 133–6, 177, 179
Özil, Mesut 118, 135, 136
Ozzy's Laguna F.C. 220

Pachuca 65–7, 197
Pachuca Athletic Club 66, 67
Panama/Panamanian 54, 55, 106, 177
Pan American Games 84, 129
Paraguay 72, 85
Patenaude, Bert 72
Pawtucket, R.I. 118
Paz, Octavio 180
Peak Azteca 173–5
Pefok, Jordan 180
Pelé vii, 14, 26, 57, 67, 82, 115, 121, 161, 170
Pep 14
Pepi, Ricardo 23, 24, 214, 226
Pérez, Verónica 212

Perspectives on the US-Mexico Rivalry: Passion and Politics in Red, White, Blue & Green (Kassing and Meân) 29–30, 139, 160, 161, 168, 211
Peru/Peruvian 57, 85
Pescador, Juan Javier 139, 140, 143
Pew Global Attitudes Survey 63
Pew Research Center 50, 192
Pharaohs of Egypt 145
Philadelphia Eagles 1
Pierce, Franklin 95
Pittsburgh Steelers 74, 168
Platini, Michel 145
Plaza de las Tres Culturas 81
Pochettino, Mauricio 27, 53, 56, 217, 218
Polk, James K. 94
Portugal/Portuguese 14, 18, 83, 103
Premier League 79, 189, 193
Priméra club 8, 9, 14, 15, 68, 71, 78, 82–5, 113, 128, 133, 212
Priméra División 67
Priméra Fuerza 68, 78
Pulisic, Christian 53, 163, 180, 216
Puskás, Ferenc 39, 40
Putin, Vladimir 114

Qatar 26, 49, 56, 84, 114, 146
Qatari World Cup 58

Ramirez, Dante 106–8
Ramírez, Ramón 173, 174
Ramos, Rafael 180
Ramos, Tab 124, 151
ranchera 51
Rancho Cucamonga, Calif. 35
Reagan, Ronald 152
Real Madrid 39, 101, 173, 193, 208
Red Sox 46, 173, 224
Reimers, Marion 34, 40, 41, 47–9, 61, 62, 85, 87, 88, 137, 141, 143, 154, 161, 192–4, 198, 204, 206, 209, 210, 214, 221
Remember the Alamo 39

Revolutionary War   93–4, 168
Reynolds, Ryan   116
Ridge, Patrick Thomas   60
Rigoni, Emiliano   220
Rio de Janeiro   69, 170
Rio Grande   78, 97, 114
Rodriguez, Juan Carlos   195
Rome   73, 77, 78
Romero, Abraham   217
Rondón, Salomón   67
Roosevelt, Teddy   145
Rose Bowl Stadium   viii, 11, 30, 104, 150, 155, 178
Rothenburg, Alan   147
Ruth & Gehrig Era Yankees   68

St. Louis   98, 120, 121, 123, 126, 127
St. Louis Kutis F.C.   120-1,
St. Louis Soccer League   117, 120
St. Louis Steamers   3, 130
St. Louis suburb of Granite City, Ill.   121, 123
St. Louis University   121, 130
Salazar, Sebastian   221
Salgado, Horacio López   127
Sanchez, Ashley   214
Sanchez, Hugo   3, 14, 128, 147, 148, 200
Sánchez, María   203
Sánchez, Oswaldo   180, 222
San Diego   19, 197, 204
San Diego Surf S.C.   218
San Francisco Soccer Football League   116
San Jose Earthquakes academy system   220
San Luis F.C.   83, 133
San Nicolás de los Garza, Nuevo León   45, 85
Santa Maria, HCMS   159
"San Zusi"   54, 55, 89, 177
Scally, Joe   218
scorn   17, 18, 25, 40, 62, 90–3, 100–3
Second World War   28, 40, 62, 78, 79, 99, 118, 119

Selecao   33
semi-professionalism/semi-pro/semi-professional   116, 117, 120, 165
Señor Colón   159
Sharp, Ronnie   83
Shaw, Jaedyn   209
Shipan, Rebecca   100
Shobe, Hunter   161
Shrader, John   220
sibling/big brother/big sister, younger brother/kid brother/punk brother   7, 23, 25, 37, 41, 42, 80, 84, 85, 87, 91, 92, 144, 154, 207, 221, 236
Simeone, Diego   57
Soca Warriors   185
Soccer America   127, 219
soccer culture   7, 147
Soccernomics   187, 191
Soccer United Marketing   49, 199
Soccer War, The (ASL)   119
Society of American Soccer History (SASH)   75, 127, 165
South America   15, 34, 57, 66, 69, 87, 103
South Florida Drug Task Force   152
South Korea   6–8, 36, 176, 201
South Side of Chicago   117
sovereignty   95, 112, 181, 186, 196
Spain/Spanish   14, 18, 65, 70, 86, 103, 131, 141, 179
Spanish-American War   145
Spanish flag   68
Stadio Nazionale del Partito Nazionale Fascista   73
Stalin   14
Star-Spangled Banner   55
Stewart, Earnie   162, 167
suburbia/suburbs/suburbanization   121, 122, 124
Summer Olympics   81, 134
Suñé, Rubén   57

Super Bowl   114
superclásico   10, 87, 156, 160, 181, 184, 225
superclásico feminil   210
Super Eagles   145
Szymanski, Stefan   187

Tariff War   141, 153
Tea Party   42
Telesistema Mexicano   80, 82
Televisa   2, 3, 8–10, 68, 82, 125, 127, 128, 150, 195
Televisión Independiente de México   82
Tello, Jorge   201, 220
Tenorio, Paul   195
Terrazas, Joaquín Soria   184
Tevez, Carlos   61
Texas   93, 94, 196, 197, 223
Texas Rangers   98
Thompson, Alyssa   209
Thompson, Gisele   209
The Three Lions   141
Tigana, Jean   145
Tlatelolco Massacre   81
Torres, Jose   177
Tottenham Hotspur   56, 136, 224
Toye, Clive   82
transnational   6, 17, 19, 135, 213
treinador de futebol   14
Trésor, Marius   145
triple domestication   122
Trittschuh, Steve   123, 124
Trost, Al   126, 127
Trump, Donald   19, 26, 42, 63, 106, 114, 153, 181, 186
Trump Administration   47, 153
T&T Football Federation   185
Turkish futbol federation   49
Türkiye *vs.* Germany   48
Turner, Matt   59
Tuzos Mesa Academy   220
Twellman, Taylor   221
Tyler, B. David   25

UEFA Champions League   190, 191, 195, 209
UNAM Pumas   3, 14
United Kingdom   14, 63
United Mexican States   94, 96
United States   vii, viii, 2, 4–5, 9–13, 26, 27, 30, 34, 36–8, 42, 46, 48–50, 54, 66, 69, 71–3, 77–9, 81–3, 86, 91, 92, 95, 97, 101, 103, 113, 115, 123, 125, 128, 130, 133, 143, 148, 152, 155, 163, 164, 166, 181, 184–7, 190, 196, 200, 207, 209, 211, 219, 226, 227
   armed forces   6, 94
   Basketball   40, 144
   Border Patrol   98
   collegiate system   207
   vs. Cuba   32
   futbol community   38
   immigrant populations in   28
   Olympic Team   121, 126, 129
   soccer fans   7, 18, 58, 67, 104, 105, 111, 121, 136, 139
   supreme court   196
   Women's National Team   x, 7, 11, 45, 123, 144, 204, 214
Universidad Tecnológica de Nezahualcóyotl   131
University of California   13
University of Massachusetts   25
University of Michigan   101
University of Virginia   165
Univision/TUDN   29, 31, 41, 47, 195, 218
Uruguay/Uruguayan   30, 70–3, 151
Uruguayan Football Association (AUF)   71
US Football Association (USFA)   73, 77, 117, 119
US Immigration Act of 1917   98
USL Championship   135, 220
US Olympic Development Program   35
US Olympic soccer team   128
US Open Cup   117, 119, 164
US Ryder Cup   6

US Soccer Federation (USSF)   3, 24, 46, 79, 131, 145, 146, 163, 174, 184–6, 196, 218
US Soccer Federation youth programs   24
USSR (Soviet Union)   3, 62

van der Heyden, Theo   82
Vaninger, Danny   127
Vasquéz, Brandon   19, 223
Vásquez, Martín   21–3, 148
Velasco, Xavier   39
Velázquez Bolio, Roberto   178
Veracruz   16, 65, 66, 94
Verlander, Justin   118
Vermes, Peter   124, 149
Vespucci, Amerigo   143
Victor, Jillian   100

Wahl, Grant   10, 34–6, 148, 166, 174, 178, 200, 215, 222, 225, 226
Waldseemüller, Martin   143
Walker, William   95, 96
Warner, Jack   184–7
Wasser, David Brett   2, 4
Weah, George   145
Wegerle, Roy   150
Welcome to Wrexham   115
Wells Fargo   221
Wembley Stadium   vi, 40, 84, 166, 170
Wenger, Arsene   145
West Bromwich Albion   67
Western Hemisphere   38, 69, 77, 184
Wilson, Pete   152
Women's Professional Soccer (WPS)   208
Women's World Cup   144, 189, 207, 209, 211
Wonder Woman   52
Wood, Bobby   134
Woosnam, Phil   82
World Cup   vii, viii, 24–6, 72, 83–4
   1930   71
   1934   73, 76, 114
   1938   77, 78
   1950   40, 83
   1958   vi
   1962   83, 84
   1966   6
   1970   3, 80, 81, 115, 125
   1974   125, 128
   1978   56, 114
   1982   2, 131
   1986   15, 54, 139, 142
   1990   15, 162
   1994   viii, ix, 11, 12, 16, 115, 124, 144, 147, 149–51, 185, 189
   1998   8, 33, 57
   2002   5, 9, 32, 84, 114, 146, 176, 224
   2010   61, 114
   2014   89
   2015   212
   2018   114, 181, 221
   2022   9, 49, 56, 57, 84, 114, 146, 176, 189
   2026   7, 41, 57, 81, 87, 88, 114, 171, 201, 217, 222, 223
Wrexham AFC   116, 118
Wrigley Field   115
Wynalda, Eric   16

Yankee Doodle Revolutionaries   144
Yanks   vii, 11, 30, 40, 44, 72, 73, 84, 115, 120, 145, 156, 157, 174, 187
yanqui culture   9
Yohannes, Lily   209
Youth National Team Hopscotch   222
Youth Soccer Revolution   121–4, 131, 151, 209

Zendejas, Alejandro ("Alex")   23, 24, 55, 215, 216, 217
Zlatan   14
zopilotes   60
Zurich   216
Zusi, Graham   54, 55

About the Author

Hal Phillips is an author, journalist, and media executive based in southern Maine. *Sibling Rivalry* represents his second book-length soccer project. Dickinson-Moses Press published the first, *Generation Zero: Founding Fathers, Hidden Histories and the Making of Soccer in America*, in July 2022. Phillips blogs on all matters futbol at www.SiblingRivalry.halphillips.net. He posts about the world at-large at www.halphillips.net.

An all-state striker at Wellesley (Mass.) High School, Phillips played four years of college soccer at Wesleyan University in Middletown, Connecticut, where he double-majored in ancient Greek history and modern American literature. He logged three years in the semi-pro, Greater Boston-based Luso-American Soccer Association, before heading north to play ten more seasons in the Maine Open League. Starting in 1997, he has owned and operated Mandarin Media, Inc., a Maine-based media consulting, content- and digital-marketing agency serving golf, hospitality, and property clients across North America, Asia-Pacific, and the UK.

Until 1997, Phillips had worked as a daily newspaper and magazine editor. The formation of Mandarin Media essentially launched his freelance journalism career. He has since contributed feature content and columns to ESPN.com, *Sports Illustrated*, *Soccer Journal*, Soccer365.com, GOLF Magazine, *Travel & Leisure*, *Golf Digest China*, LINKS Magazine, *Golf Australia*, *The Portland Press Herald* and *Sun-Journal* newspapers, *McKellar*, *The Robb Report* and dozens of additional titles worldwide, some of which still exist. He was the founder and host of the *Unsightly American Soccer Podcast* from 2009 to 2013, pioneering but effectively pre-dating the podcast movement.